Grades 4–6
Practice and Assessment

McGraw Hill Education

Bothell, WA • Chicago, IL • Columbus, OH • New York, NY

www.mheonline.com/readingwonderworks

Copyright © McGraw-Hill Education

Send all inquiries to:
McGraw-Hill Education
Two Penn Plaza
New York, New York 10121

ISBN: 978-0-02-129950-8
MHID: 0-02-129950-1

Printed in the United States of America.

4 5 6 7 8 9 RHR 18 17 16 15 14

A

CONTENTS

Phonics

CONTENTS

CONTENTS

Structural Analysis

Fluency

Other Resources

Name _____

One-Syllable Words

> The short *a* sound is spelled with the letter *a*.
>
> c**a**p p**a**n s**a**nd

A. Read the words in each row. Underline the word that has a short *a* sound. Write the word on the line.

1. <u>fact</u> five four _____fact_____
2. cold clap come _____
3. but big back _____
4. him had help _____
5. yam yes you _____
6. time two trap _____

B. Read each sentence. Underline the word that has the short *a* sound. Write the word on the line.

1. We will go in the <u>cab</u>. _____cab_____
2. I call my white cat Jim. _____
3. Will you play tag with me? _____
4. I must pack my things now. _____
5. She is glad to see me. _____
6. I will be in the band. _____

Name _____

Multi-Syllable Words

> The short *a* sound is spelled with the letter *a*.
>
> h<u>a</u>ndb<u>a</u>g   c<u>a</u>mping   <u>a</u>cted

A. Read the words in each row. Underline the word that has the short *a* sound. Then write it on the line.

1. <u>packing</u>   picking   playing   ___packing___

2. seeing   stamping   opening   _____

3. funny   yellow   sandbag   _____

4. number   today   camping   _____

5. going   catnap   people   _____

6. flapjack   little   other   _____

B. Read each sentence. Underline the word that has a short *a* sound. Then write the word on the line.

1. My <u>handbag</u> is very big.   ___handbag___

2. The backpack is on the bed.   _____

3. We will play in the bandstand.   _____

4. We will be planting fig trees.   _____

5. I like to do handstands.   _____

6. My granddad is here.   _____

Name _____

Camping With Dan and Dad

8	Dan and his dad sat on the grass.
17	Dan was sad. Dan's pal Pat was at camp.
28	"Dan, don't be sad. We can go camping, too," said Dad.
34	"Can we go rafting?" Dan asked.
45	"We can go rafting, and I can make flapjacks," Dad added.
56	Dan and Dad packed their backpacks, a raft, a map, and
69	a lamp into the van. They go to a camping place with water,
72	grass, and sand.
78	"We can camp here," said Dad.
85	Dan and Dad put up a tent.
96	Dad made stacks of flapjacks. He hands Dan a stack of
103	flapjacks. "Flapjacks are the best!" said Dan.
115	Dan and Dad drag the raft on the sand into the water.
126	Standing on the raft, Dan can see crabs. Dad can see
133	clams. Dan is glad Dad likes rafting.
144	Back on land Dan asks, "Can we plan to go camping
146	again, Dad?"
152	"That will be grand!" Dad said.

1. Underline the words in the story that have the short *a* sound.

2. Why is Dan sad?

_____

3. What do Dan and Dad see on the raft?

_____

Name _____

One-Syllable Words

> The short *i* sound is spelled with the letter *i*.
>
> br**i**m   cl**i**p   st**i**ck

A. Read the words in each row. Underline the word that has a short *i* sound. Then write the word on the line.

1. bag   <u>big</u>   back   _____big_____

2. did   dad   done   _____

3. grand   grow   grin   _____

4. plant   print   pack   _____

5. drip   drag   damp   _____

6. clap   crisp   cramp   _____

B. Read each sentence. Underline the word that has a short *i* sound. Write the word on the line to complete the sentence.

1. Fran _____hid_____ from Pat.

   sat   ran   <u>hid</u>

2. Hal and Sam are _____.

   pets   cats   twins

3. Do you like to _____?

   swim   clap   grab

4. My cat can do a funny _____.

   trick   act   walk

Name _____

Multi-Syllable Words

The short *i* sound is spelled with the letter *i*.

l<u>i</u>pst<u>i</u>ck   rabb<u>i</u>t   adm<u>i</u>t

A. Read the words in each row. Underline the word that has the short *i* sound. Write the word on the line.

1. flapjack   sandman   <u>zigzag</u>   *zigzag*

2. napkin   landmass   backtrack   _____

3. slanted   clinic   handstand   _____

4. flatland   granddad   mimic   _____

5. plastic   catnap   backpack   _____

B. Read each sentence. Underline the word or words that have a short *i* sound. Then write the word or words on the line.

1. Ants are <u>sitting</u> on the <u>anthill</u>.   *sitting*   *anthill*

2. Frank and Pip had a picnic.   _____   _____

3. Windmills are big.   _____   _____

4. Tim puts down the kickstand on his bike.   _____   _____

5. I gave my cat Flip some catnip.   _____   _____

6. Miss Black may dismiss us soon.   _____   _____

Name _____

Plant a Fig

11	It is Plant Day! Miss Vick's class will plant a fig
24	tree. It is small, but it will grow into a big tree. Nick
37	will dig a pit for it. Jill will put bits of wood around
49	it. Bill will give it a big drink of water. Water will
61	help it grow. Nick and Jill will trim and clip it. Tim
68	will pick up the clippings and twigs.
77	When the tree is big, Miss Vick's class will
86	handpick figs. The kids will pick many figs. They
98	will fill tins to the brim with figs! They will make fig
108	jam and fig snacks. The kids will visit other classes.
119	They will give figs to other kids. Then the kids will
127	eat the figs. They will lick their lips.

1. Underline words in the story that have the short *i* sound.

2. What will Miss Vick's class plant?

_____

_____

_____

3. What will the class make with the figs?

_____

_____

_____

Name _____

One-Syllable Words

> The short o sound is spelled with the letter o.
>
> st**o**p   fr**o**g   d**o**ck

A. Read the words in each row. Underline the word with the short o sound. Write the word on the line.

1. <u>flop</u>   flap   flip   ___flop___
2. sick   sack   sock   _____
3. spit   spot   span   _____
4. stick   track   rock   _____

B. Read each sentence. Underline the word that has a short o sound. Write the word on the line to complete the sentence.

1. I will _____jog_____ with a pal.

   walk   <u>jog</u>   jump

2. Cal saw the time on the _____

   clock   lamp   clip

3. Please put the _____ away.

   bag   pin   mop

4. Pat takes her fishing _____ to the pond.

   stick   rod   hat

5. The big black _____ has some gifts in it.

   sack   bin   box

Name _____

Multi-Syllable Words

> The short o sound is spelled with the letter o.
>
> st<u>o</u>mping   l<u>o</u>cking   b<u>o</u>bcat

A. Read the words in each row. Underline the word that has the short o sound. Write the word on the line.

1. <u>sandbox</u>   sanding   sandbag   _____sandbox_____

2. landfill   sobbing   rabbit   _____

3. tomcat   lipstick   backpack   _____

4. funny   landmass   gossip   _____

5. stopping   lasting   fitting   _____

6. visit   hopping   limit   _____

B. Read each sentence. Underline the word that has the short o sound. Then write the word on the line. Underline the short o sound.

1. The little black cat is <u>blocking</u> my way.   _____bl<u>o</u>cking_____

2. The robin sits in a bag.   _____

3. The bobcat ran into the tall grass.   _____

4. Sam said he would contact me today.   _____

5. We will go to the tropics.   _____

6. The ant was hopping in the sand.   _____

Name _____

A Trip to the Pond

13	Miss Todd's class is on a class trip to the pond. The pond
25	is on a hilltop. The class is looking at different plants and
26	animals.
38	"I spot a rabbit by a plant," said Robin. "It is hopping
41	near a log."
53	"I spot an anthill," said Bob. "It is by a big rock."
62	"Black ants live in the anthill," said Miss Todd.
73	"Look at that frog," said Robin. The frog hopped into the
74	pond.
85	"Hot dog!" said Don. There are six robins in the tree!"
97	"I spot a big bass swimming in the pond," said Miss Todd.
108	The kids spotted many odd animals and plants on the trip.
122	The kids felt hot. So the class sat on the grass by the pond.
132	They stopped to have snacks. The kids had packed snacks
143	in their backpacks. Bob had figs his mom had picked. Miss
157	Todd had bonbons for the class. It was a good day for a trip
160	to the pond.

1. Underline words in the story that have the short *o* sound.

2. What did Robin spot at the pond?

_____

3. Where was the anthill?

_____

Name _____

One-Syllable Words

> The short *e* sound is spelled with the letter *e*.
>
> b<u>e</u>lt   sp<u>e</u>nd   st<u>e</u>m

A. Underline the word with the short *e* sound in each row. Write the word on the line.

1. <u>sled</u>   slip   slam   _sled_____

2. last   rest   cost   _____

3. drill   drag   dwell   _____

4. help   clip   trip   _____

5. stamp   step   stop   _____

B. Underline the word with the short *e* sound in each sentence. Write the word on the line. Underline the short *e* spelling.

1. Will you <u>lend</u> me your backpack?   _lend_____

2. Can we sit on the deck?   _____

3. Sal will sell socks.   _____

4. We had a test on grasslands.   _____

5. We will take my rabbit to the vet.   _____

Name _____

Multi-Syllable Words

> The short *e* sound is spelled with the letter *e*.
>
>   b**e**drock   sm**e**lling   d**e**ntist

A. Underline the word with the short *e* sound in each row. Write the word on the line.

1. <u>spending</u>   granting   hinting   _____ *spending*

2. dismiss   bobcat   dentist   _____

3. content   picnic   rapid   _____

4. rabbit   mattress   panic   _____

5. sandbank   napkin   bedpost   _____

B. Underline the word with the short *e* sound that completes each sentence. Write the word on the line to complete the sentence.

1. Frogs live in _____ *wetlands* _____.

    landmasses   flatlands   <u>wetlands</u>

2. I will be in a spelling _____.

    clinic   contest   topic

3. I see the _____ on the grass.

    robin   tomcat   insect

4. It was a _____ day in class.

    hectic   frantic   spinning

Name _____

The Vet

13	Meg is my pet cat. We were playing tag. Meg went on top
18	of my bedpost and fell.
24	"Mom, help! Meg fell," I yelled.
35	Mom picked up Meg and felt her leg. "Meg's leg is
42	swelling. Let's get her to the vet."
56	I held Meg on my lap. We went to the vet in our van.
70	Dr. Ben looked at Meg's leg. "I can help Meg. I will do a
80	test on her leg. I will help Meg get well."
94	After the test, the vet fixed Meg's leg. He put a cast on it.
107	He said, "Let Meg rest for a bit. She has to be still."
117	"Thanks, Dr. Ben. You are the best vet!" I yelled.
132	Back home, I fed Meg cat snacks. I let Meg sit in my bed. I
144	petted Meg's neck. Meg was not well but she felt better and
151	so did I. Meg's leg is mending!

1. Underline words in the story with the short *e* sound.

2. Why did Meg go to the vet?

_____

3. What did the vet do?

_____

Name _____

One-Syllable Words

> The short *u* vowel sound is spelled with the letter *u*.
> m**u**d   d**u**g   r**u**n

A. Read each sentence. Circle the words that have the short *u* sound. Write the words with the short *u* sound on the lines.

1. The (pup) likes to (jump).   **pup**   **jump**

2. We have fun at the club.   _____   _____

3. We run to the bus stop.   _____   _____

4. I see a clump of gum.   _____   _____

B. Circle the words in the box that have the short *u* sound. Then use the words you circled. Answer the clues below.

bat	sun	pup	pig	duck	bug
hut	deck	tab	hot	(tub)	nut

1. This is something with suds.   **tub**

2. This is a dog.   _____

3. This is what you can eat for a snack.   _____

4. This is a bird.   _____

5. This is a small place to live.   _____

6. This is what you see in the sky.   _____

7. This is a fly.   _____

Name _____

Multi-Syllable Words

> The short _u_ vowel sound is spelled with the letter _u_.
>
> f<u>u</u>nny   <u>u</u>pset   h<u>u</u>ndred

A. Underline the short _u_ in each word. Then write the word on the line.

1. <u>u</u>pon _____upon_____   **4.** until _____

2. hundred _____   **5.** puppet _____

3. upset _____   **6.** number _____

B. Circle the word with the same vowel sound as _cup_ and _run_. Then write the word on the line.

1. We are _____jumping_____ rope.

(jumping)   batting   stepping

2. I see the _____ ten.

basket   rabbit   number

3. We like to sit _____ the tree.

under   bottom   backpack

4. They eat _____ at six.

flapjacks   supper   timber

5. The kids put on a _____ show.

puppet   snapshot   patted

Name _____

Working Pups

12	Working pups help us in lots of ways. Some pups do jobs
24	at home. Some pups go to see sick kids. Working pups can
35	get on a bus. They can go to lots of places.
47	Ruff and Mutt are working pups. Ruff is a big dog that
60	works with sick kids. Ruff goes to a hospital. The kids sit on
74	a rug and pet and hug Ruff. He will not jump up on them.
80	Ruff has fun with the kids.
94	Mutt has a big job, too. Mutt helps Gus. Gus is a man who
106	cannot walk. Gus trusts Mutt. Mutt can hit a button to get
112	9-1-1. She is a trusted pup.
124	Mutt and Ruff also have fun. Mutt likes it when Gus rubs
136	her back. Ruff runs after sticks and jumps in the mud. He
148	naps in the sun, too. Working pups like their jobs and help
151	lots of people!

1. Underline words in the story that have the short *u* sound.

2. What do working pups do?

_____

_____

_____

3. What does Ruff do for fun?

_____

_____

Name _____

One-Syllable Words

> Blends are consonants that work together. Some blends
> are *bl, fl, gl, br, tr, sn, sp, st, ft, mp, nt,* and *nd.* Say each
> sound in a blend.

**A. Read each word in the box. Underline the blends. Sort the
words under the correct heading.**

f<u>l</u>at	snap	last	stuff	land	pest
trip	gift	bent	glass	nest	brag

Beginning Blends   **Ending Blends**

flat _____   last _____

_____   _____

_____   _____

_____   _____

_____

**B. Read each sentence. Underline the word with a consonant
blend sound. Write the word on the line.**

1. Do you see the red <u>block</u> on top?   block _____

2. The tan cat can jump on top of it.   _____

3. They will run on the track now.   _____

4. This band is very good!   _____

5. Can you spell these words?   _____

Name _____

Multi-Syllable Words

Blends are consonants that work together. Some blends are *cl, pl, gr, tr, st, nt, ft,* and *nd.* Say each sound in a blend.

A. Read the words below. Place each word in the column that describes its consonant blend sound. Underline the letters that stand for the consonant blend sound.

| tropic | eggplant | invest | planet |
| backrest | imprint | plotted | traffic |

pl as in *plan*   *tr* as in *trap*   *nt* as in *mint*   *st* as in *last*

planet

_____   _____   _____   _____

_____   _____   _____   _____

B. Read each sentence. Underline the words with consonant blend in each sentence. Write the words on the lines.

1. Planets go around the Sun.   planet   around

2. We rented a raft.   _____   _____

3. It is the fastest jet around.   _____   _____

4. The band played on the time.   _____   _____

5. We were on a class trip.   _____   _____

6. The grasslands are grand.   _____   _____

Name _____

Just Get Fit!

12	Do you want to get fit and trim? Stand up. Do six
22	jumping jacks. Pick up two big blocks. Hold one in
32	each hand. Lift the blocks up and down ten times.
42	Next, skip, trot, jump, or run around a track. You
54	can take 100 steps up a big hill. Take a brisk walk.
66	Walking fast will help you get fit. Jog uphill or jog up
76	a slanted ramp. Swim some laps. See how many laps
79	you can swim!
89	Last, you can bend and twist, and play tag. Spend
97	time hopping, skipping, and jumping. Have some fun.
107	Clap your hands. Stamp your feet. Do not stand still.
119	Do not stop and rest. Just get fit. And do your best!

---

1. Underline words in the story that have consonant blend sounds.

2. What will walking fast help do?

_____

3. What are some things you can do to get fit?

_____

Name _____

One-Syllable Words

> When a word has a vowel, a consonant, and an *e* at the end, the first vowel is usually a long sound.
>
> g<u>a</u>m<u>e</u>   <u>e</u>v<u>e</u>   p<u>i</u>n<u>e</u>   l<u>o</u>n<u>e</u>   c<u>u</u>t<u>e</u>

A. Underline the word with the long vowel sound in each row. Write the word on the line.

1. <u>poke</u>   plant   pelt   _____poke_____

2. slat   still   skate   _____

3. crime   crop   crab   _____

4. hop   home   hunk   _____

5. fuse   flag   frog   _____

6. slim   slime   slap   _____

B. Read each sentence. Underline the word or words with the long vowel sound. Write the word or words on the line.

1. Can you tell us a funny <u>joke</u>?   _____joke_____

2. I sent a note to my best pal.   _____

3. We have six cute cats as pets.   _____

4. Dad makes me smile.   _____

5. I ate a scone for a snack.   _____   _____

Name _____

Multi-Syllable Words

> When a word has a vowel, a consonant, and an *e* at the end, the first vowel is usually a long sound.
>
> b**a**s**e**ball   compl**ete**   l**ike**ness   al**one**   c**ute**ness

A. Read the words in each row. Underline the word that has a long vowel, a consonant, and an *e* at the end. Write the word on the line.

1. <u>hopeless</u>   gossip   droplet   ____hopeless____

2. stickpin   timid   lifetime   _____

3. contest   compete   content   _____

4. music   cupid   useless   _____

5. camping   sidestep   visit   _____

B. Read each sentence. Underline the word that has a long vowel, a consonant, and an *e* at the end. Then write the word on the line.

1. I just had a big <u>pancake</u> for a snack!   ____pancake____

2. My dad's nickname is Bob.   _____

3. My dog and cat amuse me.   _____

4. She picked a red rosebud.   _____

5. The dog slept by Will's bedside.   _____

A Snake's Life

15	A snake is a long reptile. It has no legs. It slides on land. It
26	glides and swims in water. A snake has scales. Snakeskin is
38	smooth. A snake must shed its skin a few times a year.
47	Snakes have different homes. Some snakes like dry land.
61	A snake can hide in a rockpile. It can blend in with the rocks.
75	It will use the hole in the rocks for a home. A snake can
87	slide in and out of small holes. Holes and rockpiles are safe
90	homes for snakes.
102	Some snakes like water. A snake can swim and glide in a
116	lake. Snakes like the hot sun, too. A snake will use a rock to
125	take a sun bath. Snakes do not like people.
135	A snake hunts small animals, like mice, insects, and other
145	reptiles. A snake does not need to eat every day.

1. Underline the words in the story that have a long vowel sound.

2. What is a snake?

_____

3. What does a snake hunt?

_____

Name _____

One-Syllable Words

The letters *a*, *ai*, *ay*, *ea*, *ei*, *eigh*, and *ey* can stand for the long *a* sound.

<u>a</u>pe   cl**<u>ai</u>m**   pl**<u>ay</u>**   br**<u>ea</u>k**   v**<u>ei</u>l**   w**<u>eigh</u>**   pr**<u>ey</u>**

A. Underline the long *a* word in each row. Write the word on the line. Underline the letters that spell the long *a* sound.

1. track   <u>clay</u>   clap   _____clay_____

2. black   brain   bran   _____

3. vein   van   vend   _____

4. grasp   grind   great   _____

5. eve   eight   end   _____

B. Underline the long *a* word. Write the word on the line in each sentence. Underline the letters that spell the long *a* sound.

1. I see a _____snail_____ on the grass.

   bug   fly   <u>snail</u>

2. I can lift the _____ with my hands.

   glass   tray   cup

3. The _____ will glide across the ice.

   cab   bus   sleigh

4. It is a dull _____ day.

   gray   cold   warm

5. There is a _____ on my jacket.

   drip   spot   stain

Name _____

Multi-Syllable Words

The letters *a, ai, ay, ea, ei, eigh,* and *ey* can stand for the long *a* sound.

b**a**con   m**ai**nland   d**ay**time   gr**ea**tness

unv**ei**l   w**eigh**ing   ob**ey**

A. Underline the long *a* word in each row. Write the word on the line.

1. camel   <u>painted</u>   asking   _____painted_____

2. restful   rabbit   greatness   _____

3. subway   sandbag   backpack   _____

4. passing   panted   pigtail   _____

5. planting   swaying   camping   _____

6. unveiled   vastness   vented   _____

B. Underline the word with the long *a* sound in each sentence. Write the word on the line. Then underline the letters that make the long *a* sound.

1. My dog is very <u>playful</u>.   _____pl**a**yful_____

2. This bill is unpaid!   _____

3. You are weightless on the Moon.   _____

4. The fox is preying on rabbits and voles.   _____

5. We will go swimming on Sunday.   _____

6. An artist works with a paintbrush.   _____

Name _____

A Train Trip in Spain

13	Nate and his dad are in Spain. They will take a train to
16	visit Nate's grandmom!
29	"Nate, it is time to go," says Dad. "The train will leave at
40	eight o'clock. We cannot be late." Nate has been waiting for
46	this day for a long time.
59	They take a cab to the train. On the train, Nate and his
70	dad eat pancakes. The train rolls across a wide flat plain.
77	There are small homes on the plain.
87	A freight train passes their train. The freight train is
97	carrying olives. It is Spain's biggest crop. Nate snaps a
102	picture of the freight train.
114	The train stops in a small town. A man is making and
127	selling clay pots. Nate pays for a red pot. "Isn't this a great
130	gift for Grandmom!"
137	"Yes," says Dad. "Grandmom loves clay pots!"

1. Underline the words in the story that have the long *a* sound.

2. Where are Nate and his dad going to on the train?

_____

3. What did Nate buy for his grandmom?

_____

Name _____

One-Syllable Words

> The letters *i*, *igh*, *ie*, and *y* can stand for the long *i* sound.
>
> f**i**nd   h**igh**   d**ie**   fl**y**

A. Underline the word with the long *i* in each row. Write the word on the line. Underline the letters that spell the long *i* sound.

1. lip   l**ie**   _____l**ie**_____

2. might   mint   _____

3. main   mind   _____

4. bay   by   _____

5. tray   tie   _____

B. Underline the word with the long *i* to complete each sentence. Write the word on the line. Underline the letters that spell the long *i* sound.

1. That big black cat is _____w**i**ld_____ .

   tame   w**i**ld   great

2. I wake up when it is _____ .

   light   lamp   tint

3. This plum _____ tastes great!

   cake   snack   pie

4. I will _____ my wet hands.

   fix   dry   wet

5. I pulled the rope to make it _____ .

   tight   long   dull

Name _____

Multi-Syllable Words

> The letters *i*, *igh*, *ie*, and *y* can stand for the long *i* sound.
> k**i**ndness　　　day**ligh**t　　　unt**ie**　　　m**y**self

A. Underline the word with the long *i* vowel sound in each row. Write the word on the line.

1. biggest　　　picnic　　　<u>climate</u>　　　__climate__
2. potpie　　　cupcake　　　pancake　　　_____
3. limit　　　midnight　　　windmill　　　_____
4. handpick　　　topping　　　tightrope　　　_____
5. blindfold　　　stickpin　　　kickstand　　　_____
6. spilling　　　drying　　　hinting　　　_____

B. Underline the word with the long *i* sound in each sentence. Write the word on the line. Then underline the letters that make the long *i* sound.

1. It will be <u>daylight</u> at six o'clock.　　__daylight__
2. The pilot got into the big plane.　　_____
3. Please stop the bus at the stoplight.　　_____
4. Fran will untie her dog and take it for a walk.　　_____
5. The children were crying because they were sad.　　_____
6. Sid is winding up his toy.　　_____

Name _____

Day Sky, Night Sky

11	It is daylight. Look up at the sky. What can you
21	find? A magpie might be gliding by. You might see
32	kites flying high. A plane might be flying high up in
42	the sky. A flock of gulls might be flying by.
52	The sun makes the sky bright. At times you might
63	not see the sun, but it is there. Plants need sunlight.
66	We need sunlight!
78	As the sun sets, the sky gets dark. It is twilight. In
89	the night sky, there are sights to see. You might find
99	the moon in the night sky. At midnight, you might
110	sight a star shooting by. It might be a highlight of
112	your night!

---

1. Underline the words in the story that have the long *i* sound.

2. What might you find in a day sky?

_____

_____

3. What might you find in a night sky?

_____

Name _____

One-Syllable Words

> The letters *o, oa, ow,* and *oe* can stand for the long *o* sound.
> **o**ld   b**oa**t   l**ow**   t**oe**

A. Choose words from the box that have the same spelling for the long *o* in each row. Write the words on the line.

sold	float	glow	woe
grown	foe	loan	go

1. told _____**sold**_____   _____**go**_____

2. goat _____   _____

3. stow _____   _____

4. doe _____   _____

B. Underline the long *o* word that completes each sentence. Write the word on the line. Underline the letters that spell the long *o* sound.

1. The _____**road**_____ is very bumpy.

   raid   ride   <u>road</u>

2. Ned and Ana will _____ the grass on Friday.

   weigh   make   mow

3. The brown _____ is hiding in the high grasses.

   dog   doe   snake

4. It will be _____ outside when you wake up.

   cold   fine   great

Name _____

Multi-Syllable Words

> The letters *o*, *oa*, *ow*, and *oe* can stand for the long *o* sound.
>
> **o**bey   g**oa**tskin   pill**ow**   ob**oe**

A. Read the words in each row. Underline the word that has the long *o* vowel sound. Write it on the line.

1. droplet   <u>mellow</u>   contest   _mellow_

2. donate   repay   berry   _____

3. backlog   content   slowest   _____

4. comma   cocoa   coming   _____

5. program   pillbox   closet   _____

B. Underline the word with the long *o* in each sentence. Write the word on the line. Underline the letters that spell the long *o* sound.

1. A frog was <u>croaking</u> by the pond.   _cr**oa**king_

2. We went on a boating trip today.   _____

3. Mom and I are going to the store.   _____

4. The boy tiptoed by the sleeping dog.   _____

5. We sat under a big willow and slept.   _____

Name _____

Is It a Frog or a Toad?

14	How can you tell a frog from a toad? Let's take a trip in
24	my rowboat. I will show you some frogs and toads.
36	Frogs have to live by water. You can find them by a
48	coastline or in a wetland. Most grown toads live on land, but
60	some like the water, too. Frogs and toads lay eggs. The eggs
63	hatch as tadpoles.
76	A frog grows up to have slick, wet skin. A toad grows up
88	to have dry skin with bumps. A frog can swim fast because
102	of its webbed toes. Its long legs help it to jump high. A toad
116	has toes but no webs. It has short hind legs. A toad can run
129	or hop. A toad has a wide fat body. A frog does not.
140	Look, there's a frog soaking in the lake. *Croak, croak!* And
147	there's a toad hopping by the roadside!

---

1. Underline words in the story that have the long *o* sound.

2. Where do frogs have to live?

_____

3. Where do toads live?

_____

Name _____

One-Syllable Words

> The letters *e, ee, ea, ie, y,* and *ey* can stand for the long *e* sound.
>
> sh**e**   f**ee**t   b**ea**t   ch**ie**f   sunn**y**   k**ey**

A. Underline the word in each sentence with the long *e* sound. Write the word on the line. Circle the letters that spell the long *e*.

1. say   <u>key</u>   fly   _____key_____

2. weak   maid   pie   _____

3. weigh   brief   they   _____

4. steel   spy   play   _____

B. Underline the long *e* word that completes each sentence. Write the word on the line. Circle the letters that spell the long *e* sound.

1. I have to _____sneeze_____!

   stop   smile   <u>sneeze</u>

2. Let's take a _____ at this gift.

   look   peek   break

3. Will you look for my lost dog with _____?

   me   them   him

4. The riding class will be _____ today.

   big   long   brief

5. The red _____ is soft and wet.

   leaf   sand   bike

Name _____

Multi-Syllable Words

> The letters e, ee, ea, ie, y, and ey can stand for the long e sound.
>
> r**e**lay   w**ee**kend   m**ea**ltime   br**ie**fing
>
> funn**y**   hock**ey**

A. Underline the letters that make the long e sound in each word. Write the words next to the long e spelling.

r**e**late	jockey	belief	r**e**tell
windy	briefcase	seasick	needless
heating	canteen	kidney	runny

1. e   _____relate_____   _____retell_____

2. ee   _____   _____

3. ea   _____   _____

4. ie   _____   _____

5. y   _____   _____

6. ey   _____   _____

B. Underline the word that has the long e sound in each sentence. Write the word on the line. Circle the long e spelling.

1. We hiked on a <u>hilly</u> trail.   _____hill(y)_____

2. The drumbeat kept us awake.   _____

3. It's really hot today!   _____

4. The sheepskin coat is soft.   _____

5. We played hockey at five o'clock.   _____

6. She finally got relief on Sunday.   _____

Name _____

Vote for <u>Sidney</u> and <u>Eve</u>!

11	Sidney wants to be class president. He needs help to win.
20	"Eve, will you be my running mate?" Sidney said.
31	Eve smiled, "Yes. I think we will make a great team!"
42	Sidney and Eve made signs that read: *Vote for Sidney and*
54	*Eve. They are the team with a dream!* Sidney and Eve posted
61	them around the class. Sammy helped them.
72	On Election Day, Eve said, "I believe that we can work
85	together as a team. We can make rules that are just. Vote for
88	Sidney and me!"
99	Then Sidney said, "We need to treat our planet well. Let's
111	keep our city clean! Let's pick up trash! Let's plant trees! We
114	need your help!
125	"It's time to add up the votes," said Miss Reeves. All
135	twenty students voted for Sidney and Eve. The class all
137	yelled, "Yay!"

1. Underline words in the story that have the long *e* sound.

2. What did Eve say on Election Day?

_____

_____

3. What did Sidney say on Election Day?

_____

_____

Name _____

One-Syllable Words

> The letters *u_e, ew,* and *ue* can stand for the long *u* sound.
>
>   t**une**   f**ew**   c**ue**

A. Choose a word from the box that has the same spelling for long *u* as each of the words below. Write the words on the line.

> | | | | | |
> |---|---|---|---|---|
> | cute | mew | pew | fuel | cube |
> | hue | fuse | due | hew | |

1. mute   _____cute_____   _____   _____

2. few   _____   _____   _____

3. cue   _____   _____   _____

B. Underline the long *u* word that completes each sentence. Write the word on the line. Then underline the letters that spell the long *u* sound.

1. That is a _____h**uge**_____ dog!

    little   <u>huge</u>   big

2. He will ride on the _____ up the steep hill.

    mule   bus   train

3. Will Dad make a _____ dishes tonight?

    steak   few   soup

4. He said his lines on _____.

    time   top   cue

Name _____

Multi-Syllable Words

> The letters *u, u_e, ew,* and *ue* can stand for the long *u* sound.
>
> m**u**sic   ref**use**   d**ew**y   resc**ue**

A. Underline the letters that make the long *u* sound in the words below.

> continue   useless   pupil   unit
>
> amuse   duties   fewer   human

B. Underline the word that has the long *u* sound in each sentence. Write the word on the line. Underline the long *u* spelling.

1. Who is playing the tuba today?   _____tuba_____

2. I value your help.   _____

3. Today is hot and humid.   _____

4. We refueled the car.   _____

5. He was confused about where to go.   _____

6. There are fewer dogs than cats.   _____

7. The man rescued my cat.   _____

8. It was a useful book to read.   _____

Name _____

Let's Make Music!

11	Miss Yu's class has music time on Fridays. Each kid gets
23	to lead the class. Duke begins by humming a tune. What is
36	the tune? Duke will not give the class a clue. But, the class
42	guesses the name of the song!
54	Next, Hugo plays a tune on his tuba. His tuba is big!
67	Hugo plays a lot of low notes. Then Sue plays a flute. The
82	flute is tiny! It looks just like a long tube! Sue plays a lot of
94	high notes. Last, the class sings a few of their favorite songs.
106	Miss Yu cues the class when to begin by lifting her hand.
119	At the end of class, Miss Yu plays a lute. The volume is
131	low and soft. The class likes the music that Miss Yu plays.
143	All of the kids clap. They cannot wait until music class next
144	Friday!

1. Underline words in the story that have the long *u* sound.

2. Who plays the tuba?

_____

3. What does the flute look like?

_____

Name _____

One-Syllable Words

> Sometimes two or three consonants together stand for one sound.
>
> **th**in   **th**is   **ch**ap   hi**tch**

A. Read the words. Write each word in the correct column. Underline the letters that stand for the consonant sound.

| chomp | thick | snatch | that | pitch | chimp |
| hatch | thump | those | cheap | teeth | them |

th as in thin	**th as in this**	**ch as in chap**	**tch as in hitch**
<u>th</u>ick	_____	_____	_____
_____	_____	_____	_____
_____	_____	_____	_____

B. Read the sentences. Underline the word with the th, ch, or -tch sound. Write the word on the line. Underline the letters that stand for one sound.

1. I bumped my _____chin_____ on the desk.

   leg   hand   <u>ch</u>in

2. I will _____ the plan for you.

   blend   sketch   paint

3. The _____ stole some money.

   thief   people   man

4. Ned will _____ down the tree now.

   cut   hack   chop

Name _____

Multi-Syllable Words

> Sometimes two or three consonants together stand for one sound.
>
> spee**ch**less   wa**tch**man   **th**umbnail   ba**th**ing

A. Read the words in each row. Underline the word that has two or three consonants that stand for one sound. Write the word on the line.

1. <u>chatted</u>	stated	cupid	chatted
2. standup	matchbox	playmate	_____
3. transit	teacup	thumbnail	_____
4. themselves	tasted	traffic	_____
5. plastic	dispatch	pumpkin	_____
6. stopwatch	seasick	blanket	_____

B. Read the sentences. Underline the word with the *th, ch,* or *-tch* sound. Write the word on the line.

1. Please <u>unlatch</u> the lock.   unlatch

2. She got her paycheck today.   _____

3. A cat's coat will thicken when the days grow cold.   _____

4. It was so chilly today that my nose froze.   _____

5. Cleaning is a thankless job.   _____

6. My skin was itchy from the soap.   _____

Name _____

Spotlight on Athletes

12	Athletes must be fit to play in a sport. Much of an
23	athlete's time is spent on training. Some athletes run in races
34	for miles and miles. They train by running many miles every
46	week. It takes many months of training to run in a race.
55	Most athletes need to do weight training. Lifting weights
66	helps to make them strong. Some athletes need to be strong
80	to hit a home run. Or to pitch a ball at a high speed.
90	Athletes must watch what they eat. They need to eat
100	foods high in protein, such as eggs and cheese. Athletes
111	must also watch their weight. If they gain too much weight,
118	it may change the way they play.
128	Last, athletes need to have a good night's sleep. They
143	need a lot of rest so they can be on the top of their game!

1. Underline words in the story with the consonant sounds:
ch, th, -tch.

2. Why do athletes do weight training?

_____

3. What kinds of food must an athlete eat?

_____

_____

Name _____

One-Syllable Words

> Sometimes two consonants together stand for one sound.
> fi**sh**　　　**ph**oto　　　ki**ng**　　　**wh**en

A. Choose words in the box that have the same consonant sound as each of the words below. Write the words on the lines.

wash	gang	whisk	phone	whiz	sheet
wheat	photo	shack	rung	graph	hang

1. sting　_____gang_____　_____　_____

2. shield　_____　_____　_____

3. phase　_____　_____　_____

4. what　_____　_____　_____

B. Underline the word with the _sh, ph, -ng,_ or _wh-_ sound in each sentence. Write the word on the line. Circle the sound.

1. I filled my _____dish_____ with snacks.

   plate　　　hand　　　<u>dish</u>

2. The _____ of the seal pup was cute.

   play　　　photo　　　tale

3. That blue _____ is huge!

   whale　　　fly　　　snail

4. He _____ the bell to end the game.

   hit　　　rang　　　played

Name _____

Multi-Syllable Words

> Sometimes two consonants together stand for one sound.
> di**sh**rag   gra**ph**ic   ri**ng**let   buck**wh**eat

A. Read the words in each row. Underline the word with a *sh*, *ph*, *-ng*, or *wh*- consonant sound. Write the word on the line.

1. hopeful   joyful   <u>wishful</u>   _wishful_

2. helpful   ringside   sloppy   _____

3. windy   watchful   wholesale   _____

4. flapjack   catfish   reptile   _____

5. swinging   snappy   smokestack   _____

6. drifted   phonics   fellow   _____

B. Read the sentences. Underline the word that has a *sh*, *ph*, *-ng*, or *wh*- consonant sound. Write the word on the line. Circle the consonants that make one sound.

1. We found an old <u>photograph</u> in a trunk.   _photograph_

2. I picked up a pink seashell on the beach.   _____

3. The pony whinnies at the cats.   _____

4. His nephew is in a race today.   _____

5. We have ringside seats for the game.   _____

6. I will whitewash the bench today.   _____

Name _____

Stingrays Sting!

10	The sea is home to many animals. Whales and dolphins
22	live in the sea. Many fish live there, too. Stingrays are a
35	kind of fish that lives in the sea. Many stingrays live in the
40	shallow waters along the coast.
49	Stingrays are related to sharks, but look very different.
59	They have wide flat bodies. Both sharks and stingrays do
62	not have bones.
71	Stingrays eat different kinds of fish. They eat shellfish,
82	such as crabs. Some stingrays can grow to about seven feet
89	long and weigh up to 790 pounds!
100	A stingray has a whip-like tail and a sharp spine. The
111	stingray uses its spine to protect itself. Its sharp spine can
124	cut into the skin of its enemy. The cut will sting and be
125	painful!

1. Underline words in the story that have these consonant sounds: *sh, ph, -ng,* and *wh-*.

2. What sea animal is a stingray related to?

_____

3. What does a stingray look like?

_____

_____

Name _____

One-Syllable Words

> Some words have three consonants that come together, such as *scr, spr, str, thr, spl, shr,* and *squ.*
>
> **scr**ape   **spr**ing   **str**ing   **thr**ow   **spl**at   **shr**ew   **squ**at

A. Read the words in each row. Underline the word with a three-letter blend. Write the word on the line. Circle the letters that make the blend.

1. steam   <u>scream</u>   sleet   _(scr)eam_____
2. spin   space   sprain   _____
3. string   sting   stick   _____
4. thump   thrust   trust   _____
5. splice   spice   spike   _____
6. shop   shift   shrub   _____
7. squint   sink   sight   _____

B. Read each sentence. Underline the word that makes a three-letter consonant blend sound. Write the word on the line. Circle the letters that make the blend.

1. The flag has red and white <u>stripes</u>.   _(str)ipes_____
2. I need blue thread for my pants.   _____
3. Be safe and strap in your seatbelt.   _____
4. I think my socks shrunk in the wash!   _____
5. We have to go to the green square on the map.   _____
6. The bird sat in the tree and screeched at the window.   _____

Name _____

Multi-Syllable Words

> Some words have three consonants that come together at the beginning of a word to form a blend.
>
> **scr**eechy   wide**spr**ead   pin**str**ipe   **thr**owback
> **spl**ashy   **shr**ugging   **squ**eaky

A. Sort the words in the box. Write each word under the correct heading. Underline the 3-letter consonant blend.

> offspring   strapless   squarely   thrifty
>
> throwing   spraying   sunstroke   squeezing

str as in *striking*	*spr* as in *springtime*	*thr* as in *thrilling*	*squ* as in *squeaky*
strapless	_____	_____	_____
_____	_____	_____	_____

B. Underline the word that has a 3-letter blend in each sentence. Write the word on the line to complete the sentence.

1. The rain was _____ splashing _____ on the windowsill.

   sweeping   spilling   splashing

2. They are _____ the paint off the box.

   scraping   skinning   slipping

3. We had a _____ time at the picnic.

   spending   splendid   standoff

4. The theater is _____ a new film.

   looking   watching   screening

Name _____

Spring Has Sprung!

10	Kate sprinted into the kitchen. Sammy, the pet pug, was
22	scratching at the back door. He wanted to go out. Then there
29	was a scraping sound in the yard.
38	"Dad is that you?" Kate screamed through the window.
49	"We are on the porch, Kate," Dad yelled. "It's hot today,
57	Mom and I are putting up the screens."
63	Kate asked, "How can I help?"
74	Mom smiled. "You can water the plants. But put on some
80	sunscreen first. It's very sunny today."
90	Kate put on sunscreen and her striped hat. Then she
101	went out to spray the plants with the hose. Water splashed
113	on Sammy and he got wet. Then Kate squatted to look at
124	the plants. She saw that many of the plants were sprouting
135	leaves. When Kate was done, she put on the sprinkler to
138	soak the grass.
148	Soon it was lunchtime. They sat on the screened-in porch
158	and ate shrimp sandwiches. Kate told Mom and Dad about
167	the plants. Then she grinned. "Spring has sprung, today!"

1. Underline words in the story with 3-letter consonant blends.

2. What did Kate do before she went outside?

_____

3. What did Kate do when she went outside?

_____

Name _____

One-Syllable Words

> Sometimes the letters c and g have a soft sound. The letter c can make a soft /s/ sound. The letter g can make a soft /j/ sound.
>
>   <u>c</u>ell   ni<u>c</u>e   pa<u>g</u>e
>   <u>g</u>em   bad<u>ge</u>

A. Read the words in each row. Underline the word with a soft c or g in each row. Write the word on the line. Circle the letter c or g that makes the soft /s/ or /j/ sound.

1. cut   <u>since</u>   cat   _sinⓒe_

2. ridge   gave   grid   _____

3. grain   grape   fringe   _____

4. face   fact   fair   _____

5. clamp   cane   cage   _____

6. crease   cease   crest   _____

B. Underline the word with a soft c or g sound in each sentence. Write the word on the line.

1. Stan made a tasty meal with <u>rice</u>.   _rice_

2. Can you nudge him so he wakes up?   _____

3. Lin has some change to pay the bill.   _____

4. We went ice skating on the pond.   _____

5. The window pane has a smudge on it.   _____

6. We will sing and dance in the class play.   _____

Name _____

Multi-Syllable Words

> Sometimes the letters c and g have a soft sound. The
> letter c can make a soft /s/ sound. The letter g can
> make a soft /j/ sound.
>
> re**c**ent   pri**c**eless   enga**ge**
>   tra**g**ic   gad**ge**t

A. Sort the words. Write the words under the correct heading.

> magic   graceful   image   city
> menace   strangely   citrus   budget

soft c: /s/ as in ice

1. _____graceful_____

2. _____

3. _____

4. _____

soft g: /j/ as in age or ridge

5. _____

6. _____

7. _____

8. _____

**B. Read the story. Underline the words with the soft c
and soft g sound.**

> Once upon a time, there was a prince. He lived in a
> palace. It was located on a high ridge on the edge of a cliff.
> There was a village in the valley below. He went there to
> find a princess to wed. He saw a pretty woman named
> Cindy. He gave her a necklace. He convinced her to be his
> bride.

Name _____

King's Message

10   Martin Luther King, Jr., spent most of his life fighting

21 for civil rights. At that time in the United States, African

31 Americans did not have the same rights as white people.

42 King believed people of all races must be treated the same.

49 He wanted the laws to be changed.

57   King staged peaceful protests and sit-ins. Many people

67 challenged King and what he believed. King did not give

78 up. He went from city to city and gave engaging speeches.

87 Many people admired King and his message. He convinced

97 people with his speeches. King pledged that he would not

108 give up. He spoke of his dream for a better world.

119   In 1964, Congress passed the Civil Rights Act. It gave the

129 same rights to all people. King's dream had come true.

---

1. Underline the words in the passage with the soft *c* and *g* sounds.

2. What did Martin Luther King, Jr., want for all people?

_____

_____

3. What happened in 1964?

_____

_____

Name _____

One-Syllable Words

> In some letter pairs, one of the letters is silent and is not pronounced.
>
> **wr**ite   **kn**ob   **gn**u
>   la**mb**   **sc**ent

A. Choose two words from the box with the same silent letter as each of the words below. Write the words on the line.

gnome	climb	wring	knee	scab
numb	reign	knight	scene	wrote

1. wren _____wring_____   _____wrote_____

2. knot _____   _____

3. gnat _____   _____

4. comb _____   _____

5. scat _____   _____

B. Read the sentences. Underline the word with a silent letter. Write the word on the line.

1. I will <u>write</u> a note to him. _____write_____

2. I cut the cheese with a knife. _____

3. The boy signed the book. _____

4. Please pick up the crumbs from the cake. _____

5. I liked the last scene in the play. _____

6. Dad used a wrench to fix the sink. _____

Name _____

Multi-Syllable Words

In some letter pairs, one of the letters is silent and is not pronounced.

wrapped   **kn**apsack   resi**gn**

cli**mb**ing   **sc**olded

A. Read each sentence. Underline the words that have a silent letter.

1. I will be <u>climbing</u> up the big hill today.

2. He is wringing out his wet swimming trunks.

3. We have lab time in science class.

4. The athlete is kneeling at the start line.

5. The boss resigned from his job.

6. I have a wristwatch to help me tell time.

B. Read each sentence. Underline the word that has a silent letter. Write the word on the line.

1. She is a fine <u>writer</u>. _____writer_____

2. Is he knocking on the door? _____

3. Did he assign some math problems? _____

4. The plumbing in my home needs to be fixed. _____

5. This is a very scenic place with lots of trees and lakes.

   _____

6. We saw a shipwreck on the reef. _____

Name _____

Wren Knits

9	"Can you teach me to knit?" Wren asks Grandpop.
20	"I will, but it takes time. You must go slow," Grandpop
28	says. Grandpop hands Wren two knitting needles. "Hold
38	them with your thumbs and fingers. Let your wrists move."
48	Grandpop shows Wren how to make a knot and stitches.
61	Wren tries to knit. It is not easy. Wren misses a stitch, and
73	gets mad. She throws the needles on the desk. Wren makes a
81	scene and runs away. Grandpop waits. He knits.
93	Wren comes back. "I am sorry I got mad. May I try
102	again?" Grandpop keeps knitting his design. Wren sits and
113	makes a knot. She stitches. When the yarn gets knotty, Wren
123	unknots it. She takes her time. Grandpop beams. "It takes
129	time to learn a new skill."

---

1. Underline the words with the silent letter sounds: *wr, kn, gn, mb,* and *sc.*

2. What happens when Wren misses a stitch?

_____

3. What does Grandpop do when Wren runs away?

_____

Name _____

One-Syllable Words

> When the letters *er, ir, ur,* and *or* work together, they
> make the /ûr/ sound, as in *her*
>
> h**er**   sk**ir**t   f**ur**   w**or**m

**A. Read each sentence. Underline the words with the /ûr/
sound. Write the word on the line.**

1. Did you see the <u>worm</u> inching along?   _____worm_____

2. I am on the verge of getting a nasty cold.   _____

3. Lee and Jack take turns playing the game.   _____

4. Shelley dug up the dirt and put it in a pile.   _____

5. Ferns are plants that grow in the shade.   _____

**B. Underline the words with the /ûr/ sound. Write the word on
the line.**

1. The blue and white _____skirt_____ was on sale.

   <u>skirt</u>   tie   slip

2. I locked my bike to a pole by the _____.

   curb   tube   cube

3. The _____ is sitting on a tree branch.

   kitten   bat   bird

4. It takes a lot of _____ to walk a tightrope.

   spunk   nerve   guts

5. The class has a great deal of _____ to do.

   things   math   work

Name _____

Multi-Syllable Words

When the letters *er, ir, ur,* and *or* work together, they make the /ûr/ sound, as in *hermit*

h**er**mit   b**ir**dbath   b**ur**row   w**or**kday

A. Underline the word with the /ûr/ sound in each row. Write the word on the line.

1. <u>sternly</u>   stopping   solving   _____sternly_____

2. quickly   quest   quirky   _____

3. pressing   timely   hurtful   _____

4. buses   tractor   minivan   _____

5. better   bringing   briefcase   _____

6. waking   worldly   rowing   _____

B. Read the sentences. Underline the word with the /ûr/ sound in each sentence. Write the word on the line. Circle the letters that make the /ûr/ sound.

1. It is <u>urgent</u> that she gets the message.   ⬭urgent⬭ _____

2. My classmate Phil is very strange and quirky!   _____

3. The tractor got stuck in the mud.   _____

4. I felt concern for my sick pal.   _____

5. We saw a blackbird in a nest in a tree.   _____

6. She was worthy of all the praise.   _____

Name _____

Ant and Grasshopper

12	It was a hot, summer day. Ant was working in the field.
24	He was picking up kernels of wheat in the dirt. He looked
29	up when he saw Grasshopper.
39	"Chirp, chirp, *la, la, la,*" sang Grasshopper as he hopped
48	around. "Will you come and play with me, Ant?"
59	"I cannot play," said Ant as he turned to Grasshopper. "I
68	am working to put away food for the winter."
78	"Bah!" said Grasshopper. "Winter is a long way off. First,
86	come play with me. Then you can work."
96	Soon, summer turned to fall. Then fall turned to winter.
105	The fields were covered in snow. Grasshopper's tummy was
116	empty and hurting. He needed food to eat. He staggered to
128	Ant's hill. When Ant saw him, he cried, "What in the world
139	were you thinking? You did not put away food for winter!"
149	Grasshopper moaned, "I didn't have time to work. I was
153	too busy having fun."
164	"Next time you will know what to do!" Ant said sternly.
171	Then he gave Grasshopper a nice meal.

1. Underline the words in the story with the /ûr/ sound.

2. Why didn't Grasshopper have any food for the winter?

_____

3. Why didn't Ant have to worry when it was wintertime?

_____

Name _____

One-Syllable Words

> When the letters *ar* work together, they make the vowel sound /är/.
>
> c**ar**   j**ar**   st**ar**

A. Read each row of words. Underline the word with the /är/ sound. Write the word on the line.

1. <u>barge</u>	bang	badge	_____barge_____
2. back	bark	bait	_____
3. harm	hand	hatch	_____
4. shape	shake	sharp	_____
5. smell	smart	smash	_____
6. damp	ding	dark	_____

B. Read each sentence. Underline the word with the /är/ sound. Write the word on the line.

1. The <u>car</u> needs a tune up. _____car_____

2. Can you find your name on the chart? _____

3. I knitted a red and white scarf for my pal. _____

4. There is a shark alert at the beach. _____

5. The sun is a star we can see in the daytime. _____

6. Sandy got the lead part in the class play _____

7. The cart was filled with plants. _____

Name _____

Multi-Syllable Words

> When the letters *ar* work together, they make the vowel sound /är/.
>
> p**ar**ty   sp**ar**kling   g**ar**bage   landm**ar**k

A. Read each row of words. Underline the word with the /är/ sound. Write the word on the line. Circle the letters that spell the /är/ sound.

1. longest   <u>largest</u>   landmass   _____largest_____

2. cabin   canteen   cargo   _____

3. handstand   cartwheel   backflip   _____

4. pardon   paycheck   pantry   _____

5. scanty   scenic   scarlet   _____

6. garlic   gladly   grateful   _____

B. Read each sentence. Underline the word with the /är/ sound. Write the word on the line. Circle the letters that spell the /är/ sound.

1. The <u>artist</u> made a painting of a landscape.   _____artist_____

2. The postcard was sent last week from Germany.   _____

3. The leaves need to be raked in the backyard.   _____

4. There is a coffee stain on the carpet.   _____

5. They will harvest the crops soon.   _____

6. We planted beans and radishes in our garden.   _____

Name _____

The Birthday Party

10	Carla and Mark are twins. Today is their tenth birthday.
18	They are getting ready to have a party.
31	"Dad, can you take us to the market? We still need a few
40	things for the party," Carla said as she smiled."
52	"Sure thing," Dad said as he opened the car door with his
53	key.
63	At the market, Mark put charcoal, turkey dogs, and buns
75	in the shopping cart. Carla picked up a tray of tasty peach
76	tarts.
88	"Let's not forget a carton of eggs to bake the cake," Dad
91	reminded the twins.
101	When they returned home, Dad fixed up the backyard. He
114	put tables and benches on the deck. He set up the grill. Carla
119	and Mark baked the cake.
130	At 3:00 o'clock sharp, kids started to arrive by the carload!
140	Clark, the twins' dog, began barking. When everyone was in
151	the backyard, the party really got started. The kids began to
157	sing "Happy Birthday." Clark barked, too!

1. Underline the words in the story with the /är/ sound.

2. What did Carla, Mark, and Dad buy at the market?

_____

_____

3. Why did Clark begin barking?

_____

Name _____

One-Syllable Words

> When the letters *or* are together, they make the /ôr/ sound.
>
> c<u>or</u>n   s<u>ore</u>   c<u>oar</u>se

A. Read each sentence. Underline the word with the /ôr/ sound. Sort and write the words in the chart below.

1. I saw a blackbird <u>soar</u> high up in the sky.

2. Can you tell me more about the dance contest?

3. Many kids were born in the month of May in my class.

4. They had sore legs from running in the relay race.

5. The lion's roar woke the fox sleeping in a hole.

6. The storm damaged many trees.

or	ore	oar
		soar

B. Read each sentence. Underline the word with the /ôr/ sound. Write the word on the line.

1. The brave knight held a <u>sword</u> in his right hand. _____sword_____

2. The home team will score a goal soon. _____

3. The boar is a kind of wild pig. _____

4. Set the table with some knives and forks. _____

5. I like to eat my lunch on the porch. _____

Name _____

Multi-Syllable Words

> When the letters *or* are together, they make the /ôr/ sound.
>
> c**or**nmeal   sc**ore**board   h**oar**der

A. Underline the word in each row with the /ôr/ sound. Write the word on the line. Circle the letters that spell the /ôr/ sound.

1. transit   <u>transport</u>   transcend   _transp**or**t_

2. seashore   seaside   seashell   _____

3. monthly   money   morning   _____

4. excuse   explore   explode   _____

5. boarder   braided   bracelet   _____

6. vacate   valid   vapor   _____

B. Read each sentence. Underline the word with the /ôr/ sound in each sentence. Write the word on the line.

1. They went <u>aboard</u> the plane at nine o'clock. _____aboard_____

2. The shoreline has white, sandy beaches. _____

3. The storefront had a blue and green display. _____

4. The forest is dense with green pine trees. _____

5. I peeked through the porthole on the boat. _____

6. The acorns dropped from the giant oak tree. _____

Name _____

Seaports

11	A seaport is a harbor for ships, boats, and barges. Some
20	ships carry goods. Others carry people. Ships and barges
30	dock at seaports to load or unload freight and passengers.
40	Ships and barges transport goods from port to port along
49	a seaboard. Some goods are transported from around the
59	world. Nations trade things they grow and make with each
70	other. The goods a nation sells are called exports. The goods
79	a nation buys from other places are called imports.
89	Corn, wheat, and cotton are some of the crops that
98	the United States exports to places around the world.
107	The United States imports things like clothing, cars, and
108	computers.
120	All along the coasts of the United States, there are lots of
129	seaports. They are the gateways for trading. Some seaports
138	connect to rivers that can transport goods inland, too.

1. Underline words in the passage with the /ôr/ sound.

2. What crops does the United States export?

_____

_____

3. What things does the United States import?

_____

Name _____

One-Syllable Words

> When the letters *eer*, *ere*, and *ear* are together, they make the /îr/ sound.
>
> d**eer**   h**ere**   h**ear**

A. Underline the words that have the /îr/ sound in each sentence. Then sort the words in the chart below.

1. Mack <u>clears</u> his desk to write a note.

2. The deer hid behind the pine trees.

3. Can you get here by lunchtime?

4. The object is shaped like a sphere.

5. The store is near Pine and Grove streets.

6. I can steer the car down this rocky road.

eer	*ere*	*ear*
		clears

B. Underline the word that has the /îr/ sound in each sentence. Then write the word on the line.

1. We went out the <u>rear</u> door. _____rear_____

2. I shifted gears on my bike as I went up the hill. _____

3. The kids gave a big cheer for their team. _____

4. She has a smear of paint on her face. _____

5. The man combs his long beard every day. _____

6. I hear the bell ringing for class. _____

Name _____

Multi-Syllable Words

When the letters *eer, ere*, and *ear* are together, they make the /îr/ sound.

ch**eer**ful   h**ere**by   t**ear**drop

A. Underline the word with the /îr/ sound in each row. Write the word on the line. Circle the letters that spell the *îr* sound.

1. <u>severe</u>   happy   peaceful   sev(ere)

2. silly   sincere   simply   _____

3. clearest   closest   clipping   _____

4. pinkie   pioneer   pillow   _____

5. digging   digest   dearest   _____

B. Read each sentence. Underline the word with the /îr/ sound. Write the word on the line.

1. The punishment for speeding is very <u>severe</u>.   severe

2. The boy had teardrops
   painted on his face for the party.   _____

3. Fran was cheerful after winning the contest.   _____

4. The bus was veering away from the traffic.   _____

5. Miss Peach had to interfere in the game.   _____

Name _____

The <u>Deer</u> Family

10   Moose, elk, mule deer, and reindeer live in different parts

20 of the Western Hemisphere. They are all members of the

31 deer family. Deer have a keen sense of hearing, sight, and

41 smell. They can sense when there are predators nearby. Deer

52 will steer away from them. They know that danger is near!

63   Deer feed on plants in forests and in open clearings. They

69 eat grass, leaves, weeds, and twigs.

79   Male deer grow antlers. Antlers look like horns and are

89 made of bone. Deer shed their antlers each year. Female

100 reindeer are the only female deer that grow antlers. A moose

113 is the tallest of all kinds of deer. It can weigh nearly 1,800

125 pounds. A male elk's antlers can reach nearly 4 feet above its

138 head. A mule deer has large ears that are like a mule's ears.

152 You can tell a mule deer from other kinds of deer. It has a

161 white patch near its rear side, or hind legs.

---

1. Underline all the words in the story with an /îr/ sound, as in *deer*.

2. What do deer eat?

_____

_____

3. How can you tell a mule deer from other kinds of deer?

_____

_____

Name _____

One-Syllable Words

> When the letters *are, air, ear,* and *ere* are together, they make the /âr/ sound.
>
> c**are**　　　h**air**　　　w**ear**　　　th**ere**

A. Underline the word with the /âr/ sound in each row. Write the word on the line. Circle the letters with the /âr/ sound.

1. <u>hare</u>　　hate　　hand　　_____(hare)_____

2. these　　where　　this　　_____

3. land　　lamb　　lair　　_____

4. tear　　team　　term　　_____

5. fine　　fair　　fast　　_____

B. Underline the word with the /âr/ sound that completes each sentence. Write the word on the line.

1. I will _____share_____ my peanuts with you.

　　get　　　　eat　　　　<u>share</u>

2. Please sit in the _____ next to me.

　　star　　　　chair　　　　car

3. Let's split the _____ pie in half.

　　store　　　　tart　　　　pear

4. That looks like a _____ dime.

　　rare　　　　part　　　　sharp

5. Do you know _____ the class will meet today?

　　where　　　　wore　　　　worm

Name _____

Multi-Syllable Words

When the letters *are, air, ear,* and *ere* are together, they make the /âr/ sound.

c**are**ful   h**air**less   w**ear**ing   nowh**ere**

A. Underline the word with the /âr/ sound in each row. Write the word on the line. Circle the letters that spell the /âr/ sound.

1. <u>stairway</u>   donut   cupcake   st**air**way

2. away   alarm   aware   _____

3. blacken   bearish   braided   _____

4. hairy   hardly   handy   _____

5. wellness   wagon   welfare   _____

6. standstill   staircase   stampede   _____

7. nowhere   notice   nosy   _____

B. Read each sentence. Underline the word with the /âr/ sound. Write the word on the line.

1. How will you <u>prepare</u> for the spelling test?   prepare

2. The store is closed so we have to shop elsewhere.   _____

3. Alma had a bad nightmare last night.   _____

4. The plumber will repair the leak.   _____

5. Are you wearing the jeans to the park?   _____

Name _____

The Tortoise and the <u>Hare</u>

11	One day, Hare dared Tortoise to a race. Hare smugly said,
23	"I dare you to race me. I can run faster than anyone!"
34	Tortoise glared at Hare. "That's an unfair thing to say. You
47	may be fast. But I swear that I know how to beat you!"
58	Hare declared, "You cannot win. I have a flair for racing."
68	Tortoise stared at Hare. "Beware! I am prepared to race
71	you and win!"
82	The next day, the pair stepped up to the starting line.
92	They were wearing T-shirts with their names printed in red.
102	When the race began, Tortoise plodded along. Hare was far
114	ahead so he decided to have a snack and take a nap.
124	When Hare woke up, Tortoise was nowhere to be seen.
136	Hare hopped through the air. But his last hop was too late.
146	At the finish line, Tortoise was sitting in an armchair
158	eating a pear. He said to Hare, "Slowly does it every time!"
167	In despair, Hare slumped down beside the winner! "This
178	race was a real nightmare. I was unaware you were so
179	tricky."

1. Underline all the words in the story with the /âr/ sound, as in *hare.*

2. Why did Hare have a snack and take a nap during the race?

_____

3. Why did Tortoise win the race?

_____

Name _____

One-Syllable Words

> The /ou/ sound can be spelled with the letters *ou* or *ow*.
>
> c**ou**nt   t**ow**n

A. Underline the word with the /ou/ sound in each row. Write the word on the line.

1. sore   sock   <u>sound</u>   _____sound_____

2. crow   crown   cramp   _____

3. shout   shop   shock   _____

4. brink   break   brown   _____

5. trunk   trout   trail   _____

6. scout   score   scrap   _____

B. Circle the words in the box with the /ou/ sound. Write the words you circled. Answer the clues below.

> slump   howl   trout   pouch   plow
>
> (mouth)   woe   cloud   blob   you

1. This is a part of your face. _____mouth_____

2. This is what a wolf does. _____

3. This is something you use to hold money. _____

4. This is something you see in the sky. _____

5. This is something a farmer does to a field. _____

6. This is a kind of fish. _____

Name _____

Multi-Syllable Words

> The /ou/ sound can be spelled with the letters *ou* or *ow*.
>
> gr**ou**ndhog d**ow**nward

A. Read each row of words. Underline the word with the /ou/ sound. Write the word on the line. Underline the letters that spell the /ou/ sound.

1.	about	actor	advise	about
2.	stopping	spoken	shower	_____
3.	tropic	trustful	tryout	_____
4.	rainy	cloudy	sunny	_____
5.	powder	portly	provide	_____
6.	permit	proudly	parkway	_____
7.	flower	flopping	flocking	_____

B. Underline the words with the /ou/ sound. Write the word or words on the lines.

1. The cat is pouncing on the ground! pouncing ground

2. The best playground is uptown. _____ _____

3. The dog barked loudly at the prowler. _____ _____

4. Jill got two trousers and a nightgown. _____ _____

5. The hard rain is drowning the sunflowers. _____

6. The trees in the campground are sprouting leaves. _____ _____

Name _____

A <u>Powerful</u> Storm

9	Good morning, I'm Kelly Brown. I am standing outside
20	of city hall. The sound of the storm is deafening. Expect
29	pounding rain and howling winds all around town. The
41	storm is so loud that I cannot hear myself speak! There are
51	some power outages around the city and in nearby towns.
61	We hope that there will not be a power blackout.
71	This powerful storm will lose strength soon. It is now
81	moving to the south. This evening, we expect cloudy skies.
92	For all the gardeners out there, I know that your flowers
100	are drowning. Expect light showers between now and
108	Friday. Hopefully your flowers will rebound next week.
120	There will be more rain later in the month. I am predicting
129	that there will not be a drought this year!

1. Underline words in the story with the /ou/ sound.

2. What is the storm like as Kelly Brown is speaking?

_____

_____

3. What does Kelly Brown predict?

_____

Name _____

One-Syllable Words

> When the letters *oi* and *oy* are together, they make the /oi/ sound.
>
> p**oi**nt   t**oy**

A. Underline the word with the /oi/ sound in each row. Write the word on the line. Then underline the letters that spell the /oi/ sound.

1. <u>coin</u>   can   cone   _____coin_____

2. sprain   sole   soy   _____

3. bowl   boil   break   _____

4. most   must   moist   _____

5. broil   mix   bake   _____

B. Underline the word with the /oi/ sound in each sentence. Write the word on the line. Underline the letters that spell the /oi/ sound.

1. The <u>soil</u> is brown and sandy.   _____soil_____

2. The snake is coiled around a tree branch.   _____

3. The baby is playing with the toy panda.   _____

4. The grass is green and moist.   _____

5. The oil in the pan is hot.   _____

6. I always feel great joy on my birthday.   _____

Name _____

Multi-Syllable Words

When the letters *oi* and *oy* are together, they make the /oi/ sound.

p**oi**nty   b**oy**ish

A. Underline the words in the box with the /oi/ sound. Write the words on the lines below to answer the clues.

shopping	loyal	transmit	oinking	subway
annoy	hungry	<u>poison</u>	charcoal	royal

1. This will make you sick.   _____poison_____

2. This is what you do when you bother someone.   _____

3. This is a true friend.   _____

4. This is a king and queen.   _____

5. This is a sound that pigs make.   _____

B. Underline the word with the /oi/ sound in each sentence. Write the word on the line. Circle the /oi/ sound.

1. Please wrap the meat in <u>tinfoil</u>.   _____tinf(oi)l_____

2. She is employed by the city.   _____

3. This is such a joyful day!   _____

4. The voyage on the ship lasted two months.   _____

5. He is spoiling the fun at the party.   _____

6. The class was noisy at recess.   _____

Name _____

Roy's Diner

12	Roy has a diner. It is always noisy and busy because the
24	food is so tasty. Roy employs Joy and Floyd. They wait on
26	the customers.
38	"Roy, what is the dish of the day?" asked Joy on Friday.
50	"One choice is soy patties. It will be served with rice and
61	soy sauce," Roy replied. "I will also boil some beans. Then
68	I'll flash fry them in hot oil."
78	The dinner customers began to arrive at five o'clock. Joy
83	and Floyd were very helpful.
95	Mr. Troy ordered a soy burger and fries. He did not eat
97	it all.
106	"Can I wrap your leftovers in tinfoil?" asked Floyd.
115	Then Joy smiled, "I hope you enjoyed your meal!"
125	Mr. Troy left with a full tummy and his leftovers.
137	By the end of the night, Joy and Floyd had served over
139	100 meals!
149	"I am really happy. We have such loyal customers!" Roy
162	said. Then Roy invited Joy and Floyd to sit down for a tasty
170	meal! They ate soy patties with sweet corn.

1. Underline the words in the story with the /oi/ sound, as in *boy*.

2. Who does Roy employ at his diner?

_____

3. What is Roy serving tonight?

_____

Name _____

One-Syllable Words

The letters *oo, u, u_e, ew, ue,* and *ou* can make the /ü/ sound.

t<u>oo</u> fl<u>u</u> t<u>u</u>n<u>e</u> d<u>ew</u> c<u>ue</u> y<u>ou</u>

A. Read each word in the box. Write each word under the correct heading below.

clue	through	flute	threw	zoo
lute	knew	due	group	tooth

oo in *room*	*ue* in *blue*	*u_e* in *dune*	*ew* in *dew*	*ou* in *soup*
zoo	_____	_____	_____	_____
_____	_____	_____	_____	_____

B. Underline the word with the /ü/ sound in each sentence. Write the word on the line.

1. Dad uses a <u>tool</u> to fix the window. _____ tool _____

2. I used glue to make a puppet. _____

3. My dog likes to chew her bone. _____

4. I eat ice cream with a spoon. _____

5. I need a red tube of paint. _____

6. School will be closed if it snows. _____

7. She drew a cloud next to the sun. _____

8. I ate soup for lunch. _____

Name _____

Multi-Syllable Words

The letters *oo, u, u_e, ew, ue,* and *ou* can make the /ü/ sound.

t<u>oo</u>lbox   t<u>u</u>na   sal<u>ute</u>   cash<u>ew</u>   cl<u>ue</u>less   regr<u>ou</u>p

A. Underline the word with the /ü/ sound in each row. Write the word on the line.

1. getting	<u>grouping</u>	graceful	grouping
2. respond	greatness	renew	_____
3. rudely	lively	barely	_____
4. unkind	untie	untrue	_____
5. shopping	shampoo	stocking	_____
6. smoothly	smallness	sitting	_____

B. Underline the word with the /ü/ sound in each sentence. Write the word on the line. Underline the letters that spell the /ü/ sound.

1. Does your lunch <u>include</u> a snack? _____ incl<u>u</u>de _____

2. My mom withdrew from the race. _____

3. Did she give a truthful statement? _____

4. The class played kazoos at the concert. _____

5. I used a coupon to get a discount. _____

6. The red balloon floated in the sky. _____

Name _____

Kazoos, Flutes, and Tubas!

10	On a cool June night under a full moon, something
20	strange happened. A band of animals made their debut at
29	the Hollywood Bowl! It's true! The group performed on
35	Tuesday at the first summer concert.
44	The band had roosters playing flutes. There were also
54	a few raccoons playing bassoons. And a group of wild
63	baboons played tubas. There was even a goose crooning
65	happy tunes.
73	Throughout the night, the crowd clapped and cheered.
83	They were impressed by this talented group. Who knew that
88	animals could carry a tune?
100	At the end of the concert, the goose gave the final cue.
110	Some of the animals picked up kazoos and blew lively
121	tunes. Others played pairs of spoons. This put the crowd in
133	a jolly mood. Everyone got up and danced and hooted to the
134	music.

1. Underline the words in the story with a /ü/ sound, as in *zoo*.

2. What animals played tubas at the concert?

_____

3. What did the crowd do at the end?

_____

Name _____

One-Syllable Words

> When the letters *oo*, *ou*, and *u* are together, they can make the /ŭ/ sound.
>
> **loo**k   sh**ou**ld   p**u**t

A. Underline the word with the /ŭ/ sound in each row. Write the word on the line.

1. <u>hook</u>   hope   hold   **hook**

2. white   would   work   _____

3. flair   foil   foot   _____

4. pull   plot   pond   _____

5. bring   bush   bash   _____

6. crown   core   could   _____

B. Underline the word with the /ŭ/ sound in each sentence. Write the word on the line. Underline the letters with the /ŭ/ sound.

1. The <u>brook</u> is much smaller than a river.   **brook**

2. He should wear a warm coat today.   _____

3. I will push the shopping cart around the store.   _____

4. The hood on my coat will keep me dry.   _____

5. Could you help me clean up the den?   _____

6. Will you read the book with me?   _____

Name _____

Multi-Syllable Words

> When the letters *oo, ou,* and *u* are together, they can make the /ŭ/ sound.
>
>   **f**<u>**oo**</u>**tstep**   **p**<u>**u**</u>**dding**

A. Read each word in the box. Sort the words by writing each under the correct heading.

footing	pushup	bushy	bookmark	bullish
fully	sooty	bulldog	plywood	cookie

oo as in *handbook*	*u* as in *pushcart*
footing	

B. Underline the word with the /ŭ/ sound in each sentence. Write the word on the line.

1. We are baking <u>cookies</u> today. _____cookies_____

2. She used a pulley to raise the flag. _____

3. Watch your footing on the wet rock! _____

4. The kids played on the wooden horse. _____

5. The bookcase is filled to the top! _____

6. She had a red and yellow pullover top. _____

Name _____

Little Red Riding Hood

12	Little Red packed a tin of cookies. She put on her red
17	woolen cape with a hood.
28	"You should go right to Grandma's house. Do not talk to
31	strangers," said Mom.
44	Little Red set out on foot along a path by the brook. Soon,
55	a wolf appeared. "Where are you going little girl?" he said.
65	"I am going to visit my grandma," said Little Red.
77	Little Red stayed on the path, but the wolf took a shortcut.
86	When he got to Grandma's house, Grandma opened the
97	door. The old lady looked surprised. Then the wolf put her
106	in the closet! He dressed in Grandma's wool nightgown.
116	When Little Red got there, the wolf opened the door.
125	"You look different, Grandma. Your teeth are so big."
136	"The better to eat you with!" yelled the wolf. He chased
138	Little Red.
147	"Help!" cried Little Red. A nearby woodsman heard her
155	and grabbed the wolf. Little Red found Grandma.
164	"We learned a good lesson," said Grandma. "Never talk
166	to strangers!"

1. Underline words in the story that have a /ů/ sound, as in *book*.

2. What was Little Red bringing to Grandma?

_____

3. What lesson did Grandma and Little Red learn?

_____

Name _____

One-Syllable Words

> When the letters *aw, au, al, augh,* and *ough* are together, they make the /ô/ sound.
>
> l**aw**   h**au**l   b**al**d   c**augh**t   b**ough**t

A. Read each row of words. Underline the word with the /ô/ sound. Write the word on the line. Underline the letters that spell the /ô/ sound.

1. then	thin	<u>thaw</u>	_thaw_
2. lamb	launch	lunch	_____
3. stall	staff	stack	_____
4. tart	taught	teach	_____
5. scream	seek	sought	_____
6. small	smog	smart	_____
7. flew	flaw	flow	_____

B. Underline the word with the /ô/ sound in each sentence. Write the word on the line.

1. I will <u>draw</u> a picture of a horse. _draw_

2. The broken toy was not his fault. _____

3. Will you walk to the park? _____

4. I caught a cold on Monday. _____

5. We bought some ice cream at the store. _____

6. The baby just learned how to talk. _____

Name _____

Multi-Syllable Words

When the letters *aw, au, al, augh*, and *ough* are together, they make the /ô/ sound.

dr**aw**ing   bec**au**se   **al**so   d**augh**ter   th**ough**tful

A. Underline the word with the /ô/ sound in each row. Write the word on the line. Underline the letters that spell the /ô/ sound.

1. <u>clawing</u>   clipping   craving   _clawing_____

2. lately   landscape   laundry   _____

3. wasteful   walkway   waiter   _____

4. naughty   nighttime   northward   _____

5. college   coughing   catching   _____

6. awful   artist   armchair   _____

B. Underline the word with the /ô/ sound in each sentence. Write the word on the line. Underline the letters that spell the /ô/ sound.

1. The leaves turned red and yellow in <u>autumn</u>.   _autumn_____

2. We picked the smallest kitten to take home.   _____

3. How old is your daughter?   _____

4. He is a very thoughtful person.   _____

5. There was a line for the seesaw in the park.   _____

6. I can't go to the game because I am not well.   _____

7. Who is talking to your sister?   _____

8. We always take the dog to the park.   _____

Name _____

A Fawn at Dawn

11	It was dawn on a crisp autumn day. Bess and her
20	daughter Shawna were staying at a mountain cabin. Shawna
30	was awake early. She threw a shawl around herself and
40	stepped outside. The snow on the ground was beginning to
41	thaw.
53	As Shawna stood on the deck, she saw a hawk fly by.
64	Suddenly, she saw a deer and her fawn walking on the
74	lawn. They stopped and began munching on bits of grass.
85	It was the smallest fawn Shawna had ever seen! She stood
96	very still. The only thing Shawna could hear was a nearby
97	waterfall.
107	Shawna thought that the deer on the lawn were splendid.
116	At that moment, her mom stepped outside and yawned
126	loudly. Shawna froze. So did the deer. The fawn looked
138	up. The yawn caused the deer and her fawn to run away.
150	Shawna vowed to get up early the next day. She hoped to
158	see the mother deer and her fawn again.

1. Underline the words in the story with the /ô/ sound, as in *yawn*.

2. What did Shawna see as she stood on the deck of the cabin?

_____

3. What caused the deer and its fawn to run away?

_____

Name _____

Multi-Syllable Words

> A closed syllable ends with a consonant. It has a short vowel sound.
>
> n**ap**/k**in**   r**ab**/b**it**   s**un**/s**et**

A. Read each word below. Write the word on the line. Use a slash (/) to divide the word into syllables.

1. problem   _prob/lem_

2. dentist   _____

3. plastic   _____

4. custom   _____

5. catnap   _____

6. helmet   _____

7. ribbon   _____

B. Underline the word with the closed syllable in each sentence. Write the word on the line.

1. I made a wool toy for my <u>kitten</u>.   _kitten_

2. Mom stopped the car at the red signal.   _____

3. I have a test in that subject today.   _____

4. My shirt is made out of cotton.   _____

5. I placed the rubbish in the can.   _____

6. What will happen to our party plans?   _____

7. We will take ice cream on our picnic.   _____

Name _____

Multi-Syllable Words

> A closed syllable ends with a consonant. It has a short vowel sound.
>
> b**an**/d**it**   c**on**/t**ent**   h**id**/d**en**

A. Underline the word with a closed syllable in each row. Write the word on the line. Use a slash (/) to divide the word into syllables.

1. <u>mitten</u>   copy   _____mit/ten_____

2. bagel   button   _____

3. begin   contest   _____

4. skillet   hero   _____

5. hotel   happen   _____

6. trumpet   final   _____

B. Underline the word with a closed syllable in each sentence. Write the word on the line. Use a slash (/) to divide the syllables.

1. We saw the <u>contents</u> of the box.   _____con/tents_____

2. The rabbit jumped into the thick bush.   _____

3. We will leave at sunup.   _____

4. She wore a blue and gold ribbon in her hair.   _____

5. I will fill the basket with flowers.   _____

6. We drove through a tunnel.   _____

Name _____

A Rabbit at the Farm

9	The sisters Brenda and Bristol have a custom every
20	September. They take a trip with Dad to Mrs. Poppit's farm.
30	At the farm they have a picnic and pick pumpkins.
41	This year they drove to the farm on Sunday. Mrs. Poppit
46	was happy to see them.
58	"It is a splendid day," said Mrs. Poppit. "There are lots of
62	pumpkins to be picked."
73	Brenda and Bristol ran down to the field and picked five
81	big pumpkins. Mrs. Poppit's kitten, Tidbit, followed them.
91	The kitten hunted insects and played in the tall grass.
100	Then it was lunchtime. Mrs. Poppit brought a picnic
110	basket with sandwiches. They ate until they were full. Tidbit
118	took a catnap on top of a pumpkin.
128	Then all of a sudden a rabbit appeared. The rabbit
138	hopped over Tidbit's head. Tidbit jumped up and ran after
148	the rabbit. The sisters, Dad, and Mrs. Poppit chased Tidbit.
158	Bristol grabbed Tidbit, and the rabbit jumped into a hole.
167	"What a day," they cried. "We love pumpkin picking."

1. Underline words in the story with closed syllables, as in *rabbit*.

2. What were Brenda, Bristol, and Dad doing?

_____

3. What did the rabbit do after Bristol grabbed Tidbit?

_____

Name _____

Multi-Syllable Words

> An open syllable ends with a vowel and has a long vowel sound.
>
> **pa**per   **pi**lot   **o**pen

A. Underline the word with an open syllable in each row. Write the word on the line. Use a slash (/) to divide the syllables.

1. <u>silent</u>	slipper	shutting	*si/lent*
2. button	baby	burrow	_____
3. forget	expense	digest	_____
4. basic	butter	bunny	_____
5. camping	crazy	charcoal	_____
6. dipper	district	detail	_____
7. rocking	rotate	rugged	_____

B. Underline the word with an open syllable in each sentence. Write the word on the line. Use a slash (/) to divide the syllables.

1. The <u>cocoa</u> tastes great! _____*co/coa*_____

2. The robot looks like a real person! _____

3. The tiger hunts for food in the day. _____

4. Can you wait a moment for me? _____

5. The black raven sat on a rocky cliff. _____

6. The pie has a nutty flavor. _____

Name _____

Multi-Syllable Words

> An open syllable ends with a vowel and has a long vowel sound.
>
> **ba**by   **la**bor   **fa**vor

A. Underline the word with an open syllable in each row. Write the word on the line. Use a slash (/) to divide the syllables.

1. button	<u>bonus</u>	bonnet	_bo/nus_
2. cluster	catnap	climate	_____
3. pilot	pillow	picnic	_____
4. blanket	basic	basket	_____
5. employ	engine	even	_____

B. Underline the word with an open syllable in each sentence. Write the word on the line. Use a slash (/) to divide the syllables.

1. When will the puppet show <u>begin</u>? _____be/gin_____

2. My duty is to keep the classroom clean. _____

3. Jed needs to focus on the math test. _____

4. Brush your teeth so they do not decay. _____

5. Put on an apron to bake the cake. _____

6. I can't resist eating another piece of pie! _____

7. They like to listen to band music. _____

Name _____

Bird Nests

10	Birds' nests <u>provide</u> a safe place for eggs and babies.
20	Nests protect the eggs. Nests keep babies safe from hungry
31	animals and from rain or storms. Birds make cozy nests in
40	secret places, such as between branches in a tree.
53	The female, or mom, lays eggs in the nest. She sits on the
65	eggs to keep them safe and warm. When the eggs hatch, the
76	tiny babies have no feathers. They cannot fly, but they are
87	hungry. And they are vocal. They make lots of noise. The
98	mom and dad birds work hard. They feed and protect the
102	babies in the nest.
112	Then the big moment comes. The babies leave the nest
125	when they can fly. The time for the nest is over until next
132	year. Then the nesting cycle begins again.

---

1. Underline all the words with open syllables, as in *babies*.

2. What does a nest provide for birds?

_____

_____

3. When do baby birds leave the nest?

_____

Name _____

Multi-Syllable Words

> A syllable with a vowel, a consonant, and an *e* at the
> end (VC*e*) has a long vowel sound.
>
> repl**ace** dec**ide** l**one**ly

A. Underline the word with the VC*e* syllable in each row. Write the word on the line.

1. <u>consume</u>   cable   cosmic   _____**consume**_____

2. cleanup   closeup   closet   _____

3. timeless   timid   tidy   _____

4. basket   braiding   bracelet   _____

5. cement   concrete   center   _____

6. below   belong   beehive   _____

7. pilot   polite   photo   _____

B. Underline the word with the VC*e* syllable in each sentence. Write the word on the line.

1. The <u>airplane</u> departed at ten o'clock.   _____**airplane**_____

2. It will take an hour for Sara to finish her homework.   _____

3. She ate her lunch inside the lunchroom.   _____

4. Frank will complete the test by noon.   _____

5. The clown will amuse the kids.   _____

6. We played baseball in the park today.   _____

Name _____

Multi-Syllable Words

> A syllable with a vowel, a consonant, and an *e* at the end (VC*e*) has a long vowel sound.
>
> mist**ake**   handwr**ite**   brushstr**oke**   c**ute**ness

A. Underline the word with a VC*e* syllable in each row. Write the word on the line.

1. <u>advice</u>   charcoal   borrow   **advice** _____

2. seashell   seaside   seamless   _____

3. behind   backpack   backbone   _____

4. refuse   robot   return   _____

5. blindfold   blameless   blanket   _____

6. lifeboat   lifting   lightning   _____

B. Underline the words with a VC*e* syllable in each row. Write the words on the lines.

1. They <u>dislike</u> the <u>seaside</u>.   **dislike** _____   **seaside** _____

2. There is a parachute on the airplane.   _____   _____

3. Brad will complete his homework.   _____   _____

4. She will sit beside me at noontime.   _____   _____

5. I will arrive at your house by dinnertime.   _____   _____

6. That reptile has a long backbone!   _____   _____

Name _____

Donate Your Time!

13   One way you can help out in your town is to donate your
25   time. When you donate your time, you work for free. You do
28   not get wages.

39   People donate time in different ways. You may like to join
51   a group to help clean parks. Maybe you would like to help
65   in a food or clothing drive for those in need. Do you like cats
77   and dogs? Maybe you would like to donate your time at an
79   animal shelter.

91   At a shelter you may be asked to clean cages and replace
101   water pans. At mealtime, you may help feed the animals.
111   Sometimes you may even take a dog for a walk.

122   Do you want to donate your time? Ask your teacher or
132   parents to help you locate places that interest you. Read
143   about what these places do. Ask your parents to take you
155   there. Ask questions and decide if the work is right for you!

1. Underline the two-syllable words in the story with a VCe syllable, as in *timeline*.

2. What are jobs people do when they donate their time at an animal shelter?

_____

_____

3. What are some ways to donate your time?

_____

_____

Name _____

Multi-Syllable Words

When a word ends in a consonant and -*le (el, al,* or *il),*
the -*le* is always pronounced /əl/.

| tab**le** | cam**el** | met**al** | pup**il** |

**A. Underline the word with a final /əl/ syllable in each row. Write
the word on the line.**

1. holder   <u>handle</u>   highlight   _____ *handle* _____

2. mammal   mummy   meaning   _____

3. mimic   mumble   missing   _____

4. sandbag   standby   sample   _____

5. blackness   barrel   backyard   _____

6. squirrel   kitten   rabbit   _____

7. contest   cotton   council   _____

**B. Underline the word with a final /əl/ syllable in each sentence.
Write the word on the line.**

1. He can play high notes on the <u>bugle</u>.   _____ *bugle* _____

2. Please walk the horse to the stable.   _____

3. There was a twinkle in his eyes.   _____

4. I saw cattle on the ranch.   _____

5. The petal fell off of the flower.   _____

6. I will be going to France in April.   _____

Name _____

Multi-Syllable Words

When a word ends in a consonant and -le (el, al, or il), the -le is always pronounced /əl/.

| fab**le** | trav**el** | norm**al** | lent**il** |

A. Read each word in the box. Sort the words by writing each under the correct heading.

handle	final	nickel	gentle
apple	rival	purple	bagel
evil	pencil	formal	camel

-le	-el	-al	-il
handle			

B. Underline the word with an /əl/ final syllable in each sentence. Write the word on the line.

1. I ate a big <u>pickle</u> for a snack.   _____pickle_____

2. He blew a huge bubble in the air!   _____

3. I will wait until noon for you.   _____

4. Please give us a signal to start the race.   _____

5. I was able to finish my homework on time.   _____

6. Greg has a good riddle to tell.   _____

7. She lit a candle on the cake.   _____

Name _____

From Bushels to Bagels!

12	People travel far and wide to buy fresh foods at a farmers'
23	market. One seller sets up a metal table with simple displays
35	of food. Boxes are filled to the brim with peaches, pears, and
46	purple plums! You can buy bagel chips, noodle dishes, a big
58	pickle, and maple candy. You can buy one apple or a bushel
60	of them!
72	The best part about going to a farmers' market is tasting a
82	sample! There may be fresh lentil soup or homemade apple
93	strudel. You can have a little feast as you walk around!
103	One local craft artist might sell a bundle of handmade
114	towels. One may have a table with hats and gloves. At
125	another table, you may find the perfect gift. It might be
136	a candle, a painting, a wood puzzle, or a carved eagle.
144	Farmers' markets are filled with many different choices.
151	There is a little surprise for everyone!

1. Underline all the words in the passage with an /əl/ final syllable.

2. What can people buy at a farmers' market?

_____

_____

3. What kinds of things do local craft artists sell?

_____

_____

Name _____

Multi-Syllable Words

A vowel team syllable has two letters working together to form one vowel sound.

rep**ea**t	ind**ee**d	afr**ai**d	pl**ay**ful	t**ea**cher
pill**ow**	j**oy**ful	b**oa**ting	rel**ie**d	

A. Underline the word with the vowel team syllable in each row. Write the word on the line. Underline the vowel team.

1. <u>p**ea**chy</u>   planting   purple   _____p**ea**chy_____

2. camel   combing   coating   _____

3. partly   peaceful   petting   _____

4. believe   belly   blanket   _____

5. market   major   mailbox   _____

6. raspberry   raisin   radish   _____

7. leaving   lumber   little   _____

B. Underline the word in each sentence with a vowel team syllable. Write the word on the line. Underline the vowel team.

1. I am <u>really</u> tired this morning.   _____really_____

2. The freeway is jammed at rush hour!   _____

3. You can put your jacket on the coatrack.   _____

4. Can I follow you home so I do not get lost?   _____

5. She will remain after class to help.   _____

6. The girl bought a briefcase for her mother.   _____

7. He spoke loudly over the phone.   _____

8. There are red and yellow roses in the vase.   _____

Name _____

Multi-Syllable Words

> A vowel team syllable is when a syllable has two letters working together to form one vowel sound.
>
> s**ea**son   fr**ee**dom   tr**ai**ner   l**ay**er   n**au**ghty
> borr**ow**   b**oy**ish   b**oa**thouse   rel**ie**f   k**ey**hole

A. Underline the word with a vowel team syllable in each row. Write the word on the line. Underline the letters that spell the vowel team.

1. creamy   crumbs   crispy   _____cr**ea**my_____

2. sunny   sunscreen   sample   _____

3. mainly   rewrite   reptile   _____

4. booklet   bracelet   belief   _____

5. summer   subway   simple   _____

6. grateful   growing   graphite   _____

B. Underline the word with the vowel team syllable in each sentence. Write the word on the line. Underline the vowel team.

1. He had a good <u>reason</u> for being late.   _____r**ea**son_____

2. Please don't complain about the test.   _____

3. My cat is toying with the dog.   _____

4. You must look before you cross the roadway!   _____

5. She will relieve the pitcher in the next inning.   _____

6. We both agreed to work together.   _____

Name _____

The Playoff Game

12	It was a hot August day. The playoff game was unreal! It
22	started raining in the last inning. The other team boasted
31	they would beat us. But the score was tied!
40	Maureen was throwing the ball to first base. Suddenly
52	she clutched her elbow and bent over in pain! All of my
61	teammates were groaning in dismay. The relief pitcher ran
73	onto the field. I asked myself, "How will we beat the other
78	team?" We really needed Maureen.
88	Soon the game proceeded and the relief pitcher struck out
99	the other team. Now we needed to score the winning run.
112	Jessie was up at bat when the ball struck his ankle! The team
123	doctor looked at it, and then Jessie walked to first base.
135	I was up next. And I was afraid! But then I thought,
148	"Maybe I can win this game. I have to believe I can!" I
160	swung at the ball with all my might and hit a homerun!
170	"You're a hero," my noisy teammates shouted. "No, I am
173	exhausted!" I replied.

1. Underline all the multi-syllable words with a vowel team syllable.

2. What did the other team boast about?

_____

_____

3. What happened to Jessie?

_____

_____

Name _____

Multi-Syllable Words

> An *r*-controlled vowel syllable has a vowel followed by an *r*.
> p**ar**ty   ord**er**   thi**r**ty   f**or**est   sunb**urn**

A. Underline the words in the box with the *r*-controlled vowel syllable. Use the underlined words to answer the clues below.

> | | | | | | |
> |---|---|---|---|---|---|
> | minus | <u>hornet</u> | patted | marker | robot | purple |
> | hammer | rapid | forty | thirsty | person | patrol |

1. This is an insect. _____hornet_____

2. This is something you hit a nail with. _____.

3. This is a color. _____

4. This is how you feel when you want water. _____

5. This is a human being. _____

6. This is something you can draw with. _____

B. Underline the word in each sentence with the *r*-controlled vowel syllable. Write the word on the line.

1. She got a <u>silver</u> necklace as a present. _____silver_____

2. The surface was slick and shiny. _____

3. This is a perfect sunny day. _____

4. They made soup with turnips and peas. _____

5. The dog was snoring loudly throughout the night! _____

6. The circus is in town for a week. _____

Name _____

Multi-Syllable Words

> An *r*-controlled vowel syllable has a vowel followed by an *r*.
>
> m**ar**ket   spid**er**   th**ir**teen   abs**or**b   f**ur**nish

A. Underline the word in each row with the *r*-controlled vowel syllable. Write the word on the line.

1. <u>actor</u>   actress   acting   _____actor_____

2. hamster   happen   halo   _____

3. shapeless   shivered   shelving   _____

4. cloudless   snowy   stormy   _____

5. bargain   priceless   value   _____

6. daytime   morning   nighttime   _____

B. Underline the word in each sentence with the *r*-controlled vowel syllable. Write the word on the line.

1. It is a <u>dreary</u> gray day.   _____dreary_____

2. The concert will have music and dancing.   _____

3. Please do not disturb your classmate.   _____

4. Mom's garden is full of pretty roses.   _____

5. She was thirsty from jogging.   _____

6. We ate dinner late last night.   _____

Name _____

Artists

9	There are many kinds of artists. There are painters,
18	sculptors, and printmakers. Each uses different kinds of tools.
28	Painters use brushes. They paint on cloth, paper, or wood
37	or even enormous walls. Some use watercolors or tempera,
47	and some use oil paints. Some artists make sketches on
53	paper with charcoal or colored pencils.
64	A sculptor is another kind of artist. A sculptor might make
74	a statue from clay, plaster, or marble. Sculptors use different
85	kinds of carving tools, too. Some use chisels and a hammer
96	on stone or wood. Others use saws. Some even use hot
100	torches to make art.
109	A printmaker is another kind of artist. Printmakers carve
122	or scratch a picture onto a flat piece of wood or a copper
135	plate. Then ink is rolled on the plate and paper is placed on
142	top. The picture transfers onto the paper.
151	Artists works adorn many places. You can certainly see
161	watercolors in museums. But you can also see walls outside
169	covered with colorful paintings. Artist works are everywhere.

1. Underline the two-syllable words in the story with *r*-controlled vowel syllables.

2. Who are different kinds of artists?

   _____

3. Where might you see artist works?

   _____

Name _____

Plurals -*s*

Add an -*s* to a noun to make it a plural noun.

lamp + **s** = **lamps**

A. Write the letter that makes each noun a plural. Then write the plural noun on the line.

1. rock   + _____ s _____ = _____ rocks _____

2. night + _____ = _____

3. prank + _____ = _____

4. camp + _____ = _____

5. band + _____ = _____

6. drink + _____ = _____

B. Read each sentence. Fill in the blank to make the noun in bold a plural. Write the plural noun on the line.

1. The **top**___ s ___ are blue.   _____ tops _____

2. The **girl**_____ like to sing.   _____

3. There are **bell**_____ on the sled.   _____

4. Look at the **map**_____ on the desk.   _____

5. The clock has **hand**_____.   _____

6. The dog stands on two **leg**_____.   _____

7. The **plum**_____ are fresh.   _____

Name _____

Plurals -*es*

> Add an -*es* to words that end in -*ss*, -*sh*, -*ch*, and -*x* to make them plural nouns.
>
> mess + **es** = **me<u>ss</u>es**   lash + **es** = **la<u>sh</u>es**
>
> patch + **es** = **pat<u>ch</u>es**   mix + **es** = **mi<u>x</u>es**

A. Write the letters that will make each noun a plural. Then write the plural noun on the line.

1. **glass** + ___es___ = ___glasses___

2. **fox** + _____ = _____

3. **batch** + _____ = _____

4. **wish** + _____ = _____

5. **pass** + _____ = _____

6. **peach** + _____ = _____

B. Read each sentence. Make the noun in bold plural. Fill in the blank with -*s* or -*es*. Write the plural noun on the line.

1. The **beach**__es__ were crowded.   ___beaches___

2. There were many **dish**_____ of food.   _____

3. Ed saw three **fox**_____.   _____

4. The **ride**_____ were a lot of fun.   _____

5. Our teacher gave us **pass**_____ for the park.   _____

6. We saw **trick**_____ at the show.   _____

Name _____

Grand Oak Trees

11	Oak trees grow in many parts of the United States. Oaks
24	are grand plants. Some oaks can grow to be 100 feet tall! Oak
36	wood is hard and strong. It is used to make floors, boxes,
41	beds, and many other things.
52	Many oaks are planted in parks. They are good trees to
62	sit under for shade. Some people have picnic lunches under
74	oaks. Others like to climb up and sit on its branches. And
85	some people just like to take naps under a big oak.
95	Have you learned about oaks in any of your classes?
106	Acorns are seeds that grow on the branches of oaks. Some
117	cooks make tasty dishes with them. In the fall, acorns drop
129	to the ground. Some may grow into oak trees. It takes many
139	years for an acorn to become a grand oak tree.

1. Underline words in the passage that are plural nouns.

2. What things are made from oak wood?

_____

_____

_____

3. What can an acorn become?

_____

_____

Name _____

Inflectional Endings -s, -es

> The inflectional endings -s or -es can be added to the end of verbs.
> Add -es to verbs that end in *ch, sh, ss, x,* or *zz*.
>
> tap**s** clip**s** mun**ches** pu**shes**
> pa**sses** bo**xes** fi**zzes**

A. Fill in the missing ending to make the word in bold type.

1. **pats**   = pat   + _____ s _____
2. **passes** = pass + _____
3. **buzzes** = buzz + _____
4. **rushes** = rush + _____
5. **runs**   = run   + _____
6. **pushes** = push + _____
7. **pinches** = pinch + _____

B. Read each sentence. Fill in the missing ending to make the word in bold type.

1. She **misses** her stop on the bus.   miss + ____ es ____ = **misses**
2. Tom **brushes** the dust off his coat. brush + _____ = **brushes**
3. The class **plays** in the yard.   play + _____ = **plays**
4. Dad **mixes** the batter for the cake. mix   + _____ = **mixes**
5. The class **cheers** for their team.   cheer + _____ = **cheers**
6. The cat **hisses** at the dog!   hisses + _____ = **hisses**
7. Sara **fixes** the doll's dress.   fix   + _____ = **fixes**

Name _____

Inflectional Endings -*s*, -*es*

> The inflectional endings -*s* or -*es* can be added to the end of
> verbs. Add -*es* to verbs that end in *ch, sh, ss, x,* or *zz*.
>
> nap**s**   sip**s**   pun**ches**   ru**shes**
>
> mi**sses**   mi**xes**   bu**zzes**

A. Fill in the missing ending to make the word in bold type.

1. mesh + ____*es*____ = **meshes**

2. plan + _____ = **plans**

3. miss + _____ = **misses**

4. flex + _____ = **flexes**

5. hush + _____ = **hushes**

6. fizz + _____ = **fizzes**

7. lunch + _____ = **lunches**

B. Fill in the inflectional ending (-*s* or -*es*) to make the word in bold type.

1. Jess **jogs** at a fast pace.   **jog** + ___*s*___ = **jogs**

2. Ed **matches** the shapes.   **match** + _____ = **matches**

3. He **crushes** the can.   **crush** + _____ = **crushes**

4. Sue **hums** a tune.   **hum** + _____ = **hums**

5. She **passes** the ball.   **pass** + _____ = **passes**

6. Tim **mixes** the paints.   **mix** + _____ = **mixes**

Name _____

Throws, Hits, Catches, and Runs!

10	Baseball is the great American sport! There are two teams
21	with nine players on each team. Each player on a team
26	throws, hits, catches, and runs.
38	The game begins with a batter at the plate. He waits for
50	the pitcher to pitch the ball. The pitcher winds up his arm
61	and throws the ball with all his might. Sometimes the batter
72	misses the ball. The catcher then catches it. Other times the
84	batter swings and hits the ball. Then the batter runs to first
94	base. Sometimes the batter slides onto the base. The crowd
105	cheers. They are hoping the batter will make a home run.
115	The team that gets the most homeruns wins the game.
126	The baseball season runs from spring to fall. In the fall,
135	the best National League team plays the best American
145	League team. These games are the World Series. A baseball
154	fan wishes that her team will be the champs!

1. Underline verbs in the story that have the inflectional endings -s or -es.

2. What does a pitcher do?

_____

_____

3. What game is played at the end of the season?

_____

Name _____

Inflectional Endings: *-ed, -ing*

> The inflectional endings *-ed* or *-ing* can be added to some verbs.
>
> ask**ed**　　　　ask**ing**　　　　play**ed**　　　　play**ing**

A. Write the ending to make the words in bold type.

1. list　+ ____ed____ = **listed**　　　list　+ ____ing____ = **listing**

2. dress + _____ = **dressed**　　dress + _____ = **dressing**

3. milk　+ _____ = **milked**　　milk　+ _____ = **milking**

4. mix　+ _____ = **mixed**　　mix　+ _____ = **mixing**

5. press + _____ = **pressed**　　press + _____ = **pressing**

6. sprint + _____ = **sprinted**　sprint + _____ = **sprinting**

7. wish　+ _____ = **wished**　　wish　+ _____ = **wishing**

B. Read each sentence. Write the missing ending *-ed* or *-ing* to make the verb in bold type.

1. Dad and I **packed** for the trip.　　pack　+ ____ed____ = **packed**

2. Will you go **fishing** with me?　　fish　+ _____ = **fishing**

3. I **slowed** down as I ran up the hill.　slow　+ _____ = **slowed**

4. Mom is **planting** roses today.　　plant + _____ = **planting**

5. I **jumped** on top of the step.　　jump + _____ = **jumped**

6. The hens are **pecking** at their food!　peck　+ _____ = **pecking**

7. I **kicked** a ball to the dog.　　kick　+ _____ = **kicked**

Name _____

Inflectional Endings: *-ed, -ing*

> Some verbs end in a vowel and a consonant. Double the consonant when you add the ending, *-ed* or *-ing*.
>
> spot + **t** + **ed** = spot**ted**   spot + **t** + **ing** = spot**ting**

A. Write the missing endings to make the verb in bold type. Write the verb on the line.

1. **skipping**   skip + _____ p _____ + _____ ing _____ = _____ skipping _____

2. **putting**   put + _____ + _____ = _____

3. **tapped**   tap + _____ + _____ = _____

4. **gripping**   grip + _____ + _____ = _____

5. **stopped**   stop + _____ + _____ = _____

6. **grabbed**   grab + _____ + _____ = _____

7. **planning**   plan + _____ + _____ = _____

B. Fill in the missing endings *-ed* or *-ing* to make the verb in bold type.

1. Will you go **swimming** with me on Monday?

   swim + _____ m _____ + _____ ing _____ = **swimming**

2. I **dropped** my book on the desk.

   drop + _____ + _____ = **dropped**

3. She **skipped** to the park.

   skip + _____ + _____ = **skipped**

4. The dog is **digging** up Mom's roses!

   dig + _____ + _____ = **digging**

Name _____

Planning and Planting a Garden

10	Many people are interested in learning about a garden for
21	their community. It takes a lot of planning before the first
31	seed is planted. Here is how one community did it.
43	First, they needed to find a patch of land. They asked the
55	town for help. The town gave them an empty lot. Next they
65	sketched a plan. It showed them how their garden would
66	look.
75	The people wanted to grow food plants. Together they
85	listed fruits and vegetables. They planned where to plant the
95	tomatoes, beans, and peas. Then they went shopping for the
101	tools, the plants, and the seeds.
110	Some people were digging holes. Others started to plant
114	seeds. Everyone pitched in.
124	The seeds started to grow. Soon kids were pulling weeds.
130	Everyone took turns watering the plants.
139	The gardeners were happy when it rained! Water helped
151	the plants to grow. In May, they picked peas. In July, they
161	picked tomatoes and beans. They packed extra food in bags
171	and gave it away. Soon the whole community was eating
173	fresh food!

1. Underline words in the story that have the endings *-ed* and *-ing*.

2. What is the first thing to do before planting a garden?

   _____

3. When were the peas picked?

   _____

Name _____

Inflectional Endings: -ed, -ing

When a word ends with a silent *e*, drop the *e*. Then add the ending -*ed* or -*ing*.

tape − **e** + **ed** = tap**ed**   tape − **e** + **ing** = tap**ing**

A. Write the missing parts to make the word in bold.

1. **used**   = use − e + ___ed___

2. **skating** = skate − e + _____

3. **danced** = dance − e + _____

4. **pacing** = pace − e + _____

5. **mined**   = mine − _____ + _____

6. **trading** = trade − _____ + _____

7. **baked**   = bake − _____ + _____

B. Read each sentence. Write the missing parts to make the word in bold. Write the word on the line.

1. I **raced** him to park.   **race** − __e__ + __ed__ = ___raced___

2. Sal is **baking** a cake.   **bake** − ____ + ____ = _____

3. The dog **chased** the cat.   **chase** − ____ + ____ = _____

4. Dad is only **joking!**   **joke** − ____ + ____ = _____

5. I **hoped** to be on time.   **hope** − ____ + ____ = _____

6. I am **riding** Stan's bike. **ride** − ____ + ____ = _____

7. Jill **placed** the box here. **place** − ____ + ____ = _____

Name _____

Inflectional Endings: *-es, -ed*

> When a verb ends with a *y*, change the *y* to *i*. Then add the ending *-es* or *-ed*.
>
> cry – **y** + **i** + **es** = cr**ies**   cry – **y** + **i** + **ed** = cr**ied**

A. Write the missing parts to make the word in bold. Then write the word on the line.

1. **dries**   dry   – y + __i__ + __es__ = _____dries_____

2. **carried**   carry – y + _____ + _____ = _____

3. **fries**   fry   – y + _____ + _____ = _____

4. **tried**   try   – y + _____ + _____ = _____

5. **flies**   fly   – y + _____ + _____ = _____

6. **studied**   study – y + _____ + _____ = _____

7. **buries**   bury – y + _____ + _____ = _____

B. Read each sentence. Write the missing parts to make the word in bold. Write the word on the line.

1. I **dried** the dishes.   **dry**   – y + __i__ + __ed__ = _____dried_____

2. Dad **hurries** to catch the bus.   **hurry** – y + _____ + _____ = _____

3. The baby **cried** loudly.   **cry**   – y + _____ + _____ = _____

4. The dog **buried** the bone.   **bury** – y + _____ + _____ = _____

5. Pat **fries** the fish in the pan.   **fry**   – y + _____ + _____ = _____

6. Fran **studies** every day.   **study** – y + _____ + _____ = _____

Name _____

Voting

9	Voting is an important right. Today, American citizens can
20	vote when they are 18 years old. Voting laws have changed
31	over the years. At one time, women could not vote. Many
43	people tried to change this law. Changing it was a fight. But
52	women finally won the right to vote in 1920.
62	Americans vote for a new president every four years. At
73	other times, they may be voting for mayors for their towns.
82	When citizens vote, they are making decisions, too. They
93	may be changing or creating new laws for their towns. They
105	may be voting for a new park. Or they may be choosing
116	whether to build roads. Some may be voting to change tax
124	laws. Everyone tries to make the right decision.
133	Voters ask questions. Have their leaders tried to do
141	everything they promised? Have the leaders carried out
152	their jobs? Have they done their best? If they have, citizens
163	will vote for these leaders again. If not, citizens will be
174	deciding what to do. And they will be choosing new leaders!

1. Underline words in the story that have the inflectional endings *-ed, -ing*, and *-es*.

2. When do Americans vote for a new president?

   _____

3. What might happen if voters are not happy with the leader they chose?

   _____

Name _____

Plurals: *y* to *i*, add *-es*

> When a noun has a consonant followed by *y*, change the *y* to *i*. Then add the ending *-es* to make the word a plural word.
>
> baby – **y** + **i** + **es** = bab**ies**

A. Write the missing parts to change the word into a plural word. Then write the plural word on the line.

1. navy   – ___y___ + **i** + ___es___ = _____navies_____

2. spy   – _____ + **i** + _____ = _____

3. pony   – _____ + **i** + _____ = _____

4. jelly   – _____ + **i** + _____ = _____

5. city   – _____ + **i** + _____ = _____

6. penny – _____ + **i** + _____ = _____

7. belly   – _____ + **i** + _____ = _____

B. Read each sentence. Write the missing endings to make the plural in bold type.

1. The **families** had a picnic.   family – __y__ + i + __es__ = **families**

2. The **candies** are very sweet.   candy – _____ + i + _____ = **candies**

3. The **ferries** took us across the lake. ferry – _____ + i + _____ = **ferries**

4. The **nannies** went to the park.   nanny – _____ + i + _____ = **nannies**

5. We will plant some **lilies**.   lily   – _____ + i + _____ = **lilies**

6. Will you tell me some **stories?**   story – _____ + i + _____ = **stories**

7. Let's pick some **berries**.   berry – _____ + i + _____ = **berries**

Name _____

Plurals: *y* to *i*, add -*es*

> When a noun has a consonant followed by *y*, change the *y* to *i*. Then add the ending -*es* to make the word a plural word.
>
> body – **y** + **i** + **es** = bod**ies**

A. Fill in the blanks to make the plural in bold type. Write the plural on the line.

1. **countries**   country – y + ___i___ + __es__ = _____countries_____

2. **kitties**   kitty   – y + _____ + _____ = _____

3. **funnies**   funny   – y + _____ + _____ = _____

4. **libraries**   library   – y + _____ + _____ = _____

5. **parties**   party   – y + _____ + _____ = _____

6. **daisies**   daisy   – y + _____ + _____ = _____

7. **patties**   patty   – y + _____ + _____ = _____

B. Read each sentence. Write the missing endings to make the plural in bold type.

1. The **babies** are asleep.   baby   – y + __i__ + __es__ = **babies**

2. Can we pick **cherries**?   cherry – y + _____ + _____ = **cherries**

3. The **ladies** had a bake sale.   lady   – y + _____ + _____ = **ladies**

4. The **flies** were buzzing around.   fly   – y + _____ + _____ = **flies**

5. The **pansies** are yellow and white.   pansy – y + _____ + _____ = **pansies**

6. We need **supplies** for school.   supply – y + _____ + _____ = **supplies**

Name _____

Families at the Petting Farm

11	Penny and her buddy Fran are at the Ross Petting Farm
19	with their families. The buddies don't like farms.
30	"Cities are fun," says Penny. "We should go to the city."
37	"Let's try something new," her mom says.
48	Miss Ross owns the farm. She takes the families to see
59	the sheep. They walk through a field of daisies and pansies.
71	A sheep jogs up to them. Miss Ross shows Fran and Penny
82	how to pet it. "Look, her twin babies are coming!" Penny
93	cried. The baby sheep rub their heads on Penny's leg. Miss
102	Ross takes pictures of the buddies petting the babies.
113	Next, Miss Ross takes them to see the ponies. The ponies
123	come from different countries. A pony trots up to Penny.
133	"This is Tiptop. She comes from Mexico. I'll show you
140	how to brush ponies," Miss Ross explains.
151	Penny and Fran brush and feed the ponies. "This is so
161	much fun!" the buddies say. "Can we come back again?"
172	"Yes," says Miss Ross. "Then I will show you the bunnies
175	and barn kitties."

1. Underline words in the story with the plural ending *-ies.*

2. What animals do Penny and Fran see first?

_____

3. What animals do Penny and Fran see last?

_____

Name _____

Possessives

> A possessive noun tells who owns or has something.
> Add 's to a singular noun to make it a possessive noun.
>
> sister**'s** hat

A. Underline the possessive noun in each row. Write the possessive noun on the line.

1. mother	mothers	<u>mother's</u>	**mother's**
2. boy's	boy	boys	_____
3. grandma	grandma's	grandmas	_____
4. uncles	uncles	uncle's	_____
5. girl	girl's	girls	_____
6. book's	book	books	_____
7. cats	cat	cat's	_____

B. Underline the possessive noun in each sentence. Write it on the line.

1. I see a <u>bird's</u> nest. _____ **bird's**

2. Is this Mom's book on the desk? _____

3. Brad went to the doctor's office. _____

4. My dog's name is Spot. _____

5. These are my grandpa's glasses. _____

6. The pony's tail is brown. _____

7. The shop's sign is gold and red. _____

Name _____

Possessives and Plural Possessives

> A possessive noun tells who owns or has something.
> Add (') to a plural noun to make it a possessive noun.
>
> boy**s'** bikes

A. Read the nouns in the left column of the chart. Write the singular possessive and the plural possessive for each noun.

	Noun	Singular Possessive	Plural Possessive
1.	dad	dad's	dads'
2.	cow		
3.	van		
4.	girl		
5.	pig		
6.	hen		

B. Underline the plural possessive noun in each sentence. Write it on the line.

1. The cubs' mother was looking for food. _____cubs'_____

2. We had a meeting in the teachers' room. _____

3. The coats' buttons are made of gold. _____

4. Our mothers' cakes tasted great! _____

5. The teacher wanted to meet with the girls' parents. _____

6. There were a lot of eggs in the hens' nests. _____

Name _____

Hugo's Family Picnic

10	Hugo's big family is meeting at the town's park. But
18	Hugo is worried. It is getting cloudy out.
25	"Mom," said Hugo. "What if it rains?"
34	Mom replied, "Put the beach umbrellas in Dad's van.
40	Then get Grandma's box of tacos!"
50	"Good idea!" Hugo said. Soon, the van's seats were filled
53	with Hugo's family.
63	"Look!" said Dad. "I see my brothers' cars." Then Dad's
71	three brothers and their families waved and yelled.
83	The cousins lined up for a relay race in the park's field.
94	Hugo pointed, "Here is the boys' line and the girls' line."
103	The cousins began the race. Hugo's girl cousins won!
114	After the race, the kids went to their uncles' soccer game.
126	But it began raining. "What do we do now?" a cousin asked.
137	"Don't worry!" said Hugo. He ran to Dad's van and got
146	the beach umbrellas. Everyone crowded under them and ate
148	Grandma's tacos.
159	Soon, Hugo yelled. "Look! The sun is coming out. Time to
169	finish the game!" The uncles' cheers were loud and happy.

1. Underline words in the story that have possessives nouns.

2. Whose family is having a picnic in the town's park?

   _____

3. When did it start raining?

   _____

Name _____

Compound Words

A compound word is made up of two smaller words.

sun + set = sunset

A. Draw a slash (/) between the two small words within the compound word. Write the two words on the lines.

1. in/side _____in_____ _____side_____

2. himself _____ _____

3. pancake _____ _____

4. sunfish _____ _____

5. bedrock _____ _____

6. pigpen _____ _____

7. bathtub _____ _____

B. Underline the compound word in each sentence. Write the compound word on the line. Draw a slash (/) between the two small words within the compound word.

1. It was a beautiful <u>sunset</u>! _____sun/set_____

2. When is your bedtime? _____

3. Where is Mom's red handbag? _____

4. The little kids played in the sandbox. _____

5. This rug is handmade at the shop. _____

6. The kitten is a playmate for the kids. _____

7. She has a strong handshake. _____

Name _____

Compound Words

> A compound word is made up of two smaller words.
> **rain + drop = raindrop**

A. Underline the compound word in each row. Draw a slash between the two small words within the compound word. Write the compound word on the line.

1.	<u>hair/cut</u>	hilly	humming	_____haircut_____
2.	blackest	banking	back pack	_____
3.	unless	up stairs	under	_____
4.	billing	boldness	birth day	_____
5.	home work	hopping	helpful	_____
6.	summer	stringy	spring time	_____
7.	rainy	rain fall	refill	_____

B. Underline the compound word in each sentence. Write the two words that make up each compound word on the lines.

1. The <u>moonlight</u> was bright.   _____moon_____   _____light_____

2. We had a picnic by the seaside.   _____   _____

3. The butterfly was black and gold.   _____   _____

4. The snowflakes were big and cold.   _____   _____

5. I like to eat blackberries for a snack. _____   _____

6. She can do handstands on the sand.   _____   _____

7. I gave Dad a red bathrobe as a gift.   _____   _____

Name _____

From Newborn to Woodsman

9	It was wintertime. Six big storks worked overtime to
19	bring baby Paul Bunyan to his parents! Baby Paul was
32	big. When he was one week old, he could fit into his dad's
43	raincoat! Paul's feet were so big that no snowshoes fit him.
50	After two months, Paul outgrew his playhouse.
60	Each day for breakfast his mom made huge plates of
70	cornbread. At bedtime, Paul rolled around so much that he
79	flattened miles of woodlands. Soon he outgrew the house
90	where he lived with his parents. Then they moved into a
92	nearby hilltop.
103	Paul's parents did not know what to do with him. They
116	gave him an ax, a handsaw, and a fishing pole. They fed him
126	stacks of homemade blueberry pancakes. Paul used his pole to
137	catch hundreds of sunfish. He used his handsaw to cut down
149	trees. Paul put logs in the fireplace to keep the family warm.
160	Paul Bunyan grew to be twenty feet tall. He became a
171	woodsman. That's when he saved a baby ox in a snowstorm.
175	But that's another story!

1. Underline the compound words in the story.

2. How big was Paul when he was one week old?

_____

3. What did Paul eat?

_____

_____

Name _____

Contractions with Pronouns and Verbs

> A contraction is a word that is made from two words. An apostrophe (') takes the place of the letter, or letters, that are left out.
>
> she is = she**'s**

A. Read the contractions in the box. Write the contraction that stands for the two words.

> it's   I'm   he'll
>
> they'll   we've   you're

1. I am _____I'm_____   **4.** he will _____

2. it is _____   **5.** we have _____

3. you are _____   **6.** they will _____

B. Read each sentence. Write the contraction for the underlined word on the line.

1. He is feeling sick today. _____he's_____

2. I have played the game before. _____

3. You will be in the front row for the show. _____

4. He thinks they are funny! _____

5. She is going to the store now. _____

6. I think we will play for another hour. _____

Name _____

Contractions with Pronouns and Verbs

> A contraction is a word that is made from two words.
> An apostrophe (') takes the place of the letter, or
> letters, that are left out.
>
> **you will = you'll**

A. Read each row of contractions. Write the pronoun and verb that makes up the contraction on the lines.

1. she'll   _____she_____   _____will_____

2. you're   _____   _____

3. I've   _____   _____

4. he's   _____   _____

5. they've   _____   _____

6. we're   _____   _____

B. Underline the contraction in each sentence. Write the words that make up the contraction on the line.

1. He's a good friend.   _____He_____   _____is_____

2. I think I've been here before. _____   _____

3. She's coming to the party, too. _____   _____

4. They'll take a van on their trip. _____   _____

5. I'm going to the shop today.   _____   _____

6. They're going to a show.   _____   _____

Name _____

The Bundle of Sticks

11	A father watched his sons as they worked. He said to
20	himself, "I'm not happy with my sons. They're always
28	fighting. I'll give them something to think about."
40	The father gave a bundle of sticks to his first son. He
53	said, "I've a task for you. You must break this bundle in two
65	parts." The son grinned and said, "I'll break it fast. It's easy
73	to do!" But he could not do it.
83	The other brothers mocked the first son and said, "He's
95	not strong. We're stronger than he is! We'll be able to break
106	the sticks." The other sons took turns. None of them could
111	break the bundle of sticks.
123	The father gave each son one stick. "My sons, I would like
135	to see you break this stick." And they did. Then the father
147	said, "If you're of one mind, then you can do anything! But
157	if you're divided, you'll break like these sticks." From that
168	day on, the brothers got along. They've become the best of
169	friends!

---

1. Underline the contractions in the story.

2. Why did the father give the bundle of sticks to each son?

   _____

3. What is the message of the story?

   _____

Name _____

Contractions with *not*

A contraction is a word that is made up of two words. An apostrophe (') takes the place of the letter, or letters, that are left out.

is not = isn<u>'t</u>   cannot = can<u>'t</u>

A. Read each contraction. Write the words that make up the contraction on the lines.

1. aren't   <u> are </u>   <u> not </u>

2. can't   _____ _____

3. didn't   _____ _____

4. isn't   _____ _____

5. hadn't   _____ _____

6. weren't   _____ _____

7. doesn't   _____ _____

B. Read the underlined contraction in each sentence. Write the two words that make up the contraction on the lines.

1. We <u>can't</u> get to the game without a van.   <u> can </u>   <u> not </u>

2. I <u>haven't</u> seen the film yet.   _____ _____

3. She <u>wouldn't</u> eat the snack.   _____ _____

4. He <u>couldn't</u> catch the ball.   _____ _____

5. I <u>don't</u> know what time it is.   _____ _____

6. She <u>wasn't</u> finished with the test.   _____ _____

Name _____

Contractions with *not*

> A contraction is a word that is made up of two words. An apostrophe (')
> takes the place of the letter, or letters, that are left out.
>
> **would not = would<u>n't</u>**

A. Read each contraction. Write the two words that make up the contraction on the lines

1. hadn't   had _____   not _____

2. couldn't   _____   _____

3. didn't   _____   _____

4. can't   _____   _____

5. weren't   _____   _____

6. doesn't   _____   _____

7. wasn't   _____   _____

B. Underline the contraction in each sentence. Write the two words that make up the contraction on the lines.

1. I <u>didn't</u> know her name.   did _____   not _____

2. I <u>shouldn't</u> go without my mom.   _____   _____

3. We <u>can't</u> go to the bake sale today.   _____   _____

4. That puppy <u>isn't</u> for sale.   _____   _____

5. He <u>wouldn't</u> play unless Tim did.   _____   _____

6. She <u>hasn't</u> read the book yet.   _____   _____

Name _____

Should I or Shouldn't I?

8	On Sunday morning, Adam asked himself, "Should I
18	or shouldn't I?" Adam decided that he wouldn't clean his
30	room. He went out to play instead. He did this every week
33	for a month.
43	One day, his dad came into his room. "Adam, why
54	haven't you been cleaning your room? I can't see your bed!
64	Clean it up, or you can't go to the movies."
75	"I will, Dad." But Adam didn't know where to start. He
87	sat in his room and frowned. After a while, his friend, Brad,
89	walked in.
97	"Your room is a mess! This isn't good."
109	"I know," sniffed Adam. "Dad won't let me go out until I
120	clean it up. But I don't know what to do first."
126	"I will help you!" Brad said.
138	It took them two hours to clean up. And it wasn't easy!
148	After they finished, they went to a movie. When next
157	Sunday arrived, Adam asked himself, "Should I or shouldn't
167	I?" Adam didn't have to think. He said, "I should!"

1. Underline the contractions with *not* in the story.

2. Who helped Adam clean his messy room?

_____

3. Why did Adam say "I should" at the end of the story?

_____

Name _____

Comparative Endings -*er, -est*

> The ending -*er* is added to a word to compare two people, places, or things: fast + **er** = **fast<u>er</u>**
>
> The ending -*est* is added to a word to compare three or more people, places, or things: fast + **est** = **fast<u>est</u>**

A. Fill in the missing endings to make the word in bold.

1. I can run **faster** than you.

    fast   +   __er__   =   **faster**

2. My dad is the **oldest** one in the family.

    old   +   _____   =   **oldest**

3. It is **colder** in winter than in summer.

    cold   +   _____   =   **colder**

4. I have the **greatest** pet in the world!

    great   +   _____   =   **greatest**

B. Underline the word in each sentence that is comparing a person, place, or thing. Write the word on the line. Underline the ending.

1. This apple is <u>sweeter</u> than my apple.   ____sweet<u>er</u>____

2. Is your bike the newest of the five bikes?   _____

3. I am taller than Greg.   _____

4. This is the coldest winter in ten years!   _____

5. The red pillow is softer than the tan pillow.   _____

6. I have the longest hair in my class.   _____

Name _____

Comparative Endings *-er, -est*

> If *-er* or *-est* is added to a word that ends in a vowel and a consonant, double the final consonant.
>
> big + **g** + **er** = **bigger**   big + **g** + **est** = **biggest**
>
> If *-er* or *-est* is added to a word that ends in a consonant and *y*, change the *y* to *i*. Then add *-er* or *-est*.
>
> lazy − **y** + **i** + **er** = **laz<u>ier</u>**   lazy − **y** + **i** + **est** = **laz<u>iest</u>**

A. Fill in the missing parts to make the word in bold.

1. **sadder**   =   **sad**   + _____ + _____

2. **thinnest**   =   **thin**   + _____ + _____

3. **gladder**   =   **glad**   + _____ + _____

4. **wettest**   =   **wet**   + _____ + _____

5. **hotter**   =   **hot**   + _____ + _____

B. Read each sentence. Underline the comparing word. Fill in the missing parts to make the word.

1. That clown is the <u>silliest</u> of them all!

   silly   − ___y___ + ___i___ + ___est___ = ___silliest___

2. Pam is busier than Ed.

   busy   − _____ + _____ + _____ = _____

3. He is the happiest student in class!

   happy   − _____ + _____ + _____ = _____

4. The book is funnier than the movie.

   funny   − _____ + _____ + _____ = _____

Name _____

From Smallest to Biggest

11	The bee hummingbird is the smallest bird in the world. It
25	is about 2 inches long. That is about the size of two dimes! It
38	is one of the lightest birds around, too. It weighs as much as
50	a playing card! This bird can flap its wings faster than most
63	birds. It can do about 50 to 80 wing flaps per second! The
73	hummingbird can also build the tiniest nest in the world.
84	And it can lay an egg smaller than a coffee bean!
95	The ostrich is the biggest and tallest bird in the world.
107	An ostrich can grow to be 9 feet tall! That's taller than
118	any human! The ostrich is heavier than any other bird. It
130	can weigh up to 350 pounds! An ostrich cannot fly. But it
143	is speedier on land than a lot of animals. It can run over
155	40 miles an hour! The ostrich also lays the biggest egg of
166	all birds. The egg may weigh about 3 pounds! From the
175	smallest to the biggest, these birds are amazing creatures!

1. Underline the words in the story with the comparative endings
-er and *-est*.

2. What is the smallest bird in the world?

_____

3. Why is the ostrich an amazing animal?

_____

_____

Name _____

Prefixes *re-, un-, dis-*

A prefix is a word part. It is added to the beginning of a word. A prefix changes the word's meaning.

re- = "again" or "back"   re + play   = **re**play, play again

un- = "not"   un + happy = **un**happy, not happy

dis- = "not" or "away"   dis + agree = **dis**agree, opposite of agree

A. Read each meaning. Add a prefix to each base word. Then write the word on the line.

1. heat again   = _____re_____ + **heat** = _____reheat_____

2. not happy   = _____ + **happy** = _____

3. opposite of honest = _____ + **honest** = _____

4. not kind   = _____ + **kind** = _____

5. cycle again   = _____ + **cycle** = _____

B. Fill in the missing parts to make the word in bold.

1. He will **resend** the letter.

   _____re_____ + **send** = **resend**

2. I will not **disobey** my mother.

   _____ + **obey** = **disobey**

3. Mom will **uncover** the dish.

   _____ + **cover** = **uncover**

4. She needs to **replace** the button on her coat.

   _____ + **place** = **replace**

5. Ken **dislikes** cleaning his room.

   _____ + **likes** = **dislikes**

Name _____

Prefixes *pre-, non-, mis-*

A prefix is a word part. It is added to the beginning of a word. A prefix changes the word's meaning.

pre- = "before" **pre** + read = **preread,** read before

non- = "not" **non** + fat = **nonfat,** not fat

mis- = "wrong" **mis** + spell = **misspell,** spell wrong

A. Read the meaning for each word. Add a prefix to each base word. Then write the word on the line.

1. before the game = ___pre___ + **game** = ___pregame___

2. not living = _____ + **living** = _____

3. put in the wrong place = _____ + **place** = _____

4. cook before = _____ + **cook** = _____

5. lead in the wrong way = _____ + **lead** = _____

B. Underline the word with the prefix in each sentence. Then write the meaning of the word on the line.

1. My little sister is in <u>preschool</u>. ___before school___

2. Please use a nonstick pan to fry the eggs. _____

3. We had a spelling pretest. _____

4. Brett likes to read nonfiction books. _____

5. Mom prepaid for my books for class. _____

6. Grace misplaced her red hat. _____

Name _____

Reuse and Recycle

9	Everyone dislikes trash, but we need to rethink how
22	we get rid of it. The trash we throw away is making Earth
29	unsafe. We must stop mistreating our planet.
39	Plastic, metal, glass, and paper can be reused or recycled.
49	Plastic water bottles can be refilled with water. Then the
60	plastic bottle can be recycled. Better yet, use a metal water
72	bottle. It will last forever! Metal cans and glass bottles can be
82	reused to store things. Unbroken glass and metal cans may
84	be recycled.
95	We can be careful when we shop for food. Some food
104	comes prepackaged in plastic. Once you unwrap the plastic,
114	you cannot recycle that kind of plastic. Look for food
123	that comes in nonplastic wrapping. Bring your own cloth
131	shopping bag. It can be reused many times.
142	It is unlikely that trash will disappear on its own. We
153	must discover new ways to reuse and recycle things. No one
162	will disagree that it is important to save Earth!

1. Underline words in the story that have the prefixes *re-, un-, dis-,*
   pre-, non-, and *mis-*.

2. What should you do with plastic, glass, or metal things you no
   longer need?

   _____

3. Why is it important to rethink how to get rid of trash?

   _____

Name _____

Suffixes -*y*, -*ly*

A suffix is a word part. It is added to the end of a word. A suffix changes the word's meaning.

-y = "full of"   rain + **y** = **rainy,** full of rain

-ly = "in a certain way"   light + **ly** = **lightly,** in a light way

In a word ending with an *e*, drop the *e*. Then add the suffix -*y*.

juice − **e** + **y** = **juicy,** full of juice

A. Underline the suffix in each word. Write the meaning of the word on the line.

1. sand<u>y</u>   <u>full of sand</u>

2. badly   _____

3. sugary   _____

4. slowly   _____

5. tasty   _____

B. Look at the underlined words in each sentence. Write the word from above that means the same.

1. The cat behaved <u>in a bad way</u> in the car.   <u>badly</u>

2. The turtle moved <u>in a slow way</u> on the grass.   _____

3. The beach is <u>full of sand</u>.   _____

4. The drink was <u>full of sugar</u>.   _____

5. The peach was <u>full of taste</u>.   _____

Name _____

Suffixes *-ful, -less, -able*

> A suffix is a word part. It is added to the end of a word. A suffix changes the word's meaning.
>
> **-ful** = "full of" cheer**ful** = "full of cheer"
> **-less** = "without" hope**less** = "without hope"
> **-able** = "able to" enjoy**able** = "able to enjoy"

A. Fill in the missing parts to make the word in bold. Write the meaning of the word on the line.

1. **painful** = **pain** + ____ful____, means ____"full of pain"____

2. **breakable** = **break** + _____, means _____

3. **endless** = **end** + _____, means _____

4. **cheerful** = **cheer** + _____, means _____

5. **useless** = **use** + _____, means _____

6. **drinkable** = **drink** + _____, means _____

> In words that end with a silent *e*. Drop the *e*. Then add the suffix *-able*.
>
> excite – **e** + **able** = **excitable**

B. Fill in the parts to make the word in bold.

1. **valuable** = **value** – ____e____ + ____able____

2. **usable** = **use** – _____ + _____

3. **lovable** = **love** – _____ + _____

4. **believable** = **believe** – _____ + _____

5. **likable** = **like** – _____ + _____

Name _____

Grouchy Fox and the Juicy Grapes

11	One lovely day in summer, Fox saw a bunch of grapes.
22	"These grapes look tasty. I bet they are very juicy!" he
34	said. "I think they are reachable if I jump high. The grapes
39	will be enjoyable to eat."
50	The grapes were hanging on a high tree branch. Fox felt
61	cheerful. He knew he could grab them. So, Fox ran toward
72	the grapes. At the last minute, he jumped. But he jumped
76	badly and fell down!
87	Hopeful, Fox tried again. "Surely, I can get them," he said
98	to himself. But he could not reach the grapes. Soon, Fox
107	became grouchy and restless. He tried countless more times
111	and then gave up.
120	"This is hopeless," Fox thought. With a painful expression
132	on his face, Fox walked away sadly. "I know that bunch of
137	grapes is sour or tasteless!"
149	It was easy for Fox to think the grapes were sour and
156	tasteless because he could not get them.

1. Underline words in the story with the suffixes *-y*, *-ly*, *-ful*, *-less*, and *-able*.

2. Why did Fox become grouchy?

_____

3. Why did Fox think that the grapes were sour?

_____

_____

Name _____

Suffixes -ness, -ous

The suffix **-ness** means "the state of being." The suffix **-ous** means "full of." When a word ends in y, change the y to i. Then add -ness or -ous.

dark + **ness** = **dark<u>ness</u>,** state of being in the dark

joy + **ous** = **joy<u>ous</u>,** full of joy

happy – **y** + **i** + **ness** = **happ<u>iness</u>,** state of being happy

fury – **y** + **i** + **ous** = **fur<u>ious</u>,** full of fury

A. Underline the suffix in each word. Then write the word that goes with each meaning.

loud<u>ness</u>   courageous   craziness   dangerous   sadness

1. state of being loud   _____loudness_____

2. full of danger   _____

3. state of being sad   _____

4. full of courage   _____

5. state of being crazy   _____

B. Fill in the missing parts to make the word in bold.

1. The plums are full of **sweetness**.

   sweet   + _____ness_____ = **sweetness**

2. She did a **courageous** act.

   courage + _____ = **courageous**

3. There is **goodness** in his heart.

   good   + _____ = **goodness**

4. There was an **emptiness** in the house when Dad left.

   empty   – _____ + _____ + _____ = **emptiness**

Name _____

Suffixes *-ment, -ance*

> The suffix *-ment* means "the act of being."
> agree + **ment** = **agreement,** the act of agreeing
> The suffix *-ance* means "action or process."
> attend + **ance** = **attendance,** the act of attending

A. Underline the suffix in each word. Then write the word that goes with each meaning.

enjoy<u>ment</u>   punishment   allowance   movement   appearance

1. being enjoyed _____enjoyment_____

2. the act of appearing _____

3. being moved _____

4. being punished _____

5. the act of allowing _____

B. Fill in the missing parts to make the word in bold.

1. The doctor had a good **treatment.**

   treat + _____ment_____ = **treatment**

2. She gets an **allowance** every week.

   allow + _____ = **allowance**

3. The people voted for a new **government**.

   govern +_____ = **government**

4. He made an **appearance** at the party.

   appear + _____ = **appearance**

5. There is a hard **punishment** for the crime.

   punish + _____ = **punishment**

Name _____

A New Government

10	Long ago, people came from England to live in North
18	America. They were looking for freedom and happiness.
26	They made homes in the wilderness. They formed
34	colonies. But the colonies were controlled by England.
43	The colonists paid taxes to England. They thought the
52	taxes were unfair. The colonists had arguments with the
61	leaders of England. There was harsh punishment if they
65	didn't obey the laws.
74	The colonists were courageous. They wanted to form their
84	own government. They wanted to make their own laws. The
93	colonists began fighting the English to gain their freedom.
104	One day a meeting was held. All the leaders of the
113	colonies were in attendance. They wrote the Declaration of
121	Independence. This statement was of great importance. It
128	said the colonies wanted to be free.
138	On July 4, 1776, the leaders were finally in agreement.
149	They signed the declaration. Now every July 4th, there is a
158	joyous celebration. It is the birthday of our nation!

1. Underline the words in the story with the suffixes *-ness, -ous, -ment,* and *-ance.*

2. Why did people come from England to North America a long time ago?

_____

3. What statement was in the Declaration of Independence?

_____

Name _____

Suffix *-ion*

> A suffix is added at the end of a word. A suffix changes a word's meaning. The suffix *-ion* means "the act or process."
>
> subtract + **ion** = **subtraction,** process of subtracting

A. Read each meaning. Fill in the missing parts to make a word for each meaning. Then write the word on the line.

1. the act of acting   **act**   + ___ion___ = ____action____

2. the process of electing   **elect**   + _____ = _____

3. the act of predicting   **predict** + _____ = _____

4. the process of projecting **project** + _____ = _____

5. the act of expressing   **express** + _____ = _____

B. Fill in the missing parts to make the word in bold.

1. That **subtraction** problem was very hard!

   subtract + ___ion___ = **subtraction**

2. In what **direction** is the store?

   direct + _____ = **direction**

3. The class had a **discussion** about the test.

   discuss + _____ = **discussion**

4. I need to make a **correction** to the math problem.

   correct + _____ = **correction**

5. She has a big stamp **collection**.

   collect + _____ = **collection**

Name _____

Suffixes *-ion, -ation, -ition*

The suffixes *-ion, -ation,* and *-ition* all mean "the act or process of."
Sometimes these suffixes have spelling changes. When a word ends with
a silent *e,* drop the *e.* Then add *-ion, -ation,* or *-ition.*

create − **e** + **ion** = **creation**   decorate − **e** + **ation** = **decoration**

oppose − **e** + **ition** = **opposition**

A. Read each word in the box. Fill in the blanks below to make each word.

addition	combination	definition	celebration

1. add   + ___ition___ = **addition**

2. celebrate   − **e** + _____ = **celebration**

3. define   − **e** + _____ = **definition**

4. combine   − **e** + _____ = **combination**

B. Fill in the missing parts to make the word in bold.

1. The house is close to **completion**.

   complete   − ___e___ + ___ion___

2. They needed time for the test **preparation**.

   prepare   − _____ + _____

3. He wrote a fine **composition**.

   compose   − _____ + _____

4. We found a good **location** for the picnic.

   locate   − _____ + _____

Name _____

A Movie Production

10	*Lights! Camera! Action!* There is a lot of preparation that
17	goes into the production of a movie.
26	Many different people need to work together. A producer
37	gets the money to start the production. Actors try out for
50	the parts. There is a lot of competition among actors to get a
54	part in a movie!
63	A director gives direction to the actors. She makes
72	determinations about how the actors say and do their
83	parts. A camera person films the actions of the actors. Some
91	movies have animation. Artists draw the characters and
93	their actions.
103	People are also hired for the creation of sets and
112	decorations. In an action movie, there is someone who
122	finds the right location. If there are dangerous stunts, the
127	production company buys insurance protection.
137	Upon the completion of the movie, music is needed. A
147	composer writes a musical composition. It is called a score.
159	When the movie is finished, we sit back and enjoy the show!

1. Underline words in the story with suffixes *-ion*, *-ation*, and *-ition*.

2. What does a director do?

_____

_____

3. What is a movie score?

_____

_____

Name _____

Prefixes and Suffixes *un-, re-, -able, -ly, -ful*

> A prefix is added to the beginning of a base word. A suffix is added to the end of a base word. Some words can have both prefixes and suffixes added to them.
>
> **un** + help + **ful** = <u>un</u>help<u>ful</u>

A. Underline the base word in each word. Then write the word that goes with the meaning.

un<u>truth</u>ful   refillable   unusually   renewable   unkindly

1. not full of truth _____ untruthful

2. not in a usual way _____

3. able to be made new again _____

4. not in a kind way _____

5. able to be filled again _____

B. Read each sentence. Underline the word with a prefix and a suffix. Then write the base word for each word on the line.

1. I was <u>uncomfortable</u> because it was so hot. _____ comfort

2. She unexpectedly left early today. _____

3. The ink pen is refillable. _____

4. A new car is unaffordable right now. _____

5. The weather is unpredictable. _____

Name _____

Prefixes and Suffixes *un-, re-, -able, -ly, -ful*

> Some words can have both prefixes and suffixes added to them.
>
> **un** + success + **ful** = **<u>un</u>success<u>ful</u>**

A. Underline the base word in each word. Then write the word that goes with the meaning.

un<u>friend</u>ly   unskillful   unsafely   rewashable

1. not in a friendly way   _____unfriendly_____

2. not in a safe way   _____

3. able to wash again   _____

4. not skillful   _____

B. Add the prefix and suffix in parentheses ( ) to the word in bold. Write the word on the line.

1. He was not **kind (un-, -ly)** to his classmates.

   He treated his classmates _____unkindly_____.

2. She did not **thank (un-, -ful)** her friends for the gifts.

   She was _____.

3. I will **wash (re-, -able)** my apron again.

   My apron is _____.

4. The girl did not tell the **truth (un-, -ful)** to the class.

   She was _____.

5. I will **fill (re-, -able)** my water bottle again.

   My water bottle is _____.

Name _____

A Remarkable Trip

2	Dear Nate,
12	I'm having an unbelievable time at the Grand Canyon. I'm
25	staying at Bright Lodge. It is on the South Rim. I have an
35	unforgettable view of the greatest gorge on Earth. When I
47	look out my window, I see the colorful walls of the canyon.
57	When I am outside, I walk quietly and carefully. That's
68	because there are elk grazing close by! Hopefully, I will see
76	other wildlife. The Bighorn sheep seem ungraceful. But
86	they climb so well. But they are unapproachable. Since it's
94	summertime, the crowds are unavoidable. That's okay. I
103	don't mind sharing the unthinkable beauty of the canyon.
113	Today, it was unusually cool. We hiked about a mile.
120	Then the crowds unexpectedly disappeared. There were
130	delightfully cool breezes as we hiked. It was a wonderful
140	day! Unfortunately, we go home tomorrow. I wish we could
142	stay longer.
145	See you soon!
146	Vera

1. Underline the words with a prefix, a suffix, or both in the passage.

2. Where is Vera writing from?

   _____

3. What time of the year is it?

   _____

Name_____

Roots in Related Words

Look for a base word or root word in a long word. It can help you figure out the meaning of the word. The words *act, active*, and *action* are related. They all have the same root word *act*.

A. Read each row of words. Underline the word that is related to the word in bold.

1. **create**	<u>creation</u>	crayon	copy
2. **write**	whistle	writer	witness
3. **real**	rightful	redden	reality
4. **metal**	mistake	metallic	meaty
5. **company**	contact	collector	companion

B. Underline the word in each sentence that is related to the word in bold.

1. **complete**   The test was near <u>completion</u>.

2. **donate**   We gave a donation to the food drive.

3. **compete**   They will be racing in the competition.

4. **print**   The printer was out of ink.

5. **act**   They got a good reaction to the play.

Name _____

Roots in Related Words

> To figure out the meaning of a long word, look at the root or base word. The words *creative* and *creation* are related words. They have the same root word *create*.

A. Read each row of words. Underline the word that is related to the word in bold.

1. **present**	prepare	<u>presentation</u>	practice
2. **call**	recall	record	reclaim
3. **sign**	silent	silver	signal
4. **repeat**	repair	repetition	replay
5. **compose**	common	complete	composition

B. Read each sentence. Underline a word that relates to the word in bold. Write the words on the lines.

1. The <u>actor</u> **acts** in the play.

   _____actor_____   _____acts_____

2. We **cycled** in the park with our new bicycles.

   _____   _____

3. We have to finish the **final** test.

   _____   _____

4. The servant in the play **served** a meal.

   _____   _____

5. The **light** from the lightning storm was bright.

   _____   _____

Name _____

The Robot Contest

10	Kim and her family attended the robot contest in town.
22	"I want to see the robots and how they **act**," Kim said.
33	There was a lot of <u>activity</u>. At least ten robots were
43	**present**. There were all kinds of presentations. All the robots
52	were very **active.** Some played soccer. Others were actors
57	doing scenes from a play.
65	"That robot looks like a servant," Mom said.
74	"It could keep Grandma **company** and help clean!" Kim
75	exclaimed.
85	"It would make a good companion for her," Dad said.
95	People got to vote for their favorite robots. The one with
101	the most votes will win.
111	"I can't **decide**," said Kim. "This is a hard decision."
121	"The soccer robot is **able** to move in many different
129	ways," Mom exclaimed. "I've never seen such ability."
139	"Don't forget the robots that **act**," Dad said. "They sound
143	just like human actors!"
150	"All the robots should win!" said Kim.

1. Look at the boldface words in the story. Underline the nearby words that are related.

2. What were Kim and her family doing?

   _____

3. Why did they think a robot would be good for Grandma?

   _____

Name _____

Greek and Latin Roots: *astro, tele, auto, graph*

> Many English words have Greek and Latin roots. The Greek and Latin roots will give clues to the meaning of the English word.
>
> **astro** = star   **tele** = across a long distance
>
> **graph** = to write   **auto** = self

A. Read the meanings. Look at the underlined word(s). Write the word that goes with the meaning.

telephone	astronomy	telegraph	autograph

1. a machine that lets people talk <u>across a long distance</u>

   _____ telephone

2. when you <u>write</u> your name your<u>self</u>

   _____

3. a study of the <u>stars</u>

   _____

4. a machine that sends <u>written</u> messages <u>across a long distance</u>

   _____

B. Read the sentences. Underline the word with a Greek or Latin root.

1. The <u>photographer</u> takes pictures of the ocean.

2. Which television show do you like to watch?

3. I will draw with a graphite pencil.

4. The astronaut walked on the Moon.

5. The automobile drives very smoothly.

Name _____

Greek and Latin Roots: *bio, photo, micro, port*

Many English words have Greek and Latin roots. The Greek and Latin roots will give clues to the meaning of the English word.

bio = life or living thing

photo = related to or produced by light

micro = very small

port = to carry

A. Read the meanings. Look at the underlined word(s). Write the word that goes with the meaning.

biographer   transport   microscope   photograph   biology

1. a person who writes about a person's <u>life</u> _____biographer_____

2. a machine to see <u>very small</u> objects _____

3. a picture made by <u>using light</u> _____

4. the study of <u>living things</u> _____

5. <u>to carry</u> from one place to another _____

B. Read the sentences. Underline the word with a Greek or Latin root.

1. You can see stars with a <u>telescope</u>.

2. I liked the biography about Abraham Lincoln.

3. Many people use public transportation.

4. We used the microwave oven to heat the food.

5. The scientist looked at the leaf under a microscope.

6. The telephone call was from Spain.

7. The biologist was studying ocean plants.

Name _____

Telecommunications

7	Telecommunications is the way we send information
16	to one another. Today, many people use small, smart
27	telephones. It is easy to telephone or send a message. Many
36	smart phones have automatic cameras, too. You can take
48	photographs and send them to a friend in a few seconds. But
53	it wasn't always that easy.
61	Long ago, many people sent messages called telegrams.
70	They were sent through a telegraph. The telegrams were
80	electric signals sent in code over wires. Messengers on the
86	other end would deliver the telegrams.
94	Many inventors developed ways for us to communicate.
102	Samuel Morse invented the first commercial telegraph. In
112	1844, he sent the first telegram. Then in 1876, Alexander
119	Graham Bell invented the telephone. Soon afterward,
128	Emile Berliner invented a microphone. It made it easier
137	to speak into the telephone. Thomas Edison invented the
145	phonograph. It made recordings. In 1877, Thomas Edison's
154	first recorded message was: *Mary had a little lamb!*

1. Underline the words in the story with the roots: *auto*, *graph*, *micro*, *photo*, and *tele*.

2. Who invented the telephone?

_____

3. What did Thomas Edison invent to make a recording?

_____

Name _____

Speed Drill 1

Practice reading the words. Tell your teacher when you are ready to be timed.

no	that	again	kind	under
a	long	say	drink	when
eat	pretty	he	round	pick
by	one	goes	so	my
drink	pick	when	my	goes
again	long	that	round	a
he	so	under	one	eat
pretty	by	say	no	kind

Name _____

Speed Drill 2

Practice reading the words. Tell your teacher when you are ready to be timed.

she	clean	him	walk	own
this	away	is	your	keep
both	have	start	fall	always
old	made	from	ride	got
walk	both	got	is	she
this	away	old	him	start
always	keep	ride	fall	clean
have	your	from	made	own

Name _____

Speed Drill 3

Practice reading the words. Tell your teacher when you are ready to be timed.

know	said	because	much	yellow
do	me	please	can	tell
I	right	upon	help	on
about	their	not	fly	live
because	me	tell	I	can
not	yellow	right	fly	please
upon	help	on	said	know
much	about	their	live	do

Name _____

Speed Drill 4

Practice reading the words. Tell your teacher when you are ready to be timed.

did	put	want	around	little
write	call	show	who	better
it	go	am	too	his
there	must	or	small	far
go	or	write	there	did
am	who	it	better	small
put	around	want	show	little
must	call	too	far	his

Name _____

Speed Drill 5

Practice reading the words. Tell your teacher when you are ready to be timed.

buy	seven	cold	had	many
bring	now	off	does	read
where	draw	just	going	new
take	after	into	find	hold
does	bring	now	hold	take
cold	read	buy	seven	going
where	find	new	off	draw
just	after	many	into	had

Name _____

Speed Drill 6

Practice reading the words. Tell your teacher when you are ready to be timed.

laugh	don't	the	big	warm
grow	fast	us	three	once
an	sing	its	brown	went
funny	see	play	came	ran
brown	fast	see	once	came
warm	ran	don't	three	play
funny	us	laugh	the	big
sing	grow	went	its	an

Name _____

Speed Drill 7

Practice reading the words. Tell your teacher when you are ready to be timed.

ten	first	before	work	good
soon	down	what	may	how
carry	very	only	cut	shall
you	all	light	every	think
every	what	good	carry	soon
light	work	how	cut	all
think	you	may	first	very
ten	down	shall	before	only

Name _____

Speed Drill 8

Practice reading the words. Tell your teacher when you are ready to be timed.

use	black	found	let	done
myself	were	her	could	of
yes	they	jump	eight	wash
run	gave	in	and	sit
jump	myself	black	of	use
were	eight	done	they	in
found	and	wash	run	her
yes	let	sit	gave	could

Name _____

Speed Drill 9

Practice reading the words. Tell your teacher when you are ready to be timed.

best	then	pull	would	ate
has	saw	like	we	five
open	thank	never	give	why
together	hurt	up	sleep	are
like	open	saw	would	ate
has	thank	never	together	hurt
why	five	are	we	then
pull	up	sleep	give	best

Name _____

Speed Drill 10

Practice reading the words. Tell your teacher when you are ready to be timed.

with	them	our	blue	look
at	today	red	get	was
but	stop	white	over	here
to	four	any	six	make
over	get	but	today	with
at	red	here	was	make
four	to	white	our	stop
look	blue	six	them	any

Name _____

Speed Drill 11

Practice reading the words. Tell your teacher when you are ready to be timed.

come	those	been	which	these
hot	wish	well	green	ask
two	for	be	will	some
if	full	out	try	as
green	out	if	two	will
some	those	full	which	these
be	as	wish	hot	well
come	ask	try	for	been

Name _____

Speed Drill 12

Practice reading the words. Tell your teacher when you are ready to be timed.

man	day	number	each	water
time	more	another	things	way
different	even	called	through	place
years	such	part	back	used
other	most	than	place	people
also	same	more	word	day
back	word	same	years	than
other	different	way	even	another
things	place	man	through	number
most	water	such	used	called
also	people	time	each	part

Name _____

Decoding Strategy Chart

Step 1	Look for the word parts (prefixes) at the beginning of the word.
Step 2	Look for the word parts (suffixes) at the end of the word.
Step 3	In the base word, look for familiar spelling patterns. Think about the six syllable-spelling patterns you have learned.
Step 4	Sound out and blend together the word parts.
Step 5	Say the word parts fast. Adjust your pronunciation as needed. Ask yourself: "Is this a word I have heard before?" Then read the word in the sentence and ask: "Does it make sense in this sentence?"

Name _____

Progress Chart

Beginning Date: _____

Ending Date: _____

Book/Passage: _____

Number of Words Correctly Read in One Minute: _____

Words Correct Per Minute	200
	190
	180
	170
	160
	150
	140
	130
	120
	110
	100
	90
	80
	70
	60
	50
	40
	30
	20
	10

Number of Trials: 0 1 2 3 4 5

Name _____

2005 Oral Reading Fluency Data (Hasbrouck & Tindal)

Grade	Percentile	Fall WCPM*	Winter WCPM*	Spring WCPM*	Avg. Weekly Improvement**
1	90		81	111	1.9
	75		47	82	2.2
	50		23	53	1.9
	25		12	28	1.0
	10		6	15	0.6
2	90	106	125	142	1.1
	75	79	100	117	1.2
	50	51	72	89	1.2
	25	25	42	61	1.1
	10	11	18	31	0.6
3	90	128	146	162	1.1
	75	99	120	137	1.2
	50	71	92	107	1.1
	25	44	62	78	1.1
	10	21	36	48	0.8
4	90	145	166	180	1.1
	75	119	139	152	1.0
	50	94	112	123	0.9
	25	68	87	98	0.9
	10	45	61	72	0.8
5	90	166	182	194	0.9
	75	139	156	168	0.9
	50	110	127	139	0.9
	25	85	99	109	0.8
	10	61	74	83	0.7
6	90	177	195	204	0.8
	75	153	167	177	0.8
	50	127	140	150	0.7
	25	98	111	122	0.8
	10	68	82	93	0.8

*WCPM = Words Correct Per Minute   **Average words per week growth

Foundational Skills Assessment

CONTENTS

FOUNDATIONAL SKILLS ASSESSMENT

Phonics and Structural Analysis

Oral Reading Fluency Assessment

Phonics and Structural Analysis

Phonics and Structural Analysis Survey

based on **The Quick Phonics Screener**
Jan Hasbrouck, Ph.D.
© 2006-2010 JH Consulting

The purpose of the Phonics and Structural Analysis Survey (PSAS) is to provide informal diagnostic information that can be used to help (a) PLAN a student's instructional program in basic word reading skills, and (b) MONITOR THE PROGRESS or IMPROVEMENT in phonics and structural analysis skill development. The PSAS has not been normed or standardized. It is meant to be used as an informal classroom assessment tool.

Phonics and Structural Analysis

Directions for Administration and Scoring

1. Say to the student:

"I'm going to ask you to read some letters, words, and sentences to me so I can find out what kinds of words are easy for you to read and what kinds of words you still need to learn. I want you to try to do your best. We probably won't do this whole page; we'll stop if it gets too hard. Do you have any questions?"

Start the PSAS assessment where you believe the student's skills are fairly strong. For beginning readers, start with sounds or letter names.

For Skill 1, first (a) have the student tell the name of each letter. Then (b) have the student tell the sound each letter makes.

For the *NAMES* skill, have the student name the letter Q, not the *qu* digraph. For the *SOUNDS* skill, have the student give you the short sound for each of the vowels. If the student says the long sound (letter name), say: *"That is one sound that letter makes. Do you know the short sound for that letter?"* For the letter *c*, ask for the "hard sound" /k/, as in *cat*. For the letter *g* ask for the "hard sound" /g/, as in *gas*. For the letter *y* ask for the /y/ sound, as in *yes*. If the student offers a correct alternative sound for these letters, you should say, *"Yes, that is one sound for that letter. Do you know another sound that letter makes?"*

If a student reads 6/10 or more in Skill 2a, you may skip Skill 1 Letter Sounds.

2. If the student has difficulty (half or fewer correct on any skill) move up the page to an easier skill. If the student does well (more than half correct on a skill), move down to a harder skill.

3. On Skills 2–6: If the student reads all or almost all words correctly on part (a) of the skill (reading words), you may want to skip part (b) of the skill (reading sentences). If the next skill is difficult for the student, you can go back and complete the part of a previous skill that was skipped.

4. When the student is reading the words in text, only count errors on the target words (those underlined and in italics).

5. Stop the assessment when the student appears frustrated or tired. It is OK to stop in the middle of a skill. Not all skills must be administered, but try to assess as many as possible so you will have sufficient information to plan instruction or monitor progress.

Phonics and Structural Analysis

6. Mark errors and make notes or comments to help you remember how the student responded. Note that in Skill 9, students read the entire word, not syllable-by-syllable. The teacher's copy is written in syllables to facilitate marking/recording of errors within a word. For Skills 11-15, students read the entire word, and syllabication is not featured in the teacher's copy.

7. The PSAS is scored by each individual skill *only*. Record the ratio of correct responses over the total number possible, (e.g., 13/21 or 8/10 for each skill). Use the scoring chart that corresponds to each test to record PSAS results.

1. Letters		Score			Score
(a) Names	N/A not administered	/26	**(b) Sounds**		18 /21 cons. 4 /5 vowels

2. VC and CVC		Comments	Score
(a) List			8 /10
(b) Text			17 /20

3. Consonant Digraphs		Comments	Score
(a) In List			/10
(b) In Text			4 /10

8. **NOTE:** *Results from the PSAS **CAN ONLY** be used to determine a student's strengths/needs in key phonics and structural analysis skills, **NOT** his or her grade-level performance in reading.*

Phonics and Structural Analysis

	Phonics and Structural Analysis Survey, Test 1				
Skill 1(a)	b h o m d qu s k e				
	l j g u w a n i x				
Skill 1(b)	p f y c t v z r				
Skill 2(a)	sab	luf	kig	tem	dos
	pok	fal	zid	bek	mun
Skill 2(b)	Cal and Peg had a big hen. Mel and Tom got in a bus. Gus can hop and sit on the rug. Kim has a red hat.				
Skill 3(a)	teng	bock	whel	dith	thal
	shev	pash	chot	tach	rong
Skill 3(b)	That dog had a red dish. Rich and Sam ran on a long path. My ship hit a rock. When did Mick get back?				
Skill 4(a)	twib	dref	lasp	glet	tild
	renk	crut	blon	sapt	pund
Skill 4(b)	The slim frog was snug in a pink tank. Stan must bend and put up the flag in the wind.				
Skill 5(a)	fide	gake	sobe	jete	tude
	hize	mepe	wone	vabe	nute
Skill 5(b)	Rose will bake a cute white cake. Steve rode his bike for a mile to buy a fuse.				

Phonics and Structural Analysis

	Phonics and Structural Analysis Survey, Test 1				
Skill 6(a)	carn	derd	zirl	burm	borg
	tord	kurp	fird	mert	varp
Skill 6(b)	I will turn the part under her cart.				
	A dark storm will stir and hit the shore first.				
Skill 7(a)	putch	ladge	gnaf	jox	wrep
	kace	quob	tilk	lage	knek
Skill 7(b)	She wrote a grade on the quiz.				
	Gene saw a gnat near the milk.				
	Max made hot fudge.				
	Knock dirt into the center of the ditch.				

	Skill 8						
Skill 8	noat	boas	drea	leat	doon	toop	baig	traib
	nolt	folp	fay	tray	roud	cloum	soit	poin
	toyn	loy	kaud	vaut	cawn	haw	voe	doe
	rewp	hew	thal	hal	tigh	sligh		

Skill 9(a)	cabin	bother	eager	planet	cotton
	label	turkey	soggy	whisper	city
Skill 9(b)	employer	journalist	melody	cranberry	magnetic
	scavenger	endurance	customer	difference	forgetful
Skill 9(c)	kindergarten	macaroni	magnificent	agriculture	difficulty
	alligator	watermelon	television	convertible	patriotic

	Skill 10					
Skill 10	disinfect	disregard	nonhuman	nonacidic	incorrect	infinite
	preset	prehistory	resee	recycle	unreal	unafraid
	conclude	conserve	misuse	mislead	question	function
	various	serious	darkness	fitness	capable	available
	thankful	bashful	library	primary	agreement	movement

Phonics and Structural Analysis

	Phonics and Structural Analysis Survey, Test 1					
Skill 11(a)	hats	sticks	kisses	glasses	dishes	brushes
	arches	benches	axes	boxes	breezes	sizes
Skill 11(b)	flies	cries	babies	countries	ponies	stories
	elves	wolves	selves	wives	knives	shelves
Skill 12(a)	hums	snoops	tracks	fixes	catches	teaches
	played	funded	crashed	acting	swaying	gardening
Skill 12(b)	hurries	glories	quizzes	satisfies	bragged	hopped
	tried	magnified	fanning	swimming	lining	making
Skill 13(a)	boy's	dog's	child's	queen's	player's	mouse's
	birds'	girls'	men's	students'	doctors'	children's
Skill 13(b)	I'm	he'd	it's	she's	we've	they'll
	can't	didn't	couldn't	haven't	mustn't	shouldn't
Skill 14(a)	colder	faster	louder	smaller	cleaner	narrower
	slowest	roundest	warmest	freshest	smoothest	newest
Skill 14(b)	bigger	fatter	gladder	thinner	madder	wetter
	fittest	saddest	slimmest	hottest	reddest	hippest

Phonics and Structural Analysis

Phonics and Structural Analysis Survey Scoring Sheet, Test 1

1. Letters		Score				Score
(a) Names	b h o m d qu s k e l j g u w a n i x p f y c t v z r	/26	**(b) Sounds**	/b/ /h/ /o/ /m/ /d/ /kw/ /s/ /k/ /e/ /l/ /j/ /g/ /u/ /w/ /a/ /n/ /i/ /ks/ /p/ /f/ /y/ /k/ /t/ /v/ /z/ /r/		Consonants: /21 Vowels: /5

2. VC and CVC		Comments	Score
(a) In List	sab luf kig tem dos pok fal zid bek mun		/10
(b) In Text	*Cal* and *Peg had* a *big hen.* *Gus can hop* and *sit on* the *rug.* *Mel* and *Tom got in* a *bus.* *Kim has* a *red hat.*		/20

3. Consonant Digraphs		Comments	Score
(a) In List	teng bock whel dith thal shev pash chot tach rong		/10
(b) In Text	*That* dog had a red *dish.* *Rich* and Sam ran on a *long path.* My *ship* hit a *rock.* *When* did *Mick* get *back?*		/10

4. CVCC and CCVC		Comments	Score
(a) In List	twib dref lasp glet tild renk crut blon sapt pund		/10
(b) In Text	The *slim frog* was *snug* in a *pink tank.* *Stan must bend* and put up the *flag* in the *wind.*		/10

5. Silent e		Comments	Score
(a) In List	fide gake sobe jete tude hize mepe wone vabe nute		/10
(b) In Text	*Rose* will *bake a cute white cake.* *Steve rode* his *bike for a mile* to buy a *fuse.*		/10

Phonics and Structural Analysis

Phonics and Structural Analysis Survey Scoring Sheet, Test 1

6. r-Controlled Vowels		**Comments**	**Score**
(a) In List	carn derd zirl burm borg tord kurp fird mert varp		/10
(b) In Text	I will _turn_ the _part_ _under_ _her_ _cart_. A _dark_ _storm_ will _stir_ and hit the _shore_ _first_.		/10

7. Advanced Consonants (-tch, -dge, -x, qu, soft c & g, kn, gn, wr, -lk)		**Comments**	**Score**
(a) In List	putch ladge gnaf jox wrep kace quob tilk lage knek		/10
(b) In Text	She _wrote_ a grade on the _quiz_. _Gene_ saw a _gnat_ near the _milk_. _Max_ made hot _fudge_. _Knock_ dirt into the _center_ of the _ditch_.		/10

8. Vowel Teams		**Comments**	**Score**
oa, ea, oo, ai, ol, ay, ou, oi, oy, au, aw, oe, ew, al, igh	noat boas drea leat doon toop baig traib nolt folp fay tray roud cloum soit poin toyn loy kaud vaut cawn haw voe doe rewp hew thal hal tigh sligh		/30

9. Multi-Syllable		**Comments**	**Score**
(a) 2-Syllable	cab-in both-er ea-ger plan-et cot-ton la-bel tur-key sog-gy whis-per cit-y		/10
(b) 3-Syllable	em-ploy-er jour-nal-ist mel-o-dy cran-ber-ry mag-net-ic scav-eng-er en-dur-ance cus-tom-er dif-fer-ence for-get-ful		/10
(c) 4-Syllable	kin-der-gar-ten mac-a-ro-ni mag-nif-i-cent ag-ri-cul-ture dif-fi-cul-ty al-li-ga-tor wa-ter-mel-on tel-e-vi-sion con-vert-i-ble pa-tri-o-tic		/10

10. Prefixes and Suffixes					**Comments**	**Score**
dis-, non-, in-, pre-, re-, un-, con-, mis-, -tion, -ous, -ness, -able, -ful, -ary, -ment	disinfect infinite unreal mislead darkness bashful	disregard preset unafraid question fitness library	nonhuman prehistory conclude function capable primary	nonacidic resee conserve various available agreement	incorrect recycle misuse serious thankful movement		/30

Phonics and Structural Analysis

Phonics and Structural Analysis Survey Scoring Sheet, Test 1

11. Plurals (-s, -es)

					Comments	Score
(a) No spelling changes	hats	sticks	kisses	glasses		
	dishes	brushes	arches	benches		
	axes	boxes	breezes	sizes		/12
(b) With spelling changes (y to i, f, fe, to v)	flies	cries	babies	countries		
	ponies	stories	elves	wolves		
	selves	wives	knives	shelves		/12

12. Inflectional Verb Endings (-s, -es, -ed, -ing)

					Comments	Score
(a) No spelling changes	hums	snoops	tracks	fixes		
	catches	teaches	played	funded		
	crashed	acting	swaying	gardening		/12
(b) With spelling changes	hurries	glories	quizzes	satisfies		
	bragged	hopped	tried	magnified		
	fanning	swimming	lining	making		/12

13. Possessives and Contractions

					Comments	Score
(a) Possessives (singular, plural, and irregular)	boy's	dog's	child's	queen's		
	player's	mouse's	birds'	girls'		
	men's	students'	doctors'	children's		/12
(b) Contractions (pronoun-verb and with *not*)	I'm	he'd	it's	she's		
	we've	they'll	can't	didn't		
	couldn't	haven't	mustn't	shouldn't		/12

14. Comparative Endings (-er, -est)

					Comments	Score
(a) No spelling changes	colder	faster	louder	smaller		
	narrower	slowest	roundest	warmest		
	cleaner	freshest	smoothest	newest		/12
(b) With spelling changes	bigger	fatter	gladder	thinner		
	madder	wetter	fittest	saddest		
	slimmest	hottest	reddest	hippest		/12

Phonics and Structural Analysis

	Phonics and Structural Analysis Survey, Test 2
Skill 1(a)	n a j w o c u q f e p t b x v k d y
Skill 1(b)	g i s r h l z m
Skill 2(a)	pax bis kev cuv dus seg gol mab sof rit
Skill 2(b)	Ben got a big hug from Mom. Dad put the cat in the tub. Liz had a pen in the bag. She let the dog sit in the sun.
Skill 3(a)	shaf keck beng thun tash mith chon wech whan whot
Skill 3(b)	I got the duck at the pet shop When did Meg sing? That is a bath tub for a king. Sam had a chat with Chet.
Skill 4(a)	jant fusp slon swad pilf prin telt grob frug lest
Skill 4(b)	A frog slid in the sand at the pond. The swan just went to its nest to drop a twig.
Skill 5(a)	rame wote dife sove huse zule jepe fike rebe lape
Skill 5(b)	Use cones to close the lane. He gave a note to June on his bike ride home.

Phonics and Structural Analysis

	Phonics and Structural Analysis Survey, Test 2
Skill 6(a)	barm derp gird purt forb zurl sork nart wirn verm
Skill 6(b)	The first girl bought corn and pork at the farm store. Kirk could not forget the warm surf last summer.
Skill 7(a)	detch frex nulk pidge knal quap cend lige wrov gnot
Skill 7(b)	There was quite a large sign on the fridge. The chalk made her itch. Use a wrench to fix her bike. Make a knot in the center of the rope.
Skill 8	doan coast neal reat toof moop pait hain holb volt tay vay hout mout toid soip groy poy laup vaul graw craw voe poe dewn rew halk balp bigh righ
Skill 9(a)	fiddle profit ribbon morning camel robot wagon tiger bagel parlor
Skill 9(b)	elephant pedestal industry nursery trivial messenger lavender pharmacy transformer advantage
Skill 9(c)	formality identical democratic category geography illustration gymnasium exaggerate illogical apologize
Skill 10	dislodge disobey nonprofit nonstick inaccurate informal presew preview remind reset unplug unlike confer conjoin misstep mismatch hesitation reaction curious nervous goodness thickness notable payable useful careful secondary voluntary payment shipment

Phonics and Structural Analysis

Phonics and Structural Analysis Survey, Test 2						
Skill 11(a)	jars	balloons	grasses	addresses	ashes	bushes
	riches	branches	taxes	sixes	blazes	sneezes
Skill 11(b)	dries	armies	studies	parties	puppies	libraries
	calves	scarves	thieves	loaves	halves	knives
Skill 12(a)	scans	boots	snacks	teaches	flexes	rushes
	reached	staggered	tried	thinking	drawing	studying
Skill 12(b)	fries	hurries	carries	scurries	clogged	pried
	copied	unified	giving	batting	skating	creating
Skill 13(a)	cat's	writer's	mom's	chief's	animal's	woman's
	goats'	owners'	teams'	mens'	elves'	mice's
Skill 13(b)	you're	she'd	he's	we'll	it'll	they've
	don't	hadn't	aren't	weren't	wouldn't	doesn't
Skill 14(a)	taller	greater	softer	sweeter	kinder	darkest
	toughest	fewest	calmest	poorest	clearer	smartest
14(b)	flatter	sadder	slimmer	hotter	redder	gladdest
	fattest	thinnest	biggest	dimmest	wetter	fittest

Phonics and Structural Analysis

Phonics and Structural Analysis Survey Scoring Sheet, Test 2

1. Letters		Score			Score
(a) Names	n a j w o c u q f e p t b x v k d y g i s r h l z m	/26	**(b) Sounds**	/n/ /a/ /j/ /w/ /o/ /k/ /u/ /kw/ /f/ /e/ /p/ /t/ /b/ /ks/ /v/ /k/ /d/ /y/ /g/ /i/ /s/ /r/ /h/ /l/ /z/ /m/	Consonants: /21 Vowels: /5

2. VC and CVC		Comments	Score
(a) In List	pax bis kev cuv dus seg gol mab sof rit		/10
(b) In Text	*Ben* got a *big* *hug* from *Mom*. *Liz* *had* a *pen* *in* the *bag*. *Dad* *put* the *cat* *in* the *tub*. She *let* the *dog* *sit* *in* the *sun*.		/20

3. Consonant Digraphs		Comments	Score
(a) In List	shaf keck beng thun tash mith chon wech whan whot		/10
(b) In Text	I got the *duck* at the pet *shop*. *That* is a *bath* tub for a *king*. *When* did Meg *sing*? Sam had a *chat* *with* *Chet*.		/10

4. CVCC and CCVC		Comments	Score
(a) In List	jant fusp slon swad pilf prin telt grob frug lest		/10
(b) In Text	A *frog* *slid* in the *sand* at the *pond*. The *swan* *just* *went* to its *nest* to *drop* a *twig*.		/10

5. Silent e		Comments	Score
(a) In List	rame wote dife sove huse zule jepe fike rebe lape		/10
(b) In Text	*Use* *cones* to *close* the *lane*. He *gave* a *note* to *June* on his *bike* *ride* *home*.		/10

Phonics and Structural Analysis

Phonics and Structural Analysis Survey Scoring Sheet, Test 2

6. r-Controlled Vowels		Comments	Score
(a) In List	barm derp gird purt forb zurl sork nart wirn verm		/10
(b) In Text	The _first girl_ bought _corn_ and _pork_ at the _farm store_. _Kirk_ could not _forget_ the warm _surf_ last _summer._		/10

7. Advanced Consonants (-tch, -dge, -x, qu, soft c & g, kn, gn, wr, -lk)		Comments	Score
(a) In List	detch frex nulk pidge knal quap cend lige wrov gnot		/10
(b) In Text	There was _quite_ a _large sign_ on the _fridge_. The _chalk_ made her _itch_. Use a _wrench_ to _fix_ her bike. Make a _knot_ in the _center_ of the rope.		/10

8. Vowel Teams		Comments	Score
oa, ea, oo, ai, ol, ay, ou, oi, oy, au, aw, oe, ew, al, igh	doan coast neal reat toof moop pait hain holb volt tay vay hout mout toid soip groy poy laup vaul graw craw voe poe dewn rew halk balp bigh righ		/30

9. Multi-Syllable		Comments	Score
(a) 2-Syllable	fid-dle prof-it rib-bon morn-ing cam-el ro-bot wa-gon ti-ger ba-gel parl-or		/10
(b) 3-Syllable	el-e-phant ped-e-stal in-dus-try nurs-er-y triv-i-al mes-sen-ger lav-en-der phar-ma-cy trans-form-er ad-van-tage		/10
(c) 4-Syllable	for-mal-i-ty i-den-ti-cal dem-o-crat-ic cat-e-go-ry ge-og-ra-phy il-lus-tra-tion gym-na-si-um ex-ag-ger-ate il-log-i-cal a-pol-o-gize		/10

10. Prefixes and Suffixes		Comments	Score
dis-, non-, in-, pre-, re-, un-, con-, mis-, -tion, -ous, -ness, -able, -ful, -ary, -ment	dislodge disobey nonprofit nonstick inaccurate informal presew preview remind reset unplug unlike confer conjoin misstep mismatch hesitation reaction curious nervous goodness thickness notable payable useful careful secondary voluntary payment shipment		/30

Phonics and Structural Analysis

11. Plurals (-*s*, -*es*)

					Comments	Score
(a) No spelling changes	jars	balloons	grasses	addresses		
	ashes	bushes	riches	branches		
	taxes	sixes	blazes	sneezes		/12
(b) With spelling changes (*y* to *i*, *f*, *fe*, to *v*)	dries	armies	studies	parties		
	puppies	libraries	calves	scarves		
	thieves	loaves	halves	knives		/12

12. Inflectional Verb Endings (-*s*, -*es*, -*ed*, -*ing*)

					Comments	Score
(a) No spelling changes	scans	boots	snacks	teaches		
	flexes	rushes	reached	staggered		
	boxed	thinking	drawing	studying		/12
(b) With spelling changes	fries	hurries	carries	scurries		
	clogged	pried	copied	unified		
	giving	batting	skating	creating		/12

13. Possessives and Contractions

					Comments	Score
(a) Possessives (singular, plural, and irregular)	cat's	writer's	mom's	chief's		
	animal's	woman's	goats'	owners'		
	teams'	mens'	elves'	mice's		/12
(b) Contractions (pronoun-verb and with *not*)	you're	she'd	he's	we'll		
	it'll	they've	don't	hadn't		
	aren't	weren't	wouldn't	doesn't		/12

14. Comparative Endings (-*er*, -*est*)

					Comments	Score
(a) No spelling changes	taller	greater	softer	sweeter		
	kinder	darkest	toughest	fewest		
	calmest	poorest	clearer	smartest		/12
(b) With spelling changes	flatter	sadder	slimmer	hotter		
	redder	gladdest	fattest	thinnest		
	biggest	dimmest	wetter	fittest		/12

Phonics and Structural Analysis

	Phonics and Structural Analysis Survey, Test 3				
Skill 1(a)	f s o b u z j y m				
	k v d x q e n a w				
Skill 1(b)	r c l t h p i g				
Skill 2(a)	wog	hab	rud	tas	ren
	pes	lib	bok	fim	nug
Skill 2(b)	Jan and Kip ran a lap. Cam had to get the tan cup. Mom and Dad let Tom sit in the hut. Val put the lid on.				
Skill 3(a)	leth	shim	whun	chot	whog
	ting	koch	thap	dush	zock
Skill 3(b)	Put that dog in a bath. Did Ling pack his mesh bag? Check for a puck. He got sick with a rash.				
Skill 4(a)	dweb	tand	zont	vink	twum
	sted	plam	prin	clof	busk
Skill 4(b)	Rick and Kent must go past the flag. Bess and Brad held a clam and a crab.				
Skill 5(a)	waze	libe	hene	lome	fune
	zise	dete	fave	roke	hupe
Skill 5(b)	Gale and Steve dive into the lake with Dave. Cole broke the vase and put the blame on Clive.				

Phonics and Structural Analysis

	Phonics and Structural Analysis Survey, Test 3				
Skill 6(a)	mirn	turs	sark	hurn	ferd
	zorf	gerp	corg	birt	harl
Skill 6(b)	Worms curl up in the firm dirt to avoid birds.				
	Gert bought dark red shorts, a skirt, and a shirt.				
Skill 7(a)	bex	gnep	todge	quib	pice
	wral	filk	rutch	goft	knaf
Skill 7(b)	Gina went to fetch a silk wrap.				
	Greg did not know the name of the lodge on the trip.				
	The quick bird left its cage.				
	The ax broke when it hit a gnarl on the branch.				

	Skill 8							
Skill 8	zoat	toast	steab	peach	cood	spoon	haid	sail
	rolg	mold	nay	spray	roup	house	boin	moist
	poy	enjoy	raut	pause	gawf	dawn	foe	boe
	prew	stew	palt	salt	nigh	right		

	Skill 9(a)				
Skill 9(a)	behind	pilot	lemon	summer	target
	rotate	global	rapid	olive	channel
Skill 9(b)	energy	counselor	establish	fantastic	cosmetic
	persistence	scorpion	poetry	orphanage	hesitate
Skill 9(c)	caterpillar	immaculate	significant	relationship	monopoly
	semicircle	memorial	majority	obedient	capitalize

	Skill 10					
Skill 10	disable	display	nonfiction	nonsense	inactive	indirect
	predate	predict	reread	replace	uncut	unknown
	connect	confer	misfile	misfit	option	mention
	nervous	poisonous	happiness	sadness	reliable	laughable
	restful	thoughtful	ordinary	solitary	ailment	pavement

Phonics and Structural Analysis

	Phonics and Structural Analysis Survey, Test 3					
Skill 11(a)	cars	tops	classes	bosses	flashes	wishes
	lunches	inches	faxes	prefixes	blazes	crazes
Skill 11(b)	spies	cities	berries	bodies	candies	ladies
	loaves	calves	scarves	wharves	wives	hooves
Skill 12(a)	clips	fools	knocks	meshes	jinxes	coaches
	waited	fizzed	floated	hurrying	dusting	straying
Skill 12(b)	tries	studies	rallies	remedies	dragged	chugged
	fried	certified	hiding	splitting	reducing	writing
Skill 13(a)	cow's	pilot's	dad's	teacher's	farmer's	sailor's
	boys'	babies'	armies'	monkeys'	women's	thieves'
Skill 13(b)	I'd	she'll	you'd	you'll	we've	they're
	isn't	wasn't	couldn't	wouldn't	haven't	weren't
Skill 14(a)	warmer	quicker	harder	fresher	wilder	crisper
	cleanest	kindest	roughest	fastest	steepest	weakest
14(b)	dimmer	fitter	redder	sadder	thinner	hipper
	flattest	tannest	hottest	wettest	slimmest	fattest

Phonics and Structural Analysis

Phonics and Structural Analysis Survey Scoring Sheet, Test 3

1. Letters		Score			Score
(a) Names	f s o b u z j y m k v d x q e n a w r c l t h p i g	 /26	**(b) Sounds**	/f/ /s/ **/o/** /b/ **/u/** /z/ /j/ /y/ /m/ /k/ /v/ /d/ /ks/ /kw/ **/e/** /n/ **/a/** /w/ /r/ /k/ /l/ /t/ /h/ /p/ **/i/** /g/	Consonants: /21 Vowels: /5

2. VC and CVC		Comments	Score
(a) In List	wog hab rud tas ren pes lib bok fim nug		/10
(b) In Text	_Jan_ and _Kip_ _ran_ a _lap_. _Cam_ _had_ to _get_ the _tan_ _cup_. _Mom_ and _Dad_ _let_ _Tom_ _sit_ _in_ _Val_ _put_ the _lid_ _on_. the _hut_.		/20

3. Consonant Digraphs		Comments	Score
(a) In List	leth shim whun chot whog ting koch thap dush zock		/10
(b) In Text	Put _that_ dog in a _bath_. Did _Ling_ _pack_ his _mesh_ bag? _Check_ for a _puck_. He got _sick_ _with_ a _rash_.		/10

4. CVCC and CCVC		Comments	Score
(a) In List	dweb tand zont vink twum sted plam prin clof busk		/10
(b) In Text	_Rick_ and _Kent_ _must_ go _past_ the _flag_. _Bess_ and _Brad_ _held_ a _clam_ and a _crab_.		/10

5. Silent e		Comments	Score
(a) In List	waze libe hene lome fune zise dete fave roke hupe		/10
(b) In Text	_Gale_ and _Steve_ _dive_ into the _lake_ with _Dave_. _Cole_ _broke_ the _vase_ and put the _blame_ on _Clive_.		/10

Phonics and Structural Analysis

Phonics and Structural Analysis Survey Scoring Sheet, Test 3

6. r-Controlled Vowels		Comments	Score
(a) In List	mirn turs sark hurn ferd zorf gerp corg birt harl		/10
(b) In Text	_Worms curl_ up in the _firm dirt_ to avoid _birds_. _Gert_ bought _dark_ red _shorts_, a _skirt_, and a _shirt_.		/10

7. Advanced Consonants (-tch, -dge, -x, qu, soft c & g, kn, gn, wr, -lk)		Comments	Score
(a) In List	bex gnep todge quib pice wral filk rutch foge knaf		/10
(b) In Text	_Gina_ went to _fetch_ a _silk wrap_. Greg did not _know_ the name of the _lodge_ on the trip. The _quick_ bird left its _cage_. The _ax_ broke when it hit a _gnarl_ on the branch.		/10

8. Vowel Teams		Comments	Score
oa, ea, oo, ai, ol, ay, ou, oi, oy, au, aw, oe, ew, al, igh	zoat toast steab peach cood spoon haid sail rolg mold nay spray roup house boin moist poy enjoy raut pause gawf dawn foe boe prew stew palt salt nigh right		/30

9. Multi-Syllable		Comments	Score
(a) 2-Syllable	be-hind pi-lot lem-on sum-mer tar-get ro-tate glob-al rap-id ol-ive chan-nel		/10
(b) 3-Syllable	en-er-gy coun-se-lor es-tab-lish fan-tas-tic cos-met-ic per-sist-ence scor-pi-on po-et-ry or-phan-age hes-i-tate		/10
(c) 4-Syllable	cat-er-pil-lar im-mac-u-late sig-nif-i-cant re-la-tion-ship mo-nop-o-ly sem-i-cir-cle me-mo-ri-al ma-jor-i-ty o-be-di-ent cap-i-tal-ize		/10

10. Prefixes and Suffixes						Comments	Score
dis-, non-, in-, pre-, re-, un-, con-, mis-, -tion, -ous, -ness, -able, -ful, -ary, -ment	disable indirect uncut misfit happiness thoughtful	display predate unknown option sadness ordinary	nonfiction predict connect mention reliable solitary	nonsense reread confer nervous laughable ailment	inactive replace misfile poisonous restful pavement		/30

Phonics and Structural Analysis

Phonics and Structural Analysis Survey Scoring Sheet, Test 3

11. Plurals (-s, -es)

					Comments	Score
(a) No spelling changes	cars	tops	classes	bosses		
	flashes	wishes	lunches	inches		
	faxes	prefixes	blazes	crazes		/12
(b) With spelling changes (y to i, f, fe to v)	spies	cities	berries	bodies		
	candies	ladies	loaves	calves		
	scarves	wharves	wives	hooves		/12

12. Inflectional Verb Endings (-s, -es, -ed, -ing)

					Comments	Score
(a) No spelling changes	clips	fools	knocks	meshes		
	jinxes	coaches	waited	fizzed		
	floated	hurrying	dusting	straying		/12
(b) With spelling changes	tries	studies	rallies	remedies		
	dragged	chugged	fried	certified		
	hiding	splitting	reducing	writing		/12

13. Possessives and Contractions

					Comments	Score
(a) Possessives (singular, plural, and irregular)	cow's	pilot's	dad's	teacher's		
	farmer's	sailor's	boys'	babies'		
	armies'	monkeys'	women's	thieves'		/12
(b) Contractions (pronoun-verb and with not)	I'd	she'll	you'd	you'll		
	we've	they're	isn't	wasn't		
	couldn't	wouldn't	haven't	weren't		/12

14. Comparative Endings (-er, -est)

						Comments	Score
(a) No spelling changes	warmer	quicker	harder	fresher	wilder		
	crisper	cleanest	kindest	roughest	fastest		
	steepest	weakest					/12
(b) With spelling changes	dimmer	fitter	redder	sadder	thinner		
	hipper	flattest	tannest	hottest	wettest		
	slimmest	fattest					/12

Phonics and Structural Analysis

<table>
<tr><td colspan="2">Phonics and Structural Analysis Survey, Test 4</td></tr>
<tr><td>Skill 1(a)</td><td>e   qu   c   s   w   m   f   u   j
p   k   h   x   a   z   t   v   n</td></tr>
<tr><td>Skill 1(b)</td><td>b   g   r   i   y   o   d   l</td></tr>
<tr><td>Skill 2(a)</td><td>sim   ral   jod   til   rom
lem   dun   feg   vad   sut</td></tr>
<tr><td>Skill 2(b)</td><td>Jon sat on a log.
Jin has a bug on her bag.
Kit had to get a cab.
Viv can lug the bag on a jet.</td></tr>
<tr><td>Skill 3(a)</td><td>chud   seng   lith   whap   thub
fosh   gack   shan   vich   mong</td></tr>
<tr><td>Skill 3(b)</td><td>Jack was in a rush.   We can chat.
When did you wash those?   That duck was on a path.</td></tr>
<tr><td>Skill 4(a)</td><td>stod   spuf   bral   griv   glup
tras   flen   blit   crog   jesk</td></tr>
<tr><td>Skill 4(b)</td><td>Brit and Brad will swim past the raft in the pond.
Glen has dust on the brim of his best hat.</td></tr>
<tr><td>Skill 5(a)</td><td>lefe   cobe   lope   vime   pume
gude   kede   paze   zite   nade</td></tr>
<tr><td>5(b)</td><td>Steve wants to hide his flute and bike at home.
Eve hopes that the rake and the twine are on sale.</td></tr>
</table>

Phonics and Structural Analysis

	Phonics and Structural Analysis Survey, Test 4
Skill 6(a)	burb lork horm garn pert sirm cerk firl furd jard
Skill 6(b)	Kurt lives on a farm that sells corn and chard. Fern likes more circles on her purse and shirt.
Skill 7(a)	wrom fuge wox bedge kitch salk knev foce quiv gnas
Skill 7(b)	The girls walk by the edge of the quiet river. Did you know that a gnome is small? Can you wrap the parcel? Mitch planted a box of sage seeds.
Skill 8	hoak goat gream meal joot spoon mait paint spold fold fayn tray boun groun toid spoil poyt oyster naut auto daw claw loe toe bew stew dalt calm lighs tight
Skill 9(a)	fiction money lettuce dentist vacant pumpkin coffee fifteen hamster scholar
Skill 9(b)	basketball turbulent improvise humorous photograph computer strawberry highlighter defiant remember
Skill 9(c)	experiment discovery macaroni impossible convertible harmonica elevator activated biology horizontal
Skill 10	disappear disagree nonverbal nonlife incapable inactive preheat preschool reknit replay unveil unlock concede concur misread mistreat attention induction fabulous enormous fairness awareness enjoyable adorable peaceful hopeful dietary literary statement payment

Phonics and Structural Analysis

	Phonics and Structural Analysis Survey, Test 4					
Skill 11(a)	mugs	bricks	guesses	actresses	rashes	marshes
	watches	porches	suffixes	hoaxes	blazes	prizes
Skill 11(b)	fries	bunnies	lillies	supplies	families	patties
	shelves	halves	knives	wives	loaves	scarves
Skill 12(a)	mops	drips	coats	waxes	crashes	wishes
	rushed	nailed	heated	playing	sketching	pitching
Skill 12(b)	flies	denies	copies	glorifies	dried	planned
	grabbed	slipped	clapping	hiding	sliding	organizing
Skill 13(a)	principal's	king's	child's	flower's	giant's	worker's
	drivers'	directors'	ducks'	sheep's	ladies'	children's
Skill 13(b)	I'll	you've	they'll	he's	we're	it's
	hasn't	doesn't	shouldn't	aren't	couldn't	mustn't
Skill 14(a)	poorer	shorter	richer	harder	colder	prouder
	neatest	longest	coldest	loudest	dampest	slickest
14(b)	dimmer	tanner	bigger	wetter	redder	hotter
	saddest	thinnest	gladdest	flattest	maddest	fittest

Phonics and Structural Analysis

Phonics and Structural Analysis Survey Scoring Sheet, Test 4

1. Letters

(a) Names						Score	(b) Sounds						Score
e	qu	c	s	w	m		/e/	/kw/	/k/	/s/	/w/	/m/	Consonants:
f	u	j	p	k	h		/f/	**/u/**	/j/	/p/	/k/	/h/	/21
x	a	z	t	v	n		/ks/	**/a/**	/z/	/t/	/v/	/n/	
b	g	r	i	y	o		/b/	/g/	/r/	**/i/**	/y/	**/o/**	Vowels:
d	l					/26	/d/	/l/					/5

2. VC and CVC

					Comments	Score
(a) In List	sim ral jod til rom lem dun feg vad sut					/10
(b) In Text	_Jon_ _sat_ _on_ a _log_. _Jin_ _has_ a _bug_ _on_ her _bag_. _Kit_ _had_ to _get_ a _cab_. _Viv_ _can_ _lug_ the _bag_ _on_ a _jet_.					/20

3. Consonant Digraphs

					Comments	Score
(a) In List	chud seng lith whap thub fosh gack shan vich mong					/10
(b) In Text	_Jack_ was in a _rush_. We _can_ _chat_. _When_ did you _wash_ _those_? _That_ _duck_ was on a _path_.					/10

4. CVCC and CCVC

					Comments	Score
(a) In List	stod spuf bral griv glup tras flen blit crog jesk					/10
(b) In Text	_Brit_ and _Brad_ will _swim_ _past_ the _raft_ in the _pond_. _Glen_ has _dust_ on the _brim_ of his _best_ hat.					/10

5. Silent e

					Comments	Score
(a) In List	lefe cobe lope vime pume gude kede paze zite nade					/10
(b) In Text	_Steve_ wants to _hide_ his _flute_ and _bike_ at _home_. _Eve_ _hopes_ that the _rake_ and the _twine_ are on _sale_.					/10

Phonics and Structural Analysis

Phonics and Structural Analysis Survey Scoring Sheet, Test 4

6. r-Controlled Vowels					Comments	Score
(a) In List	burb pert furd	lork sirm jard	horm cerk	garn firl		/10
(b) In Text	*Kurt* lives on a *farm* that sells *corn* and *chard*. *Fern* likes *more* *circles* on *her* *purse* and *shirt*.					/10

7. Advanced Consonants (-tch, -dge, -x, qu, soft c & g, kn, gn, wr, -lk)					Comments	Score
(a) In List	wrom kitch quiv	fuge salk gnas	wox knev	bedge foce		/10
(b) In Text	The girls *walk* by the *edge* of the *quiet* river. Did you *know* that a *gnome* is small? Can you *wrap* the *parcel*? *Mitch* planted a *box* of *sage* seeds.					/10

8. Vowel Teams								Comments	Score
oa, ea, oo, **ai, ol, ay,** **ou, oi, oy,** **au, aw, oe,** **ew, al, igh**	hoak paint toid claw lighs	goat spold spoil loe tight	gream fold poyt toe	meal fayn oyster bew	joot tray naut stew	spoon boun auto dalt	mait groun daw calm		/30

9. Multi-Syllable					Comments	Score
(a) 2-Syllable	fic-tion va-cant ham-ster	mon-ey pump-kin schol-ar	let-tuce cof-fee	den-tist fif-teen		/10
(b) 3-Syllable	bas-ket-ball pho-to-graph de-fi-ant	tur-bu-lent com-put-er re-mem-ber	im-pro-vise straw-ber-ry	hu-mor-ous high-light-er		/10
(c) 4-Syllable	ex-per-i-ment con-vert-i-ble bi-ol-o-gy	dis-cov-er-y har-mon-i-ca hor-i-zon-tal	mac-a-ro-ni el-e-va-tor	im-pos-si-ble ac-ti-va-ted		/10

10. Prefixes and Suffixes						Comments	Score
dis-, non-, **in-, pre-, re-,** **un-, con-,** **mis-, -tion,** **-ous, -ness,** **-able, -ful,** **-ary, -ment**	disappear inactive unveil mistreat fairness hopeful	disagree preheat unlock attention awareness dietary	nonverbal preschool concede induction enjoyable literary	nonlife reknit concur fabulous adorable statement	incapable replay misread enormous peaceful payment		/30

Phonics and Structural Analysis

Phonics and Structural Analysis Survey Scoring Sheet, Test 4

11. Plurals (-s, -es)

					Comments	Score
(a) No spelling changes	mugs	bricks	guesses	actresses		
	rashes	marshes	watches	porches		
	suffixes	hoaxes	blazes	prizes		/12
(b) With spelling changes (*y* to *i*, *fe*, *fe* to *v*)	fries	bunnies	lillies	supplies		
	families	patties	shelves	halves		
	knives	wives	loaves	scarves		/12

12. Inflectional Verb Endings (-s, -es, -ed, -ing)

					Comments	Score
(a) No spelling changes	mops	drips	coats	waxes		
	crashes	wishes	rushed	nailed		
	heated	playing	sketching	pitching		/12
(b) With spelling changes	flies	denies	copies	glorifies		
	dried	planned	grabbed	slipped		
	clapping	hiding	sliding	organizing		/12

13. Possessives and Contractions

					Comments	Score
(a) Possessives (singular, plural, and irregular)	principal's	king's	child's	flower's		
	giant's	worker's	drivers'	directors'		
	ducks'	sheep's	ladies'	children's		/12
(b) Contractions (pronoun-verb and with *not*)	I'll	you've	they'll	he's		
	we're	it's	hasn't	doesn't		
	shouldn't	aren't	couldn't	mustn't		/12

14. Comparative Endings (-er, -est)

					Comments	Score
(a) No spelling changes	poorer	shorter	richer	harder		
	colder	prouder	neatest	longest		
	coldest	loudest	dampest	slickest		/12
(b) With spelling changes	dimmer	tanner	bigger	wetter		
	redder	hotter	saddest	thinnest		
	gladdest	flattest	maddest	fittest		/12

Phonics and Structural Analysis

	Phonics and Structural Analysis Survey, Test 5				
Skill 1(a)	h o f n s i w p a				
	k b v y c t l qu m				
Skill 1(b)	e j d r u x z g				
Skill 2(a)	col	hin	rul	caz	dup
	jep	gat	hos	vig	tez
Skill 2(b)	Gus and Pat had to cut the ham. Jan sat on the mat Ted and Vin fed the dog in the den. Rob had to get the wet mop.				
Skill 3(a)	nath	thop	whek	duth	shib
	dush	rach	deng	chil	zeck
Skill 3(b)	Check which map is hung. Jen can wash a sock or hat. A ship hit the dock. What did Tom do with that jug?				
Skill 4(a)	rund	fleb	clav	gosp	keld
	gred	zost	trul	skal	fint
Skill 4(b)	Fred had to stop and grab the flag by hand. Ross will miss his swim at camp.				
Skill 5(a)	vate	cupe	wote	sine	veke
	jipe	mobe	gade	lune	tefe
Skill 5(b)	Luke came to get fake pine cones at the sale. The dog made a pile of bones in the hole.				

Phonics and Structural Analysis

Phonics and Structural Analysis Survey, Test 5

Skill 6(a)	warl vurb pern serd lirp tarf mort cirv dorv nurk
Skill 6(b)	Dirk hurt his leg on a sharp and hard corner. She bore the dirt for the ferns with a fork.
Skill 7(a)	knil nage natch celm wrib vedge quen belk drox gnaz
Skill 7(b)	Madge and I talk at lunch. Ginny was quick to put away her pencil. I know how to patch a hole. Max wrote about a gnat.
Skill 8	poat toast fea seal loof book waip mail trolk bolt blay cay lour south voit coin koy noy raun haut taw baw loel moep yewn rew galk halk digh thigh
Skill 9(a)	lucky credit napkin problem frantic salad medal athlete blister cement
Skill 9(b)	conclusion melody tomato generate slippery syllable acceptance cabinet horizon family
Skill 9(c)	operator manufacture preoccupied captivity secretary facilitate impossible territory calculator incredible
Skill 10	discontent dismiss nonliving nonmeat inflame insincere preset precede review retell unclear unrest conceal conjoin misbehave misplace ignition creation precious cautious kindness wilderness miserable portable grateful powerful monetary necessary equipment settlement

Phonics and Structural Analysis

Phonics and Structural Analysis Survey, Test 5

Skill 11(a)	mats	smocks	dresses	kisses	ashes	wishes
	churches	arches	axes	mailboxes	sizes	mazes
Skill 11(b)	dries	trophies	groceries	cities	pennies	duties
	calves	loaves	selves	knives	thieves	hooves
Skill 12(a)	jogs	shoots	wrecks	mixes	pushes	rises
	shouted	added	laughed	bursting	staying	digesting
Skill 12(b)	replies	marries	defies	worries	fried	solved
	drummed	skidded	picturing	dropping	rotating	cycling
Skill 13(a)	waiter's	dancer's	writer's	farmer's	baby's	parent's
	pets'	foxes'	visitors'	teachers'	oxen's	men's
Skill 13(b)	I've	you'd	he'll	they're	she's	we'd
	can't	weren't	wouldn't	hasn't	shouldn't	isn't
Skill 14(a)	firmer	taller	longer	calmer	odder	smarter
	fairest	wildest	smallest	youngest	loudest	coldest
14(b)	madder	bigger	fitter	thinner	fatter	flatter
	gladdest	slimmest	reddest	hottest	dimmest	tannest

Phonics and Structural Analysis

Phonics and Structural Analysis Survey Scoring Sheet, Test 5

1. Letters

		Score									Score
(a) Names	h o f n s i w p a k b v y c t l qu m e j d r u x z g	/26	**(b) Sounds**	/h/ /o/ /f/ /n/ /s/ /i/ /w/ /p/ /a/ /k/ /b/ /v/ /y/ /k/ /t/ /l/ /kw/ /m/ /e/ /j/ /d/ /r/ /u/ /ks/ /z/ /g/						Consonants: /21 Vowels: /5

2. VC and CVC

		Comments	Score
(a) In List	col hin rul caz dup jep gat hos vig tez		/10
(b) In Text	*Gus* and *Pat* *had* to *cut* the *ham*. *Jan* *sat* *on* the *mat*. *Ted* and *Vin* *fed* the *dog* *in* the *den*. *Rob* *had* to *get* the *wet* *mop*.		/20

3. Consonant Digraphs

		Comments	Score
(a) In List	nath thop whek duth shib dush rach deng chil zeck		/10
(b) In Text	*Check* *which* map is *hung*. A *ship* hit the *dock*. Jen can *wash* a *sock* or hat. *What* did Tom do *with* *that* jug?		/10

4. CVCC and CCVC

		Comments	Score
(a) In List	rund fleb clav gosp keld gred zost trul skal fint		/10
(b) In Text	*Fred* had to *stop* and *grab* the *flag* by *hand*. *Ross* *will* *miss* his *swim* at *camp*.		/10

5. Silent e

		Comments	Score
(a) In List	vate cupe wote sine veke jipe mobe gade lune tefe		/10
(b) In Text	*Luke* *came* to get *fake* *pine* *cones* at the *sale*. The dog *made* a *pile* of *bones* in the *hole*.		/10

Phonics and Structural Analysis

Phonics and Structural Analysis Survey Scoring Sheet, Test 5

6. r-Controlled Vowels

			Comments	Score
(a) In List	warl vurb pern serd lirp tarf mort cirv dorv nurk			/10
(b) In Text	*Dirk* *hurt* his leg on a *sharp* and *hard* *corner*. She *bore* the *dirt* *for* the *ferns* with a *fork*.			/10

7. Advanced Consonants (-tch, -dge, -x, qu, soft c & g, kn, gn, wr, -lk)

			Comments	Score
(a) In List	knil nage natch celm wrib vedge quen belk drox gnaz			/10
(b) In Text	*Madge* and I *talk* at lunch. *Ginny* was *quick* to put away her *pencil*. I *know* how to *patch* a hole. *Max* *wrote* about a *gnat*.			/10

8. Vowel Teams

oa, ea, oo, ai, ol, ay, ou, oi, oy, au, aw, oe, ew, al, igh								Comments	Score
	poat toast fea seal loof book waip mail trolk bolt blay cay lour south voit coin koy noy raun haut taw baw loel moep yewn rew galk halk digh thigh									/30

9. Multi-Syllable

			Comments	Score
(a) 2-Syllable	luck-y cred-it nap-kin prob-lem fran-tic sal-ad med-al ath-lete blis-ter ce-ment			/10
(b) 3-Syllable	con-clu-sion mel-o-dy to-ma-to gen-er-ate slip-per-y syl-la-ble ac-cept-ance cab-i-net ho-ri-zon fam-i-ly			/10
(c) 4-Syllable	op-er-a-tor man-u-fac-ture pre-oc-cu-pied cap-tiv-i-ty sec-re-tar-y fa-cil-i-tate im-pos-si-ble ter-ri-to-ry cal-cu-la-tor in-cred-i-ble			/10

10. Prefixes and Suffixes

dis-, non-, in-, pre-, re-, un-, con-, mis-, -tion, -ous, -ness, -able, -ful, -ary, -ment					Comments	Score
discontent insincere unclear misplace kindness powerful	dismiss preset unrest ignition wilderness monetary	nonliving precede conceal creation miserable necessary	nonmeat review conjoin precious portable equipment	inflame retell misbehave cautious grateful settlement		/30

Phonics and Structural Analysis

Phonics and Structural Analysis Survey Scoring Sheet, Test 5

11. Plurals (-s, -es)

					Comments	Score
(a) No spelling changes	mats	smocks	dresses	kisses		
	ashes	wishes	churches	arches		
	axes	mailboxes	sizes	mazes		/12
(b) With spelling changes (*y* to *i*, *f*, *fe* to *v*)	dries	trophies	groceries	cities		
	pennies	duties	calves	loaves		
	selves	knives	thieves	hooves		/12

12. Inflectional Verb Endings (-s, -es, -ed, -ing)

					Comments	Score
(a) No spelling changes	jogs	shoots	wrecks	mixes		
	pushes	rises	shouted	added		
	laughed	bursting	staying	digesting		/12
(b) With spelling changes	replies	marries	defies	worries		
	fried	solved	drummed	skidded		
	picturing	dropping	rotating	cycling		/12

13. Possessives and Contractions

					Comments	Score
(a) Possessives (singular, plural, and irregular)	waiter's	dancer's	writer's	farmer's		
	baby's	parent's	pets'	foxes'		
	visitors'	teachers'	oxen's	men's		/12
(b) Contractions (pronoun-verb and with *not*)	I've	you'd	he'll	they're		
	she's	we'd	can't	weren't		
	wouldn't	hasn't	shouldn't	isn't		/12

14. Comparative Endings (-er, -est)

						Comments	Score
(a) No spelling changes	firmer	taller	longer	calmer	odder		
	smarter	fairest	wildest	smallest	youngest		
	loudest	coldest					/12
(b) With spelling changes	madder	bigger	fitter	thinner	fatter		
	flatter	gladdest	slimmest	reddest	hottest		
	dimmest	tannest					/12

Phonics and Structural Analysis

	Phonics and Structural Analysis Survey, Test 6				
Skill 1(a)	g r b z m y u p j l i o e w h x d s				
Skill 1(b)	f c qu v a t n k				
Skill 2(a)	ked	tob	nes	buk	fak
	dif	nal	pum	zop	pib
Skill 2(b)	The big bag was in the hut. Can you hit the bug on my leg? Dan and his dad won a hat. The cat sat on his lap.				
Skill 3(a)	thal	teck	wath	vock	kish
	shub	whid	whef	mang	gech
Skill 3(b)	Tom got a ring at a shop. Which fish did Mom pick? Deb is a chess whiz. Then he sang a song.				
Skill 4(a)	scaf	cemp	jusk	flot	vunt
	brek	glat	swid	solt	hink
Skill 4(b)	I plan to get a golf club and a ball. Stop and grab the pink lamp from my hand.				
Skill 5(a)	seme	beve	tane	koze	lume
	hafe	pude	nive	lote	fide
Skill 5(b)	The haze will fade from the lake in time for games. Mike made a joke to make us smile.				

Phonics and Structural Analysis

	Phonics and Structural Analysis Survey, Test 6						
Skill 6(a)	surn	terb	sirt	gort	carg		
	darm	lorp	virn	nerk	murd		
Skill 6(b)	I saw a bird dart by the porch and turn to the water.						
	The jar over there is more dirty than the urn.						
Skill 7(a)	sotch	hudge	plax	nace	knef		
	jolk	pige	wral	quap	gnaz		
Skill 7(b)	Get a quart of milk.						
	The box will not budge.						
	It will gnaw on the giant red pencil.						
	I had a scratch on my knee and my wrist.						
Skill 8	toaf	hoax	steab	jeans	doot	stool	taim	paid
	stol	mold	glay	fay	foud	soun	rois	joit
	gloy	joy	vaud	laun	daw	jaw	loe	foe
	tew	knew	shal	talk	trigh	migh		
Skill 9(a)	actor	quiver	magic	improve	package		
	booklet	radish	bucket	soccer	finger		
Skill 9(b)	optional	talkative	excellence	bakery	demolish		
	butterfly	possible	hydrogen	favorite	cucumber		
Skill 9(c)	exaggerate	aluminum	delivery	citizenship	elevator		
	category	anybody	accidental	particular	helicopter		
Skill 10	dislocate	dislike	nonfat	nonslip	invisible	inaccurate	
	preview	pretest	refill	repay	unfair	undo	
	construct	convict	misspell	mistake	action	section	
	furious	numerous	business	illness	knowable	valuable	
	hopeful	restful	visionary	honorary	payment	treatment	

Phonics and Structural Analysis

Phonics and Structural Analysis Survey, Test 6						
Skill 11(a)	fans	pets	mattresses	glasses	blushes	sashes
	beaches	couches	sixes	hoaxes	glazes	snoozes
Skill 11(b)	skies	carries	ponies	studies	copies	butterflies
	elves	thieves	wolves	shelves	halves	knives
Skill 12(a)	hangs	strolls	skips	relaxes	launches	polishes
	asked	yelled	pelting	helping	starting	delaying
Skill 12(b)	applies	dries	identifies	worries	cried	supplied
	begged	stubbed	getting	timing	believing	recycling
Skill 13(a)	rider's	gardener's	uncle's	sheriff's	nurse's	fighter's
	experts'	horses'	friends'	artists'	people's	geese's
Skill 13(b)	I'm	you're	he'd	she'll	it's	they've
	didn't	haven't	wasn't	shouldn't	couldn't	mustn't
Skill 14(a)	softer	sharper	kinder	brighter	quieter	harsher
	poorest	newest	smallest	deepest	coolest	sweetest
14(b)	hotter	slimmer	sadder	hipper	redder	madder
	tallest	fittest	wettest	thinnest	biggest	tannest

Phonics and Structural Analysis

Phonics and Structural Analysis Survey Scoring Sheet, Test 6

1. Letters		Score			Score
(a) Names	g r b z m y u p j l i o e w h x d s f c qu v a t n k	 /26	**(b) Sounds**	/g/ /r/ /b/ /z/ /m/ /y/ /u/ /p/ /j/ /l/ /i/ /o/ /e/ /w/ /h/ /ks/ /d/ /s/ /f/ /k/ /kw/ /v/ /a/ /t/ /n/ /k/	Consonants: /21 Vowels: /5

2. VC and CVC		Comments	Score
(a) In List	ked tob nes buk fak dif nal pum zop pib		/10
(b) In Text	The *big bag was in* the *hut*. *Can* you *hit* the *bug on* my *leg*? *Dan* and *his dad won* a *hat*. The *cat sat on his lap*.		/20

3. Consonant Digraphs		Comments	Score
(a) In List	thal teck wath vock kish shub whid whef mang gech		/10
(b) In Text	Tom got a *ring* at a *shop*. *Which fish* did Mom *pick*? Deb is a *chess whiz*. *Then* he *sang* a *song*.		/10

4. CVCC and CCVC		Comments	Score
(a) In List	scaf cemp jusk flot vunt brek glat swid solt hink		/10
(b) In Text	I *plan* to get a *golf club* and a *ball*. *Stop* and *grab* the *pink lamp from* my *hand*.		/10

5. Silent e		Comments	Score
(a) In List	seme beve tane koze lume hafe pude nive lote fide		/10
(b) In Text	The *haze* will *fade* from the *lake* in *time* for *games*. *Mike made* a *joke* to *make* us *smile*.		/10

Phonics and Structural Analysis

Phonics and Structural Analysis Survey Scoring Sheet, Test 6

6. r-Controlled Vowels		Comments	Score
(a) In List	surn terb sirt gort carg darm lorp virn nerk murd		/10
(b) In Text	I saw a *bird dart* by the *porch* and *turn* to the *water*. The *jar over* there is *more dirty* than the *urn*.		/10

7. Advanced Consonants (-tch, -dge, -x, qu, soft c & g, kn, gn, wr, -lk)		Comments	Score
(a) In List	sotch hudge plax nace knef jolk pige wral quap gnaz		/10
(b) In Text	Get a *quart* of *milk*. The *box* will not *budge*. It will *gnaw* on the *giant* red *pencil*. I had a *scratch* on my *knee* and my *wrist*.		/10

8. Vowel Teams		Comments	Score
oa, ea, oo, **ai, ol, ay,** **ou, oi, oy,** **au, aw, oe,** **ew, al, igh**	toaf hoax steab jeans doot stool taim paid stol mold glay fay foud soun rois joit gloy joy vaud laun daw jaw loe foe tew knew shal talk trigh migh		/30

9. Multi-Syllable		Comments	Score
(a) 2-Syllable	ac-tor quiv-er mag-ic im-prove pack-age book-let rad-ish buck-et soc-cer fin-ger		/10
(b) 3-Syllable	op-tion-al talk-a-tive ex-cel-lence bak-er-y de-mol-ish but-ter-fly pos-si-ble hy-dro-gen fa-vor-ite cu-cum-ber		/10
(c) 4-Syllable	ex-ag-ger-ate a-lu-mi-num de-liv-er-y cit-i-zen-ship el-e-va-tor cat-e-go-ry an-y-bod-y ac-ci-den-tal par-tic-u-lar hel-i-cop-ter		/10

10. Prefixes and Suffixes					Comments	Score
dis-, non-, **in-, pre-, re-,** **un-, con-,** **mis-, -tion,** **-ous, -ness,** **-able, -ful,** **-ary, -ment**	dislocate inaccurate unfair mistake business restful	dislike preview undo action illness visionary	nonfat pretest construct section knowable honorary	nonslip refill convict furious valuable payment	invisible repay misspell numerous hopeful treatment	/30

Phonics and Structural Analysis

Phonics and Structural Analysis Survey Scoring Sheet, Test 6					Comments	Score
11. Plurals (-s, -es)						
(a) No spelling changes	fans	pets	mattresses	glasses		
	blushes	sashes	beaches	couches		
	sixes	hoaxes	glazes	snoozes		/12
(b) With spelling changes (y to i, f, fe, to v)	skies	carries	ponies	studies		
	copies	butterflies	elves	thieves		
	wolves	shelves	halves	knives		/12

12. Inflectional Verb Endings (-s, -es, -ed, -ing)					Comments	Score
(a) No spelling changes	hangs	strolls	skips	relaxes		
	launches	polishes	asked	yelled		
	pelting	helping	starting	delaying		/12
(b) With spelling changes	applies	dries	identifies	worries		
	cried	supplied	begged	stubbed		
	getting	timing	believing	recycling		/12

13. Possessives and Contractions					Comments	Score
(a) Possessives (singular, plural, and irregular)	rider's	gardener's	uncle's	sheriff's		
	nurse's	fighter's	experts'	horses'		
	friends'	artists'	people's	geese's		/12
(b) Contractions (pronoun-verb and with _not_)	I'm	you're	he'd	she'll		
	it's	they've	didn't	haven't		
	wasn't	shouldn't	couldn't	mustn't		/12

14. Comparative Endings (-er, -est)					Comments	Score
(a) No spelling changes	softer	sharper	kinder	brighter		
	quieter	harsher	poorest	newest		
	smallest	deepest	coolest	sweetest		/12
(b) With spelling changes	hotter	slimmer	sadder	hipper		
	redder	madder	tallest	fittest		
	wettest	thinnest	biggest	tannest		/12

Fluency
Assessment

Our Great Forests

Long ago, most of the eastern United States was a big forest. The land was covered with trees. Today big parts of this forest are gone. People cut down the trees as they moved west. They used the trees to make farms and cities. Now people plant new forests. They want to put back some of the trees that were cut down.

There are three kinds of forests in the United States. In one kind the trees lose their leaves in the fall. In a second kind, the trees stay green all year. The third kind is a mixed forest. It has trees that lose their leaves and trees that stay green.

If you visit a forest, look at the trees. See if you can tell what kind they are.

✔ Why are people planting new forests?

✔ What are two types of forest in the United States?

Name: _____ Date: _____

Our Great Forests

11	Long ago, most of the eastern United States was a big
21	forest. The land was covered with trees. Today big parts
33	of this forest are gone. People cut down the trees as they
44	moved west. They used the trees to make farms and cities.
55	Now people plant new forests. They want to put back some
62	of the trees that were cut down.
72	There are three kinds of forests in the United States.
86	In one kind the trees lose their leaves in the fall. In a second
98	kind, the trees stay green all year. The third kind is a
110	mixed forest. It has trees that lose their leaves and trees that
112	stay green.
126	If you visit a forest, look at the trees. See if you can tell
130	what kind they are.

✔ Why are people planting new forests?

✔ What are two types of forest in the United States?

Words Read	–	Errors	=	WCPM

☐ **Fall (94 WCPM)**
☐ **Winter (112 WCPM)**
☐ **Spring (123 WCPM)**

WCPM	/	Words Read	=	Accuracy %

PROSODY				
	L1	L2	L3	L4
Reading in Phrases	O	O	O	O
Pace	O	O	O	O
Syntax	O	O	O	O
Self-correction	O	O	O	O
Intonation	O	O	O	O

Working Dogs

Dogs make wonderful pets. They are fun to play with, and they can be very friendly as well. But did you know that dogs can have jobs, too? Many dogs work. They help people in important ways.

Some dogs are trained to help blind people get around. They are called seeing-eye dogs. Other dogs are trained to help deaf people. They can alert their owners to sounds. The sound may be a fire alarm or a doorbell.

Most dogs have an excellent sense of smell. That is why police officers use them to locate people who are lost or hurt. Dogs also herd animals. They know how to make sheep and cows move along. They help to protect the animals as well. Even though dogs like to play, they are hard workers, too!

✔ What are "seeing-eye dogs"?
✔ Name two types of jobs dogs can have.

Name: _____ Date: _____

Working Dogs

10	Dogs make wonderful pets. They are fun to play with,
22	and they can be very friendly as well. But did you know
33	that dogs can have jobs, too? Many dogs work. They help
37	help people in important ways.
47	Some dogs are trained to help blind people get around.
58	They are called seeing-eye dogs. Other dogs are trained to
68	help deaf people. They can alert their owners to sounds.
78	The sound may be a fire alarm or a doorbell.
89	Most dogs have an excellent sense of smell. That is why
100	police officers use them to locate people who are lost or
110	hurt. Dogs also herd animals. They know how to make
120	sheep and cows move along. They help to protect the
131	animals as well. Even though dogs like to play, they are
134	hard workers, too!

 What are "seeing-eye dogs"?

 Name two types of jobs dogs can have.

Words Read	–	Errors	=	WCPM

☐ **Fall (94 WCPM)**
☐ **Winter (112 WCPM)**
☐ **Spring (123 WCPM)**

WCPM	/	Words Read	=	Accuracy %

PROSODY

	L1	L2	L3	L4
Reading in Phrases	O	O	O	O
Pace	O	O	O	O
Syntax	O	O	O	O
Self-correction	O	O	O	O
Intonation	O	O	O	O

Kurt Goes to School

Mark had a playful dog named Kurt. Kurt was a nice dog, but he had a problem. He disturbed people when they were eating by putting his paws on the table and barking.

"Kurt will have to go to dog school," Mark's father declared.

Kurt had to stay at the school for three days. Mark missed him. He could not wait until Kurt would come home.

Finally, Mark and his dad went to pick up Kurt. While they ate lunch, Kurt sat quietly. He did not put his paws on the table. He did not bark.

Mark's father noted, "See, Mark. Kurt is now a well-behaved dog." Mark was just happy to have his furry pal back.

When they got home, Mark talked to Kurt. "From now on, I'm the only one who goes to school," he said. Kurt wagged his tail.

✔ What is Kurt's problem?

✔ How does Mark's dad solve the problem?

Name: _____ Date: _____

Kurt Goes to School

11	Mark had a playful dog named Kurt. Kurt was a nice
22	dog, but he had a problem. He disturbed people when they
33	were eating by putting his paws on the table and barking.
43	"Kurt will have to go to dog school," Mark's father
44	declared.
55	Kurt had to stay at the school for three days. Mark
65	missed him. He could not wait until Kurt would come
66	home.
77	Finally, Mark and his dad went to pick up Kurt. While
90	they ate lunch, Kurt sat quietly. He did not put his paws on
96	the table. He did not bark.
105	Mark's father noted, "See, Mark. Kurt is now a
116	well-behaved dog." Mark was just happy to have his furry
118	pal back.
128	When they got home, Mark talked to Kurt. "From now
140	on, I'm the only one who goes to school," he said. Kurt
143	wagged his tail.

✔ What is Kurt's problem?

✔ How does Mark's dad solve the problem?

Words Read	–	Errors	=	WCPM

☐ **Fall (94 WCPM)**
☐ **Winter (112 WCPM)**
☐ **Spring (123 WCPM)**

WCPM	/	Words Read	=	Accuracy %

PROSODY				
	L1	L2	L3	L4
Reading in Phrases	O	O	O	O
Pace	O	O	O	O
Syntax	O	O	O	O
Self-correction	O	O	O	O
Intonation	O	O	O	O

Slow as a Sloth

Sloths live in the rainforests of Central and South America. They are very slow moving. They may stay in the same tree for most of their lives. They can live for 30 years. They do not need much food because they are so slow. Sloths eat fruit, buds, and twigs.

There are two types of sloths. One has two toes on each foot. The other type has three toes. They are about the size of a small dog. Their fur is gray and brown. Their faces look like they are smiling.

Their long arms and big claws help them hang from branches. Sloths may sleep for as long as 20 hours a day. While sleeping, they put their heads between their arms. This helps to hide them from predators. At night they are awake, looking for food.

✔️ Where do sloths live?

✔️ Why do sloths eat so little?

Name: _____ Date: _____

Slow as a Sloth

9	Sloths live in the rainforests of Central and South
20	America. They are very slow moving. They may stay in the
33	same tree for most of their lives. They can live for 30 years.
44	They do not need much food because they are so slow.
50	Sloths eat fruit, buds, and twigs.
62	There are two types of sloths. One has two toes on each
74	foot. The other type has three toes. They are about the size
87	of a small dog. Their fur is gray and brown. Their faces look
91	like they are smiling.
101	Their long arms and big claws help them hang from
113	branches. Sloths may sleep for as long as 20 hours a day.
122	While sleeping, they put their heads between their arms.
133	This helps to hide them from predators. At night they are
137	awake, looking for food.

✓ Where do sloths live?

✓ Why do sloths eat so little?

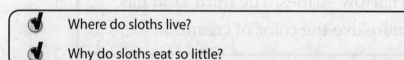

Words Read	–	Errors	=	WCPM

☐ **Fall (94 WCPM)**
☐ **Winter (112 WCPM)**
☐ **Spring (123 WCPM)**

WCPM	/	Words Read	=	Accuracy %

PROSODY				
	L1	L2	L3	L4
Reading in Phrases	O	O	O	O
Pace	O	O	O	O
Syntax	O	O	O	O
Self-correction	O	O	O	O
Intonation	O	O	O	O

Why Do Zebras Have Stripes?

Herds of zebras are found on the plains of Africa. They look like small horses. In fact, they are related to horses. But they do not have the colors of horses we know. Instead, they have stripes that are black and white. Every zebra has its own design.

Stripes help keep zebras cool. They also help to protect the animals. How? When zebras stand in a herd, their stripes seem to blend together. This makes it hard for a lion. It cannot see just one zebra. The herd may look like one big blob.

There are three types of zebras. Each type has stripes that are a little different. One kind has wide stripes that fade to gray. A second kind has narrow stripes. The third kind has white stripes that look more like the color of cream.

⏺ What animal does a zebra look like?

⏺ How do its stripes help the zebra?

Name: _____ Date: _____

Why Do Zebras Have Stripes?

11	Herds of zebras are found on the plains of Africa. They
23	look like small horses. In fact, they are related to horses. But
35	they do not have the colors of horses we know. Instead, they
46	have stripes that are black and white. Every zebra has its
48	own design.
58	Stripes help keep zebras cool. They also help to protect
68	the animals. How? When zebras stand in a herd, their
80	stripes seem to blend together. This makes it hard for a lion.
92	It cannot see just one zebra. The herd may look like one
94	big blob.
105	There are three types of zebras. Each type has stripes that
117	are a little different. One kind has wide stripes that fade to
128	gray. A second kind has narrow stripes. The third kind has
138	white stripes that look more like the color of cream.

✓ What animal does a zebra look like?

✓ How do its stripes help the zebra?

Words Read	–	Errors	=	WCPM

☐ **Fall (94 WCPM)**
☐ **Winter (112 WCPM)**
☐ **Spring (123 WCPM)**

WCPM	/	Words Read	=	Accuracy %

PROSODY				
	L1	L2	L3	L4
Reading in Phrases	O	O	O	O
Pace	O	O	O	O
Syntax	O	O	O	O
Self-correction	O	O	O	O
Intonation	O	O	O	O

Phillip Steps Up

Phillip Palmer was a quiet student. He completed his work and got good grades, but he just never had much to say.

One day, Phillip's class was working in groups on different projects. A boy in his group said to another boy, "That's not the way to do it. Why can't you do it the right way?" His voice sounded mean and nasty.

Phillip became angry. "You are being a bully," he said to the boy. "You cannot treat people that way because we have learned to respect and help each other."

The boy was surprised since no student had ever talked to him that way. He wanted to say something mean to Phillip. But he stopped when he saw his fierce and determined face.

"I'm sorry," said the boy. He was more respectful the rest of the time.

✔ What upsets Phillip?

✔ How does Phillip help a classmate?

Name: _____ Date: _____

Phillip Steps Up

9	Phillip Palmer was a quiet student. He completed his
20	work and got good grades, but he just never had much
22	to say.
31	One day, Phillip's class was working in groups on
42	different projects. A boy in his group said to another boy,
56	"That's not the way to do it. Why can't you do it the right
63	way?" His voice sounded mean and nasty.
74	Phillip became angry. "You are being a bully," he said to
85	the boy. "You cannot treat people that way because we have
92	learned to respect and help each other."
102	The boy was surprised since no student had ever talked
113	to him that way. He wanted to say something mean to
123	Phillip. But he stopped when he saw his fierce and
125	determined face.
136	"I'm sorry," said the boy. He was more respectful the rest
139	of the time.

✔ What upsets Phillip?

✔ How does Phillip help a classmate?

Words Read	–	Errors	=	WCPM

☐ **Fall (94 WCPM)**
☐ **Winter (112 WCPM)**
☐ **Spring (123 WCPM)**

WCPM	/	Words Read	=	Accuracy %

PROSODY				
	L1	L2	L3	L4
Reading in Phrases	O	O	O	O
Pace	O	O	O	O
Syntax	O	O	O	O
Self-correction	O	O	O	O
Intonation	O	O	O	O

Flood Rescue

Jack, his mother, and sister watched as rain fell in torrents. Since they lived at the top of a steep hill, Jack's family was lucky

"Cory's family lives right near the stream!" cried Jack. "Can we help them?" he asked.

"Of course," said Jack's mom. "Luckily my cell phone is working, and I can call them right now."

It wasn't long before Cory's family was knocking at the door. They were soaking wet and were glad to get into some dry clothes. Soon it was time for bed.

From his window, Jack watched the storm. Soon, the whole house was quiet.

Jack woke up early. He looked out the window and down the hill. He saw that the stream had flooded. Just then he heard the sound of motorboats.

"Phew!" said Jack. "Looks like everyone will be rescued."

☝ Why is Jack's family safe from the storm?

☝ Why is Jack worried about Cory's family?

Name: _____ Date: _____

Flood Rescue

10	Jack, his mother, and sister watched as rain fell in
22	torrents. Since they lived at the top of a steep hill, Jack's
25	family was lucky
34	"Cory's family lives right near the stream!" cried Jack.
40	"Can we help them?" he asked.
50	"Of course," said Jack's mom. "Luckily my cell phone is
58	working, and I can call them right now."
68	It wasn't long before Cory's family was knocking at the
80	door. They were soaking wet and were glad to get into some
88	dry clothes. Soon it was time for bed.
97	From his window, Jack watched the storm. Soon, the
101	whole house was quiet.
112	Jack woke up early. He looked out the window and down
124	the hill. He saw that the stream had flooded. Just then he
129	heard the sound of motorboats.
138	"Phew!" said Jack. "Looks like everyone will be rescued."

 Why is Jack's family safe from the storm?

 Why is Jack worried about Cory's family?

Words Read	–	Errors	=	WCPM

☐ **Fall (94 WCPM)**
☐ **Winter (112 WCPM)**
☐ **Spring (123 WCPM)**

WCPM	/	Words Read	=	Accuracy %

PROSODY				
	L1	L2	L3	L4
Reading in Phrases	O	O	O	O
Pace	O	O	O	O
Syntax	O	O	O	O
Self-correction	O	O	O	O
Intonation	O	O	O	O

Learning Something New

The program Amy watched in class was amazing. She never knew how important bats were. She discovered that bats help to pollinate flowers. They also eat tons of insects that damage crops and harm people. Bats were now Amy's new favorite animal.

That weekend Amy was at a picnic and heard people talking about bats.

"They are ugly and dangerous pests," one woman said. "They should be destroyed." Amy was upset when other people agreed with the woman. She had to say something.

"Bats are helpful," Amy said. "You don't see many mosquitoes bothering us at this picnic. That's because bats live around here. They eat insects at night. They won't bite you either. If they fly close to you, they will just dart away. They are chasing a tasty bug."

Amy was able to change their opinions about bats.

👆 What animal is Amy interested in?

👆 What does Amy do at the picnic?

Name: _____ Date: _____

Learning Something New

9	The program Amy watched in class was amazing. She
18	never knew how important bats were. She discovered that
29	bats help to pollinate flowers. They also eat tons of insects
39	that damage crops and harm people. Bats were now Amy's
42	new favorite animal.
52	That weekend Amy was at a picnic and heard people
55	talking about bats.
64	"They are ugly and dangerous pests," one woman said.
73	"They should be destroyed." Amy was upset when other
83	people agreed with the woman. She had to say something.
92	"Bats are helpful," Amy said. "You don't see many
101	mosquitoes bothering us at this picnic. That's because bats
112	live around here. They eat insects at night. They won't bite
125	you either. If they fly close to you, they will just dart away.
131	They are chasing a tasty bug."
140	Amy was able to change their opinions about bats.

✔ What animal is Amy interested in?

✔ What does Amy do at the picnic?

Words Read	–	Errors	=	WCPM

☐ **Fall (94 WCPM)**
☐ **Winter (112 WCPM)**
☐ **Spring (123 WCPM)**

WCPM	/	Words Read	=	Accuracy %

PROSODY				
	L1	L2	L3	L4
Reading in Phrases	O	O	O	O
Pace	O	O	O	O
Syntax	O	O	O	O
Self-correction	O	O	O	O
Intonation	O	O	O	O

Greyhounds

Greyhounds are dogs that can run very fast. Some of them run in races. Most greyhounds can race for just a few years. Then homes must be found for them. Special groups help them find homes.

A group that helps greyhounds find homes is called an *adoption group*. There are adoption groups for all kinds of dogs and cats. There are even groups for horses.

The people who help in these groups love animals. They are hopeful that each one will find a good home. They want to make sure the homes give good care.

Sometimes it is hard to find homes for greyhounds. They are cute but big. Many of them grow up on a racetrack. (In some states, greyhound racing is an organized sport.) They have never lived in a home. They have not lived with a family. Some adoption groups work with the greyhounds. They help them get ready to live in a home.

✔ How long can greyhounds be racing dogs?

✔ Why can it be difficult to find homes for greyhounds?

Name: _____ Date: _____

Greyhounds

10	Greyhounds are dogs that can run very fast. Some of
22	them run in races. Most greyhounds can race for just a few
32	years. Then homes must be found for them. Special groups
36	help them find homes.
46	A group that helps greyhounds find homes is called an
56	*adoption group.* There are adoption groups for all kinds of
65	dogs and cats. There are even groups for horses.
75	The people who help in these groups love animals. They
87	are hopeful that each one will find a good home. They want
95	to make sure the homes give good care.
104	Sometimes it is hard to find homes for greyhounds.
117	They are cute but big. Many of them grow up on a racetrack.
126	(In some states, greyhound racing is an organized sport.)
138	They have never lived in a home. They have not lived with
147	a family. Some adoption groups work with the greyhounds.
157	They help them get ready to live in a home.

✓ How long can greyhounds be racing dogs?

✓ Why can it be difficult to find homes for greyhounds?

Words Read	–	Errors	=	WCPM

☐ **Fall (94 WCPM)**
☐ **Winter (112 WCPM)**
☐ **Spring (123 WCPM)**

WCPM	/	Words Read	=	Accuracy %

PROSODY				
	L1	L2	L3	L4
Reading in Phrases	O	O	O	O
Pace	O	O	O	O
Syntax	O	O	O	O
Self-correction	O	O	O	O
Intonation	O	O	O	O

Space Age Science

The space program is exciting. Astronauts have visited the moon. They have gone around Earth many times in the shuttle. They also have helped build the space station. The space program has allowed us to explore Mars and other planets.

Many people like the space program. However, they wonder what it does for them. In fact, the space program is a part of many things. Some are things we use everyday. To send people into space, scientists had to create new technology. The new tools and products they made helped astronauts live in space. They also helped people on Earth.

Solar panels came from the space program. Freeze-dried food and water filters did as well. We have power tools without cords because of the space program. Equipment made for astronauts also has helped fight fires on Earth. The computer mouse came from the space program, too. We can thank the space program for making long-distance phone calls easier as well.

👋 Why does the author view the space program as "exciting"?

👋 How does the space program help people on Earth?

Name: _____ Date: _____

Space Age Science

8	The space program is exciting. Astronauts have visited
19	the moon. They have gone around Earth many times in the
28	shuttle. They also have helped build the space station.
38	The space program has allowed us to explore Mars and
40	other planets.
48	Many people like the space program. However, they
60	wonder what it does for them. In fact, the space program is
71	a part of many things. Some are things we use everyday.
81	To send people into space, scientists had to create new
90	technology. The new tools and products they made helped
100	astronauts live in space. They also helped people on Earth.
109	Solar panels came from the space program. Freeze-dried
120	food and water filters did as well. We have power tools
128	without cords because of the space program. Equipment
138	made for astronauts also has helped fight fires on Earth.
147	The computer mouse came from the space program, too.
157	We can thank the space program for making long-distance
162	phone calls easier as well.

✓ Why does the author view the space program as "exciting"?

✓ How does the space program help people on Earth?

Words Read	–	Errors	=	WCPM

☐ **Fall (94 WCPM)**
☐ **Winter (112 WCPM)**
☐ **Spring (123 WCPM)**

WCPM	/	Words Read	=	Accuracy %

PROSODY				
	L1	L2	L3	L4
Reading in Phrases	O	O	O	O
Pace	O	O	O	O
Syntax	O	O	O	O
Self-correction	O	O	O	O
Intonation	O	O	O	O

The Welcome Club

Kevin and Ally noticed that their town was becoming bigger. More people were moving in. "There are two new families in my neighborhood," Kevin said. "And I see new faces at school."

"Some of the kids are from other countries," Ally added. "It must be hard to learn a new language. It's hard enough being in a new school."

"I have an idea," Kevin said. "Let's see how we can help the new kids." And that is how the Welcome Club was born.

Kevin and Ally talked to their friends. Many of them wanted to help. They talked to their teacher. Then their principal helped them with a plan. When new students were about to start school, the principal informed the Welcome Club. The club ate lunch with them. They took them on a tour. They answered questions and helped them find places. The Welcome Club became the new students' first friends.

👆 What is the Welcome Club?

👆 How does Kevin and Ally's principal help the Welcome Club?

Name: _____ Date: _____

The Welcome Club

9	Kevin and Ally noticed that their town was becoming
19	bigger. More people were moving in. "There are two new
29	families in my neighborhood," Kevin said. "And I see new
32	faces at school."
42	"Some of the kids are from other countries," Ally added.
54	"It must be hard to learn a new language. It's hard enough
59	being in a new school."
71	"I have an idea," Kevin said. "Let's see how we can help
83	the new kids." And that is how the Welcome Club was born.
93	Kevin and Ally talked to their friends. Many of them
103	wanted to help. They talked to their teacher. Then their
113	principal helped them with a plan. When new students were
122	about to start school, the principal informed the Welcome
134	Club. The club ate lunch with them. They took them on a
143	tour. They answered questions and helped them find places.
152	The Welcome Club became the new students' first friends.

 What is the Welcome Club?

 How does Kevin and Ally's principal help the Welcome Club?

Words Read	–	Errors	=	WCPM

☐ **Fall (94 WCPM)**
☐ **Winter (112 WCPM)**
☐ **Spring (123 WCPM)**

WCPM	/	Words Read	=	Accuracy %

PROSODY				
	L1	L2	L3	L4
Reading in Phrases	O	O	O	O
Pace	O	O	O	O
Syntax	O	O	O	O
Self-correction	O	O	O	O
Intonation	O	O	O	O

The Campaign

Tyra thought that the school elections were silly. Three students wanted to be president of the fourth grade. Posters were going up in the halls. Many students were wearing paper tags that read "Vote For" with a name written in.

The candidates also were telling students why they should be president. Tyra had not heard one good reason from any of them. One candidate wanted shorter school days. Another wanted more options during lunch. The third promised no homework if elected.

"None of them have the power to fulfill any of these promises," Tyra muttered. "We need a serious candidate." And suddenly that candidate became Tyra.

Tyra told others she wanted to make a difference. She wanted to start a recycling program in school. She wanted to partner with other schools to find ways to help their community. Tyra did not think that anyone would take her seriously. But they did. Tyra was soon the class president.

👆 Why does Tyra think none of the candidates are serious?

👆 Who wins the fourth-grade election?

Name: _____ Date: _____

The Campaign

9	Tyra thought that the school elections were silly. Three
19	students wanted to be president of the fourth grade. Posters
29	were going up in the halls. Many students were wearing
40	paper tags that read "Vote For" with a name written in.
48	The candidates also were telling students why they
58	should be president. Tyra had not heard one good reason
67	from any of them. One candidate wanted shorter school
76	days. Another wanted more options during lunch. The third
81	promised no homework if elected.
92	"None of them have the power to fulfill any of these
100	promises," Tyra muttered. "We need a serious candidate."
106	And suddenly that candidate became Tyra.
116	Tyra told others she wanted to make a difference. She
126	wanted to start a recycling program in school. She wanted
137	to partner with other schools to find ways to help their
147	community. Tyra did not think that anyone would take her
157	seriously. But they did. Tyra was soon the class president.

 Why does Tyra think none of the candidates are serious?

Who wins the fourth-grade election?

Words Read	–	Errors	=	WCPM

☐ **Fall (94 WCPM)**
☐ **Winter (112 WCPM)**
☐ **Spring (123 WCPM)**

WCPM	/	Words Read	=	Accuracy %

PROSODY

	L1	L2	L3	L4
Reading in Phrases	O	O	O	O
Pace	O	O	O	O
Syntax	O	O	O	O
Self-correction	O	O	O	O
Intonation	O	O	O	O

Moon Mysteries

The moon is the biggest (and most familiar) object in our night sky. But how much do we really know about the moon? Throughout history, people have made up stories about the moon, but most are not true. For example, there is no "man in the moon." The face we think we see is formed by shadows on mountains and in craters.

Over many years, we have learned a lot about our moon. Many scientists think the moon was formed from Earth. It happened millions of years ago. An object about the size of Mars hit Earth when it was still forming. The material knocked off from Earth became the moon. Once in orbit, the moon's gravity helped stop Earth from wobbling.

Although the moon is dry, scientists now think there is water on the moon. A spacecraft sent to the moon detected water vapor. This may come from ice deep in dark craters.

✔️ What is the "man in the moon"?

✔️ What theory do scientists have about the moon's creation?

Name: _____ Date: _____

Moon Mysteries

11	The moon is the biggest (and most familiar) object in our
22	night sky. But how much do we really know about the
30	moon? Throughout history, people have made up stories
42	about the moon, but most are not true. For example, there is
55	no "man in the moon." The face we think we see is formed
62	by shadows on mountains and in craters.
73	Over many years, we have learned a lot about our moon.
83	Many scientists think the moon was formed from Earth. It
94	happened millions of years ago. An object about the size of
104	Mars hit Earth when it was still forming. The material
115	knocked off from Earth became the moon. Once in orbit, the
122	moon's gravity helped stop Earth from wobbling.
132	Although the moon is dry, scientists now think there is
143	water on the moon. A spacecraft sent to the moon detected
154	water vapor. This may come from ice deep in dark craters.

✓ What is the "man in the moon"?

✓ What theory do scientists have about the moon's creation?

Words Read	–	Errors	=	WCPM

☐ **Fall (94 WCPM)**
☐ **Winter (112 WCPM)**
☐ **Spring (123 WCPM)**

WCPM	/	Words Read	=	Accuracy %

PROSODY				
	L1	L2	L3	L4
Reading in Phrases	O	O	O	O
Pace	O	O	O	O
Syntax	O	O	O	O
Self-correction	O	O	O	O
Intonation	O	O	O	O

Wrong Number

Mr. Bayville did not like telephones. In particular, he disliked cell phones. He certainly did not think they were "smart" phones. "Cell phones are dangerous," he would say. Then he would say that people crashed their cars because of cell phones. Or that people walked into walls because of cell phones.

At the library, Mr. Bayville read about the invention of the telephone. He read about Alexander Graham Bell's first phone call. Bell had called his assistant Thomas Watson from another room. His first words were, "Mr. Watson, come here. I want to see you."

To get rid of the telephone, Mr. Bayville built a one-person time machine. He set the clock for March 10, 1876, and climbed in. The machine whirred and shook. In just a few moments, Mr. Bayville was in the room with Mr. Watson. Over the wire, Bell's voice could be heard, calling for Mr. Watson.

"Don't answer that call," Mr. Bayville shouted. "It's a wrong number."

👆 What does Mr. Bayville dislike?

👆 What text evidence proves this story is not realistic?

Name: _____ Date: _____

Wrong Number

9	Mr. Bayville did not like telephones. In particular, he
19	disliked cell phones. He certainly did not think they were
27	"smart" phones. "Cell phones are dangerous," he would
37	say. Then he would say that people crashed their cars
47	because of cell phones. Or that people walked into walls
51	because of cell phones.
61	At the library, Mr. Bayville read about the invention of
70	the telephone. He read about Alexander Graham Bell's first
79	phone call. Bell had called his assistant Thomas Watson
88	from another room. His first words were, "Mr. Watson,
95	come here. I want to see you."
105	To get rid of the telephone, Mr. Bayville built a
116	one-person time machine. He set the clock for March 10,
125	1876, and climbed in. The machine whirred and shook.
137	In just a few moments, Mr. Bayville was in the room with
147	Mr. Watson. Over the wire, Bell's voice could be heard,
151	calling for Mr. Watson.
160	"Don't answer that call," Mr. Bayville shouted. "It's a
162	wrong number."

✔ What does Mr. Bayville dislike?

✔ What text evidence proves this story is not realistic?

Words Read	–	Errors	=	WCPM

☐ **Fall (94 WCPM)**
☐ **Winter (112 WCPM)**
☐ **Spring (123 WCPM)**

WCPM	/	Words Read	=	Accuracy %

PROSODY				
	L1	L2	L3	L4
Reading in Phrases	O	O	O	O
Pace	O	O	O	O
Syntax	O	O	O	O
Self-correction	O	O	O	O
Intonation	O	O	O	O

Ancient Farming

The Andes mountains of Peru are changing. Weather patterns are more extreme. Farmers who live high in the mountains find it hard to grow crops in the ways they are used to. So, many farmers are looking to the past.

Hundreds of years ago farmers in the Andes grew their crops on mounds of earth. The crops were watered with canals. The ruins of the canals can be seen still. Farmers are now repairing the canals. They are building up the mounds. In some places where the old ways are being used, crops have increased.

The farmers are also planting some of the crops their ancestors grew. These plants are stronger. They grow better in the highest parts of the mountains. The plants will grow in spite of frost, floods, and drought. One of these crops is a small pink potato. The potatoes can be stored for up to two years. Then, they still can be eaten.

👆 How are the Andes changing?

👆 How did farmers in the Andes change their methods?

Name: _____ Date: _____

Ancient Farming

8	The Andes mountains of Peru are changing. Weather
18	patterns are more extreme. Farmers who live high in the
30	mountains find it hard to grow crops in the ways they are
40	used to. So, many farmers are looking to the past.
50	Hundreds of years ago farmers in the Andes grew their
60	crops on mounds of earth. The crops were watered with
72	canals. The ruins of the canals can be seen still. Farmers are
82	now repairing the canals. They are building up the mounds.
93	In some places where the old ways are being used, crops
95	have increased.
105	The farmers are also planting some of the crops their
114	ancestors grew. These plants are stronger. They grow better
125	in the highest parts of the mountains. The plants will grow
138	in spite of frost, floods, and drought. One of these crops is a
150	small pink potato. The potatoes can be stored for up to two
157	years. Then, they still can be eaten.

✔ How are the Andes changing?

✔ How did farmers in the Andes change their methods?

Words Read	–	Errors	=	WCPM

☐ **Fall (94 WCPM)**
☐ **Winter (112 WCPM)**
☐ **Spring (123 WCPM)**

WCPM	/	Words Read	=	Accuracy %

PROSODY				
	L1	L2	L3	L4
Reading in Phrases	O	O	O	O
Pace	O	O	O	O
Syntax	O	O	O	O
Self-correction	O	O	O	O
Intonation	O	O	O	O

Not Interested

Joel entered his new school and looked for his classroom. He had seen the school a couple of weeks ago when he had come to register with his dad. He liked what he saw because there were students from many different backgrounds. They all seemed to be really involved in their school.

In his class, Joel saw the familiar things. Some students were quiet while others liked to joke around. Some had little trouble with the work and some struggled. And he noticed that most were friendly, but there was always at least one kid who was not.

He met this kid at lunch. Because he was new, the kid thought Joel was an easy target. He made fun of Joel's clothes and the way he wore his hair. He made fun of Joel's old school, too.

Joel sighed. Having moved a lot, he was used to it. Joel stared at the kid for a long moment. Then he said, "I'm not interested."

✔ What new situation is Joel dealing with?

✔ What does Joel mean when he says he is "not interested"?

Name: _____ Date: _____

Not Interested

10	Joel entered his new school and looked for his classroom.
23	He had seen the school a couple of weeks ago when he had
35	come to register with his dad. He liked what he saw because
43	there were students from many different backgrounds. They
52	all seemed to be really involved in their school.
62	In his class, Joel saw the familiar things. Some students
73	were quiet while others liked to joke around. Some had little
83	trouble with the work and some struggled. And he noticed
94	that most were friendly, but there was always at least one
98	kid who was not.
110	He met this kid at lunch. Because he was new, the kid
121	thought Joel was an easy target. He made fun of Joel's
134	clothes and the way he wore his hair. He made fun of Joel's
137	old school, too.
148	Joel sighed. Having moved a lot, he was used to it.
160	Joel stared at the kid for a long moment. Then he said,
163	"I'm not interested."

✔ What new situation is Joel dealing with?

✔ What does Joel mean when he says he is "not interested"?

Words Read	–	Errors	=	WCPM

☐ **Fall (94 WCPM)**
☐ **Winter (112 WCPM)**
☐ **Spring (123 WCPM)**

WCPM	/	Words Read	=	Accuracy %

PROSODY				
	L1	L2	L3	L4
Reading in Phrases	O	O	O	O
Pace	O	O	O	O
Syntax	O	O	O	O
Self-correction	O	O	O	O
Intonation	O	O	O	O

Wildlife and the Bay

Many animals live in and around the bay not far from my town. We live on the Oregon coast. The blue sea makes a fine home for wildlife. Tiny and big fish live in the water, along with crabs and sea stars. Even small sharks swim along the shore. Mammals such as sea otters live there too. Birds cluster on the rocky cliffs above the bay.

The sea otters are strong swimmers and divers. They make their homes on the shore. But they spend most of their time in the water. Sea otters eat fish, mussels, and clams. It's fun to watch them crack open clams with rocks. They use their stomachs as a dining table. After a meal, they spend a long time cleaning their faces and whiskers.

Eagles make their homes on the cliffs above the bay. They lay their eggs in large nests made of sticks. After the eggs hatch, the mother and father leave the chicks. They fly off to catch fish for their babies.

👆 Where does the narrator live?

👆 Where do sea otters spend most of their time?

Name: _____ Date: _____

Wildlife and the Bay

12	Many animals live in and around the bay not far from my
24	town. We live on the Oregon coast. The blue sea makes a
36	fine home for wildlife. Tiny and big fish live in the water,
46	along with crabs and sea stars. Even small sharks swim
57	along the shore. Mammals such as sea otters live there too.
66	Birds cluster on the rocky cliffs above the bay.
75	The sea otters are strong swimmers and divers. They
87	make their homes on the shore. But they spend most of their
99	time in the water. Sea otters eat fish, mussels, and clams. It's
110	fun to watch them crack open clams with rocks. They use
122	their stomachs as a dining table. After a meal, they spend a
129	long time cleaning their faces and whiskers.
140	Eagles make their homes on the cliffs above the bay. They
152	lay their eggs in large nests made of sticks. After the eggs
164	hatch, the mother and father leave the chicks. They fly off to
169	catch fish for their babies.

✔ Where does the narrator live?

✔ Where do sea otters spend most of their time?

Words Read	–	Errors	=	WCPM

☐ **Fall (94 WCPM)**
☐ **Winter (112 WCPM)**
☐ **Spring (123 WCPM)**

WCPM	/	Words Read	=	Accuracy %

PROSODY				
	L1	L2	L3	L4
Reading in Phrases	O	O	O	O
Pace	O	O	O	O
Syntax	O	O	O	O
Self-correction	O	O	O	O
Intonation	O	O	O	O

Snakes That Stay Off the Ground

Some people think that all snakes live on the ground. That is not true. Snakes can live in the water and up in trees, too.

Water snakes have lived in many places in the world. They often prey on fish and other animals that live in the same area. These snakes can swim just like fish. To defend themselves, water snakes will puff up their heads and open their mouths. This makes them look large and fierce. They also can give off a bad smell as a defense.

Some snakes live in trees. These green or brown snakes are difficult to see. Their color patterns blend in with the dappled leaves of the tree. Some tree snakes can be very small and thin. These snakes are able to blend in with vines growing on a tree. Other tree snakes can flatten themselves and glide from tree to tree. Tree snakes usually prey on birds and frogs.

So whenever you think about snakes, look up as well as down! Snakes are not always on the ground.

✔️ Where can snakes live?

✔️ How can water snakes protect themselves?

Name: _____ Date: _____

Snakes That Stay Off the Ground

10	Some people think that all snakes live on the ground.
23	That is not true. Snakes can live in the water and up in
25	trees, too.
35	Water snakes have lived in many places in the world.
47	They often prey on fish and other animals that live in the
58	same area. These snakes can swim just like fish. To defend
68	themselves, water snakes will puff up their heads and open
78	their mouths. This makes them look large and fierce. They
88	also can give off a bad smell as a defense.
98	Some snakes live in trees. These green or brown snakes
109	are difficult to see. Their color patterns blend in with the
120	dappled leaves of the tree. Some tree snakes can be very
132	small and thin. These snakes are able to blend in with vines
142	growing on a tree. Other tree snakes can flatten themselves
153	and glide from tree to tree. Tree snakes usually prey on
156	birds and frogs.
167	So whenever you think about snakes, look up as well as
175	down! Snakes are not always on the ground.

✓ Where can snakes live?

✓ How can water snakes protect themselves?

Words Read	–	Errors	=	WCPM

☐ **Fall (94 WCPM)**
☐ **Winter (112 WCPM)**
☐ **Spring (123 WCPM)**

WCPM	/	Words Read	=	Accuracy %

PROSODY				
	L1	L2	L3	L4
Reading in Phrases	O	O	O	O
Pace	O	O	O	O
Syntax	O	O	O	O
Self-correction	O	O	O	O
Intonation	O	O	O	O

The Photo Album

Maribel wanted to know about her family history. She knew her family originally came from Mexico. But she was not sure exactly where they had lived. Everyone seemed to be too busy to answer her questions. Some who did listen just said they didn't know.

On a weekend trip to see her aunt and uncle, there was a thunderstorm. It was too rainy to go outside, so Maribel decided to ask her aunt and uncle about her family history.

"Your great-grandmother and great-grandfather came from a little town outside of Mexico City," her uncle said. "Your grandfather was a teacher. He taught in a high school in Los Angeles for many years."

"What did they look like?" Maribel asked.

"I can show you," her aunt said. She went into the bedroom and came back with a large photo album. She sat with Maribel and went through page after page of family photos. Maribel saw her great-grandparents, grandparents, and cousins. By the end of the weekend, Maribel proudly knew the history of her family.

✔ What does Maribel want to find out?

✔ Why does Maribel ask her aunt and uncle questions instead of playing?

Name: _____ Date: _____

The Photo Album

9	Maribel wanted to know about her family history. She
19	knew her family originally came from Mexico. But she was
29	not sure exactly where they had lived. Everyone seemed to
40	be too busy to answer her questions. Some who did listen
45	just said they didn't know.
58	On a weekend trip to see her aunt and uncle, there was a
68	thunderstorm. It was too rainy to go outside, so Maribel
79	decided to ask her aunt and uncle about her family history.
86	"Your great-grandmother and great-grandfather came
97	from a little town outside of Mexico City," her uncle said.
108	"Your grandfather was a teacher. He taught in a high school
114	in Los Angeles for many years."
121	"What did they look like?" Maribel asked.
132	"I can show you," her aunt said. She went into the
143	bedroom and came back with a large photo album. She sat
153	with Maribel and went through page after page of family
160	photos. Maribel saw her great-grandparents, grandparents,
170	and cousins. By the end of the weekend, Maribel proudly
176	knew the history of her family.

✔ What does Maribel want to find out?

✔ Why does Maribel ask her aunt and uncle questions instead of playing?

Words Read	–	Errors	=	WCPM

☐ **Fall (94 WCPM)**
☐ **Winter (112 WCPM)**
☐ **Spring (123 WCPM)**

WCPM	/	Words Read	=	Accuracy %

PROSODY				
	L1	L2	L3	L4
Reading in Phrases	O	O	O	O
Pace	O	O	O	O
Syntax	O	O	O	O
Self-correction	O	O	O	O
Intonation	O	O	O	O

Chinese New Year

The Chinese New Year begins with the first new moon in the year. It ends 15 days later when the moon is full. The date of the New Year changes every year. This is because the Chinese add an extra month every few years to their calendar.

The New Year is also known as the Spring Festival. In China, this festival is an important holiday. During a traditional New Year celebration, almost all business stops. People focus on their homes and family. Houses are cleaned and food prepared to honor ancestors.

Throughout the 15 days, many feasts are held. On the first night, one fish is left and not eaten. This fish is a symbol of abundance. People eat long noodles in the first five days as a symbol of long life. The Lantern Festival is held on the last night. Children carry lanterns through the streets. For the feast on that night, round dumplings are served. They are a symbol of the full moon and the family.

✔ Why does the date of the Chinese New Year change?

✔ What is another name for the Chinese New Year?

Name: _____ Date: _____

Chinese New Year

10	The Chinese New Year begins with the first new moon
23	in the year. It ends 15 days later when the moon is full.
34	The date of the New Year changes every year. This is
44	because the Chinese add an extra month every few years
47	to their calendar.
58	The New Year is also known as the Spring Festival. In
67	China, this festival is an important holiday. During a
75	traditional New Year celebration, almost all business stops.
85	People focus on their homes and family. Houses are cleaned
91	and food prepared to honor ancestors.
101	Throughout the 15 days, many feasts are held. On the
114	first night, one fish is left and not eaten. This fish is a
124	symbol of abundance. People eat long noodles in the first
136	five days as a symbol of long life. The Lantern Festival is
146	held on the last night. Children carry lanterns through the
156	streets. For the feast on that night, round dumplings are
168	served. They are a symbol of the full moon and the family.

✔ Why does the date of the Chinese New Year change?

✔ What is another name for the Chinese New Year?

Words Read	–	Errors	=	WCPM

☐ **Fall (94 WCPM)**
☐ **Winter (112 WCPM)**
☐ **Spring (123 WCPM)**

WCPM	/	Words Read	=	Accuracy %

PROSODY				
	L1	L2	L3	L4
Reading in Phrases	O	O	O	O
Pace	O	O	O	O
Syntax	O	O	O	O
Self-correction	O	O	O	O
Intonation	O	O	O	O

Toothbrush Trivia

The toothbrush, like the one you use everyday, has been in use for only about 75 years. The modern toothbrush has nylon bristles. It was invented in 1938. So how did people clean their teeth before that time?

Amazingly, ancient forms of toothbrushes have been found that are over five thousand years old! They are thin twigs with one end chewed. The chewing made the end into a brush. The stick was then rubbed against the teeth to clean them.

In the late 1400s, the Chinese invented a toothbrush that used bristles. The bristles were made from hog hair. The rough hairs came from the back of a hog's neck. They were put on a handle made of bone or bamboo.

Before World War II, people did not take care of their teeth like we do today. Soldiers in the war were given toothbrushes. These were modern brushes with nylon bristles. The soldiers were told to brush their teeth. People heard what the soldiers did. So they began to use toothbrushes on their own teeth.

👆 How old are the earliest toothbrushes?

👆 What caused more people to use toothbrushes in the twentieth century?

Name: _____ Date: _____

Toothbrush Trivia

10	The toothbrush, like the one you use everyday, has been
21	in use for only about 75 years. The modern toothbrush has
32	nylon bristles. It was invented in 1938. So how did people
38	clean their teeth before that time?
45	Amazingly, ancient forms of toothbrushes have been
56	found that are over five thousand years old! They are thin
66	twigs with one end chewed. The chewing made the end
78	into a brush. The stick was then rubbed against the teeth to
80	clean them.
90	In the late 1400s, the Chinese invented a toothbrush that
100	used bristles. The bristles were made from hog hair. The
112	rough hairs came from the back of a hog's neck. They were
121	put on a handle made of bone or bamboo.
132	Before World War II, people did not take care of their
143	teeth like we do today. Soldiers in the war were given
150	toothbrushes. These were modern brushes with nylon
160	bristles. The soldiers were told to brush their teeth. People
170	heard what the soldiers did. So they began to use
175	toothbrushes on their own teeth.

 How old are the earliest toothbrushes?

 What caused more people to use toothbrushes in the twentieth century?

Words Read	–	Errors	=	WCPM

☐ **Fall (94 WCPM)**
☐ **Winter (112 WCPM)**
☐ **Spring (123 WCPM)**

WCPM	/	Words Read	=	Accuracy %

PROSODY				
	L1	L2	L3	L4
Reading in Phrases	O	O	O	O
Pace	O	O	O	O
Syntax	O	O	O	O
Self-correction	O	O	O	O
Intonation	O	O	O	O

Fireball

Rico loved stargazing. He spent a few hours every clear night watching the skies. His sister thought he was wasting time, but Rico knew he wasn't. As he patiently watched, he saw amazing sights. He had seen the streak of a comet's tail and watched a space station whiz by.

Rico's favorite nights for watching the skies were when there was a meteor shower. These happened about four times a year. On one August night, he planned to see the Perseid shower, so he invited his sister to watch too.

"How boring!" his sister said. "You just sit and watch the sky?"

"Just try it," Rico said. At last, he convinced her to watch the sky with him.

After an hour, Rico's sister was bored and grumbling. She threatened to leave when suddenly a bright flash appeared and a fireball zipped across the sky. Rico and his sister could hear it crackle and sizzle as it burned. Then it disappeared over the horizon. Rico's sister was amazed. She would never again think that watching the sky was boring.

✓ What does Rico like to do?

✓ How does Rico's sister change at the end of the passage?

Name: _____ Date: _____

Fireball

10	Rico loved stargazing. He spent a few hours every clear
20	night watching the skies. His sister thought he was wasting
31	time, but Rico knew he wasn't. As he patiently watched, he
43	saw amazing sights. He had seen the streak of a comet's tail
50	and watched a space station whiz by.
59	Rico's favorite nights for watching the skies were when
68	there was a meteor shower. These happened about four
80	times a year. On one August night, he planned to see the
90	Perseid shower, so he invited his sister to watch too.
100	"How boring!" his sister said. "You just sit and watch
102	the sky?"
114	"Just try it," Rico said. At last, he convinced her to watch
118	the sky with him.
128	After an hour, Rico's sister was bored and grumbling. She
137	threatened to leave when suddenly a bright flash appeared
149	and a fireball zipped across the sky. Rico and his sister could
160	hear it crackle and sizzle as it burned. Then it disappeared
170	over the horizon. Rico's sister was amazed. She would never
178	again think that watching the sky was boring.

✓ What does Rico like to do?

✓ How does Rico's sister change at the end of the passage?

Words Read	–	Errors	=	WCPM

☐ **Fall (94 WCPM)**
☐ **Winter (112 WCPM)**
☐ **Spring (123 WCPM)**

WCPM	/	Words Read	=	Accuracy %

PROSODY				
	L1	L2	L3	L4
Reading in Phrases	O	O	O	O
Pace	O	O	O	O
Syntax	O	O	O	O
Self-correction	O	O	O	O
Intonation	O	O	O	O

Just One Rule

Long ago, there was a small village that had been established by people who did not like to be told what to do. So their village had no rules or regulations.

Everything was fine for a while. Then arguments began to break out. One woman complained that her neighbor did not get rid of his garbage fast enough. Another woman accused her neighbor of playing loud music late at night. Someone else announced that the big plastic flamingo he had put in his front yard had been stolen.

Finally, the people had a meeting. Everyone talked and shouted at once. At last, one man asked for quiet and said, "Someone has to conduct this meeting or we won't get anything done. It might as well be me." They all agreed and were quiet.

The man said, "I propose just one rule. Don't do anything to anyone else that you wouldn't want done to you. If you have a problem, then have a talk with me. But remember that I am not in charge." So everyone was happy after "Not in Charge" took charge.

✔ Why did the village have no rules?

✔ Why does the one rule make everyone happy?

Name: _____ Date: _____

Just One Rule

10	Long ago, there was a small village that had been
22	established by people who did not like to be told what to
31	do. So their village had no rules or regulations.
40	Everything was fine for a while. Then arguments began
50	to break out. One woman complained that her neighbor did
60	not get rid of his garbage fast enough. Another woman
70	accused her neighbor of playing loud music late at night.
79	Someone else announced that the big plastic flamingo he
88	had put in his front yard had been stolen.
97	Finally, the people had a meeting. Everyone talked and
109	shouted at once. At last, one man asked for quiet and said,
119	"Someone has to conduct this meeting or we won't get
131	anything done. It might as well be me." They all agreed and
133	were quiet.
144	The man said, "I propose just one rule. Don't do anything
156	to anyone else that you wouldn't want done to you. If you
167	have a problem, then have a talk with me. But remember
178	that I am not in charge." So everyone was happy after
183	"Not in Charge" took charge.

✔ Why did the village have no rules?

✔ Why does the one rule make everyone happy?

Words Read	–	Errors	=	WCPM

☐ **Fall (94 WCPM)**
☐ **Winter (112 WCPM)**
☐ **Spring (123 WCPM)**

WCPM	/	Words Read	=	Accuracy %

PROSODY				
	L1	L2	L3	L4
Reading in Phrases	O	O	O	O
Pace	O	O	O	O
Syntax	O	O	O	O
Self-correction	O	O	O	O
Intonation	O	O	O	O

Too Many Cats

Mr. Bixby had two big orange cats that he was very proud of. One had a magnificent long and bushy tail. The other cat was beautiful, with fur the color of marmalade jam.

The cats in the town knew that Mr. Bixby loved cats. So they were careful not to bother the birds around his home. They did not meow around his open window late at night.

One day, there was a big storm with several inches of rain. Many parts of the town were flooded. Mr. Bixby was fortunate that his house was on a hill, so his home was high and dry.

The day after the storm, Mr. Bixby went down into his basement. He was startled to find that the basement was full of many cats. "There are too many cats in here," he cried. "Where did they all come from?"

Mr. Bixby finally figured out why the cats were in the basement. They came to get away from the flood. So he began to call all of the townspeople. Everyone was thrilled their cats had been found safe and sound.

👆 How are Mr. Bixby's cats alike?

👆 Where do the cats go to escape the flood?

Name: _____ Date: _____

Too Many Cats

11	Mr. Bixby had two big orange cats that he was very
21	proud of. One had a magnificent long and bushy tail.
31	The other cat was beautiful, with fur the color of
33	marmalade jam.
45	The cats in the town knew that Mr. Bixby loved cats. So
56	they were careful not to bother the birds around his home.
67	They did not meow around his open window late at night.
78	One day, there was a big storm with several inches of
89	rain. Many parts of the town were flooded. Mr. Bixby was
102	fortunate that his house was on a hill, so his home was high
104	and dry.
115	The day after the storm, Mr. Bixby went down into his
126	basement. He was startled to find that the basement was full
138	of many cats. "There are too many cats in here," he cried.
144	"Where did they all come from?"
155	Mr. Bixby finally figured out why the cats were in the
166	basement. They came to get away from the flood. So he
176	began to call all of the townspeople. Everyone was thrilled
184	their cats had been found safe and sound.

✔ How are Mr. Bixby's cats alike?

✔ Where do the cats go to escape the flood?

Words Read	–	Errors	=	WCPM

☐ **Fall (94 WCPM)**
☐ **Winter (112 WCPM)**
☐ **Spring (123 WCPM)**

WCPM	/	Words Read	=	Accuracy %

PROSODY				
	L1	L2	L3	L4
Reading in Phrases	O	O	O	O
Pace	O	O	O	O
Syntax	O	O	O	O
Self-correction	O	O	O	O
Intonation	O	O	O	O

Paul's Big Problem

Paul Breen felt discouraged. He had been selling fruit, jams, and preserves for a long time. Paul's fruit shop was the best in town. Then a new store, Joy's Veggie Nook, opened up in a small mall nearby. Now Joy seemed to be stealing Paul's customers because his shop had fewer customers each day. He had heard that Joy's store was crowded.

Paul went to talk to Joy. "I am not getting any new customers," he complained. "And the customers I always have had are now coming to you for their healthy snacks."

Joy thought for a moment and then beamed. "I think I can help you out. Why don't we join your fruits with my vegetables? Your shop is roomier than what I have here and can certainly hold two businesses. Customers will buy your fruits, my veggies, and healthy salads from both of us."

Paul thought for a moment. Then he grinned. "We have found the perfect solution!"

What is Paul's problem?

How is the problem solved?

Name: _____ Date: _____

Paul's Big Problem

9	Paul Breen felt discouraged. He had been selling fruit,
20	jams, and preserves for a long time. Paul's fruit shop was
31	the best in town. Then a new store, Joy's Veggie Nook,
43	opened up in a small mall nearby. Now Joy seemed to be
51	stealing Paul's customers because his shop had fewer
60	customers each day. He had heard that Joy's store
62	was crowded.
74	Paul went to talk to Joy. "I am not getting any new
82	customers," he complained. "And the customers I always
93	have had are now coming to you for their healthy snacks."
104	Joy thought for a moment and then beamed. "I think I
116	can help you out. Why don't we join your fruits with my
127	vegetables? Your shop is roomier than what I have here and
136	can certainly hold two businesses. Customers will buy your
146	fruits, my veggies, and healthy salads from both of us."
156	Paul thought for a moment. Then he grinned. "We have
160	found the perfect solution!"

✓ What is Paul's problem?

✓ How is the problem solved?

Words Read	–	Errors	=	WCPM

☐ **Fall (110 WCPM)**
☐ **Winter (127 WCPM)**
☐ **Spring (139 WCPM)**

WCPM	/	Words Read	=	Accuracy %

PROSODY				
	L1	L2	L3	L4
Reading in Phrases	O	O	O	O
Pace	O	O	O	O
Syntax	O	O	O	O
Self-correction	O	O	O	O
Intonation	O	O	O	O

Trees or Gems?

Although both trees and gems are beneficial, or useful, trees are more beneficial. Gems are shiny and pretty. They can be made into necklaces and rings. Hard gems can be used in tools. But trees have even more uses. Trees give us paper and wood. They give us food as well, such as fruit and nuts. Birds and other animals live in trees. Trees also give us air to breathe.

Some people want to protect old trees that are still standing. Others say that aged trees need to be cleared away and young trees planted. The way to solve this argument is to cut only portions of a forest and leave others intact. That saves more trees and creates a healthy forest.

Many think that trees do not need to be protected because they are renewable. But as we cut them, we must replant them. That is the best way to save trees.

✔ Why does the author view trees as important?

✔ In the author's view, what is the best way to save trees?

Name: _____ Date: _____

Trees or Gems?

9	Although both trees and gems are beneficial, or useful,
19	trees are more beneficial. Gems are shiny and pretty. They
30	can be made into necklaces and rings. Hard gems can be
42	used in tools. But trees have even more uses. Trees give us
54	paper and wood. They give us food as well, such as fruit
65	and nuts. Birds and other animals live in trees. Trees also
70	give us air to breathe.
80	Some people want to protect old trees that are still
91	standing. Others say that aged trees need to be cleared away
102	and young trees planted. The way to solve this argument is
114	to cut only portions of a forest and leave others intact. That
122	saves more trees and creates a healthy forest.
132	Many think that trees do not need to be protected
143	because they are renewable. But as we cut them, we must
153	replant them. That is the best way to save trees.

✓ Why does the author view trees as important?

✓ In the author's view, what is the best way to save trees?

Words Read	–	Errors	=	WCPM

☐ **Fall (110 WCPM)**
☐ **Winter (127 WCPM)**
☐ **Spring (139 WCPM)**

WCPM	/	Words Read	=	Accuracy %

PROSODY				
	L1	L2	L3	L4
Reading in Phrases	O	O	O	O
Pace	O	O	O	O
Syntax	O	O	O	O
Self-correction	O	O	O	O
Intonation	O	O	O	O

A Faster Way to Travel

People have always wanted to travel faster. Long ago, people were limited to how fast they could go by their own feet. Then people found that they could travel faster by boat (if there was water nearby). Soon they learned to make canoes and sailboats.

On land, people tamed wild horses. This meant they could ride much faster than they could walk. Yet, they were still limited by how much they could carry. The wheel and the invention of carts and wagons solved this problem. Wagons loaded with goods could be pulled by horses.

Wheels and carts finally led to the invention of trains and cars. Then people could travel much farther. A trip of many months took just a few days. The invention of airplanes made travel even faster. People could travel halfway around the world in a little more than a day. Now people look to the stars. How fast and far can they go in the future?

✔️ Name two advances that made travel faster.

✔️ Why did people tame wild horses?

Name: _____ Date: _____

A Faster Way to Travel

9	People have always wanted to travel faster. Long ago,
21	people were limited to how fast they could go by their own
32	feet. Then people found that they could travel faster by boat
42	(if there was water nearby). Soon they learned to make
45	canoes and sailboats.
54	On land, people tamed wild horses. This meant they
65	could ride much faster than they could walk. Yet, they were
76	still limited by how much they could carry. The wheel and
85	the invention of carts and wagons solved this problem.
94	Wagons loaded with goods could be pulled by horses.
105	Wheels and carts finally led to the invention of trains and
116	cars. Then people could travel much farther. A trip of many
126	months took just a few days. The invention of airplanes
135	made travel even faster. People could travel halfway around
149	the world in a little more than a day. Now people look to the
160	stars. How fast and far can they go in the future?

 Name two advances that made travel faster.

 Why did people tame wild horses?

Words Read	–	Errors	=	WCPM

☐ **Fall (110 WCPM)**
☐ **Winter (127 WCPM)**
☐ **Spring (139 WCPM)**

WCPM	/	Words Read	=	Accuracy %

PROSODY

	L1	L2	L3	L4
Reading in Phrases	O	O	O	O
Pace	O	O	O	O
Syntax	O	O	O	O
Self-correction	O	O	O	O
Intonation	O	O	O	O

Surrender at Yorktown

Jeremy urged his horse to go faster as he raced through the Virginia countryside in 1781. He had heard that General Lord Cornwallis had surrendered to General George Washington in Yorktown. He wondered if the war was nearly over.

Jeremy soon reached his uncle's farm. Bursting through the door, he delivered the momentous news. His uncle made him sit down and take several deep breaths before telling more.

Jeremy had heard the story from a spectator who had watched the ceremony. "He told me that Cornwallis was not there," Jeremy panted. "He pretended to be ill. He sent his second in command instead. The British soldiers were sullen as well. Some threw their weapons down in disgust."

However, the surrender had happened, and it was still surrender. This was a major victory for the American Patriots. But Jeremy and his family would have to wait until 1783 for the Treaty of Paris to be signed. The treaty granted the colonies their independence.

👆 What news does Jeremy have for his uncle?

👆 What text evidence shows that Jeremy is excited?

Name: _____   Date: _____

Surrender at Yorktown

11	Jeremy urged his horse to go faster as he raced through
21	the Virginia countryside in 1781. He had heard that General
28	Lord Cornwallis had surrendered to General George
37	Washington in Yorktown. He wondered if the war was
39	nearly over.
47	Jeremy soon reached his uncle's farm. Bursting through
56	the door, he delivered the momentous news. His uncle
66	made him sit down and take several deep breaths before
68	telling more.
78	Jeremy had heard the story from a spectator who had
88	watched the ceremony. "He told me that Cornwallis was not
99	there," Jeremy panted. "He pretended to be ill. He sent his
108	second in command instead. The British soldiers were sullen
117	as well. Some threw their weapons down in disgust."
126	However, the surrender had happened, and it was still
135	surrender. This was a major victory for the American
146	Patriots. But Jeremy and his family would have to wait until
158	1783 for the Treaty of Paris to be signed. The treaty granted
162	the colonies their independence.

✓ What news does Jeremy have for his uncle?

✓ What text evidence shows that Jeremy is excited?

Words Read	–	Errors	=	WCPM

☐ **Fall (110 WCPM)**
☐ **Winter (127 WCPM)**
☐ **Spring (139 WCPM)**

WCPM	/	Words Read	=	Accuracy %

PROSODY				
	L1	L2	L3	L4
Reading in Phrases	O	O	O	O
Pace	O	O	O	O
Syntax	O	O	O	O
Self-correction	O	O	O	O
Intonation	O	O	O	O

The Silk Road

The Silk Road was not made of silk. Nor was it truly a road. It was an ancient trade route. The Silk Road linked China and India with the Roman Empire. Silk was just one of the treasures that the caravans, or groups of travelers and traders, carried. They also brought gems, jade, and glass to the West. Horses and exotic foods were traded as well. The caravans returned with Roman gold. Three major routes made up the Silk Road. They snaked across deserts and over mountains for more than 2,800 miles.

Traveling the road was dangerous. Traders had to watch out for bandits who would rob them. There were also tribes who threatened the caravans. Tribal leaders often demanded money. If the traders did not pay, they could not pass.

The Silk Road continued as a major trade route for hundreds of years. More than just a way to sell goods, the Silk Road connected people. The road became a way to exchange new ideas.

✔ Why was the Silk Road important?

✔ How was the Silk Road dangerous?

Name: _____ Date: _____

The Silk Road

13	The Silk Road was not made of silk. Nor was it truly a
24	road. It was an ancient trade route. The Silk Road linked
35	China and India with the Roman Empire. Silk was just one
46	of the treasures that the caravans, or groups of travelers and
56	traders, carried. They also brought gems, jade, and glass to
67	the West. Horses and exotic foods were traded as well. The
75	caravans returned with Roman gold. Three major routes
86	made up the Silk Road. They snaked across deserts and over
92	mountains for more than 2,800 miles.
101	Traveling the road was dangerous. Traders had to watch
112	out for bandits who would rob them. There were also tribes
120	who threatened the caravans. Tribal leaders often demanded
131	money. If the traders did not pay, they could not pass.
141	The Silk Road continued as a major trade route for
153	hundreds of years. More than just a way to sell goods, the
163	Silk Road connected people. The road became a way to
166	exchange new ideas.

✔ Why was the Silk Road important?

✔ How was the Silk Road dangerous?

Words Read	–	Errors	=	WCPM

☐ **Fall (110 WCPM)**
☐ **Winter (127 WCPM)**
☐ **Spring (139 WCPM)**

WCPM	/	Words Read	=	Accuracy %

PROSODY				
	L1	L2	L3	L4
Reading in Phrases	O	O	O	O
Pace	O	O	O	O
Syntax	O	O	O	O
Self-correction	O	O	O	O
Intonation	O	O	O	O

A Living Museum

When the Pilgrims landed on the coast of North America, they did not have homes to move into. They had to build a colony. There were no stores for them to buy food. So they had to grow their own food. They made their own clothing as well.

People today can see what life was like for the pilgrims. They can visit Plimoth Plantation in Massachusetts. An English village has been built here to show people what life was like in 1627. This was only seven years after the colonists arrived. At the time, there were about 160 people living there.

People at the site dress like the colonists did in 1627. They show visitors how the colonists led their daily lives. They also invite visitors to join in activities such as cooking and gardening.

There also are many animals in the village. These are the same types of animals that the colonists had. They include rare breeds of cattle, goats, chickens, and sheep.

👆 What is Plimoth Plantation?

👆 What text evidence shows that life for the Pilgrims was hard?

Name: _____ Date: _____

A Living Museum

10	When the Pilgrims landed on the coast of North America,
23	they did not have homes to move into. They had to build a
35	colony. There were no stores for them to buy food. So they
46	had to grow their own food. They made their own clothing
48	as well.
59	People today can see what life was like for the pilgrims.
67	They can visit Plimoth Plantation in Massachusetts. An
77	English village has been built here to show people what
89	life was like in 1627. This was only seven years after the
99	colonists arrived. At the time, there were about 160 people
101	living there.
112	People at the site dress like the colonists did in 1627.
122	They show visitors how the colonists led their daily lives.
133	They also invite visitors to join in activities such as cooking
135	and gardening.
146	There also are many animals in the village. These are the
156	same types of animals that the colonists had. They include
164	rare breeds of cattle, goats, chickens, and sheep.

✔ What is Plimoth Plantation?

✔ What text evidence shows that life for the Pilgrims was hard?

Words Read	–	Errors	=	WCPM

☐ **Fall (110 WCPM)**
☐ **Winter (127 WCPM)**
☐ **Spring (139 WCPM)**

WCPM	/	Words Read	=	Accuracy %

PROSODY				
	L1	L2	L3	L4
Reading in Phrases	O	O	O	O
Pace	O	O	O	O
Syntax	O	O	O	O
Self-correction	O	O	O	O
Intonation	O	O	O	O

Abigail Rests

Abigail was tired of tending to the herb garden. It was a hot day, and she had been working since early morning. She had fetched water for her mother then fed the chickens. From there she had gone to the garden. Now the sun was high.

Abigail peeked into the small wood-frame house where her mother had just finished baking bread.

"Mother, may I please have a few moments to go to the stream to rest?" Abigail asked. "It is very warm, and I would like some cool water."

Her mother said yes and cautioned her to be careful. Abigail skipped away before her mother could change her mind. She quickly followed the path down to the water where there was shade and a cool place to relax.

Abigail remained for about an hour. She enjoyed listening to the birds' chatter and watching a young deer come for a drink. At last, she felt refreshed. She knew it was time to go back to work.

👆 Why was Abigail tired?

👆 What does Abigail ask her mother?

Name: _____ Date: _____

Abigail Rests

11	Abigail was tired of tending to the herb garden. It was
22	a hot day, and she had been working since early morning.
33	She had fetched water for her mother then fed the chickens.
44	From there she had gone to the garden. Now the sun
46	was high.
55	Abigail peeked into the small wood-frame house where
62	her mother had just finished baking bread.
74	"Mother, may I please have a few moments to go to the
85	stream to rest?" Abigail asked. "It is very warm, and I
90	would like some cool water."
100	Her mother said yes and cautioned her to be careful.
109	Abigail skipped away before her mother could change her
119	mind. She quickly followed the path down to the water
129	where there was shade and a cool place to relax.
138	Abigail remained for about an hour. She enjoyed listening
150	to the birds' chatter and watching a young deer come for a
163	drink. At last, she felt refreshed. She knew it was time to go
166	back to work.

✔ Why was Abigail tired?

✔ What does Abigail ask her mother?

Words Read	–	Errors	=	WCPM

☐ **Fall (110 WCPM)**
☐ **Winter (127 WCPM)**
☐ **Spring (139 WCPM)**

WCPM	/	Words Read	=	Accuracy %

PROSODY				
	L1	L2	L3	L4
Reading in Phrases	O	O	O	O
Pace	O	O	O	O
Syntax	O	O	O	O
Self-correction	O	O	O	O
Intonation	O	O	O	O

A Wildlife Project

Leon's group was having trouble coming up with a topic for its class project. The group had to focus on something local and use some form of technology.

"Let's do local wildlife," Leon said. There was a groan. The group didn't think Leon's idea was interesting at all. The group changed its mind after Leon told more about his idea.

On Saturday, Leon, his classmates, and some adults took a hike. The children used a camera and a cell phone to take pictures and videos. Later, they used a computer to put together their work. They had filmed a close-up of a hawk swooping through the sky. They had pictures of deer, squirrels, and even a fox. There was also a video of a flock of wild turkeys.

The presentation to the class went well. Everyone was surprised at how much wildlife could be seen in the area. They also liked the way the pictures and videos were done. It was more like a movie than a class project.

✔ What problem does Leon's group have?

✔ What does Leon's group do during their hike?

Name: _____ Date: _____

A Wildlife Project

10	Leon's group was having trouble coming up with a topic
21	for its class project. The group had to focus on something
28	local and use some form of technology.
38	"Let's do local wildlife," Leon said. There was a groan.
48	The group didn't think Leon's idea was interesting at all.
58	The group changed its mind after Leon told more about
60	his idea.
69	On Saturday, Leon, his classmates, and some adults took
82	a hike. The children used a camera and a cell phone to take
92	pictures and videos. Later, they used a computer to put
104	together their work. They had filmed a close-up of a hawk
113	swooping through the sky. They had pictures of deer,
126	squirrels, and even a fox. There was also a video of a flock
129	of wild turkeys.
138	The presentation to the class went well. Everyone was
149	surprised at how much wildlife could be seen in the area.
160	They also liked the way the pictures and videos were done.
170	It was more like a movie than a class project.

✔ What problem does Leon's group have?

✔ What does Leon's group do during their hike?

Words Read	–	Errors	=	WCPM

☐ **Fall (110 WCPM)**
☐ **Winter (127 WCPM)**
☐ **Spring (139 WCPM)**

WCPM	/	Words Read	=	Accuracy %

PROSODY				
	L1	L2	L3	L4
Reading in Phrases	O	O	O	O
Pace	O	O	O	O
Syntax	O	O	O	O
Self-correction	O	O	O	O
Intonation	O	O	O	O

Snakes of Many Colors

You might think snakes do not need protection, but they do. Pigs and mongooses prey on snakes. Large birds, such as the serpent eagle, think snakes are good to eat. Even other snakes, such as the King Cobra, hunt other snakes.

Snakes often use color to protect themselves. The bright colors of some snakes warn enemies that the snake is poisonous. Other snakes, such as the Mangrove snake, only pretend to be poisonous. The Pueblan milk snake has bright red, black, and white scales. They are arranged in bands. It looks like another kind of snake that is poisonous. Other animals leave it alone.

Snakes also use their colors to hide themselves. For example, the bright green cat snake lives high in a tree in the rainforest. The snake stays coiled around a branch during the day. It looks just like a vine. This fools animals that might want to make it their dinner.

These snakes need their colorful scales to stay safe. After all, it is a dangerous world—even for a snake.

✔ Why do snakes need protection?

✔ How do snakes use color to help themselves?

Name: _____ Date: _____

Snakes of Many Colors

10	You might think snakes do not need protection, but they
20	do. Pigs and mongooses prey on snakes. Large birds, such
31	as the serpent eagle, think snakes are good to eat. Even
41	other snakes, such as the King Cobra, hunt other snakes.
50	Snakes often use color to protect themselves. The bright
60	colors of some snakes warn enemies that the snake is
69	poisonous. Other snakes, such as the Mangrove snake, only
79	pretend to be poisonous. The Pueblan milk snake has bright
90	red, black, and white scales. They are arranged in bands. It
100	looks like another kind of snake that is poisonous. Other
104	animals leave it alone.
113	Snakes also use their colors to hide themselves. For
126	example, the bright green cat snake lives high in a tree in the
135	rainforest. The snake stays coiled around a branch during
147	the day. It looks just like a vine. This fools animals that
154	might want to make it their dinner.
164	These snakes need their colorful scales to stay safe. After
174	all, it is a dangerous world—even for a snake.

✔ Why do snakes need protection?

✔ How do snakes use color to help themselves?

Words Read	–	Errors	=	WCPM

☐ **Fall (110 WCPM)**

☐ **Winter (127 WCPM)**

☐ **Spring (139 WCPM)**

WCPM	/	Words Read	=	Accuracy %

PROSODY				
	L1	L2	L3	L4
Reading in Phrases	O	O	O	O
Pace	O	O	O	O
Syntax	O	O	O	O
Self-correction	O	O	O	O
Intonation	O	O	O	O

Flying to Help

Pilots fly planes. Some pilots help people in danger by flying to places where people need help. They use their planes to help find people lost in parks. They also dump water and chemicals to put out fires. They bring supplies to the firefighting crew as well.

Pilots need special skills to do their job. For example, pilots who fly to help find people must have fine eyesight. They may have to spot a person from far away. They may have to land in canyons or deep valleys to drop off supplies. Pilots who help to put out fires must be able to respond quickly and focus on safety.

Flying to a fire is dangerous. For example, flames can burn the plane if it flies too low. The air may be filled with smoke, which makes it hard for the pilot to see and breathe.

Flying a plane to put out a fire or to find missing people is not easy. Sometimes it is not safe. But it is a job that helps many people. These brave pilots should be thanked for all they do.

- ✔ What is the author's view of pilots?
- ✔ Why is flying to a fire dangerous?

Name: _____ Date: _____

Flying to Help

10	Pilots fly planes. Some pilots help people in danger by
20	flying to places where people need help. They use their
31	planes to help find people lost in parks. They also dump
42	water and chemicals to put out fires. They bring supplies to
47	the firefighting crew as well.
57	Pilots need special skills to do their job. For example,
68	pilots who fly to help find people must have fine eyesight.
80	They may have to spot a person from far away. They may
92	have to land in canyons or deep valleys to drop off supplies.
104	Pilots who help to put out fires must be able to respond
109	quickly and focus on safety.
119	Flying to a fire is dangerous. For example, flames can
133	burn the plane if it flies too low. The air may be filled with
145	smoke, which makes it hard for the pilot to see and breathe.
158	Flying a plane to put out a fire or to find missing people
173	is not easy. Sometimes it is not safe. But it is a job that helps
183	many people. These brave pilots should be thanked for all
185	they do.

👍 What is the author's view of pilots?

👍 Why is flying to a fire dangerous?

Words Read	–	Errors	=	WCPM

☐ **Fall (110 WCPM)**
☐ **Winter (127 WCPM)**
☐ **Spring (139 WCPM)**

WCPM	/	Words Read	=	Accuracy %

PROSODY

	L1	L2	L3	L4
Reading in Phrases	O	O	O	O
Pace	O	O	O	O
Syntax	O	O	O	O
Self-correction	O	O	O	O
Intonation	O	O	O	O

Victor Discovers History

Victor had no interest in history and did not see any value in learning about the past. "The past is past," he would often proclaim. "I should only be concerned with what is happening now."

One Saturday Victor had nothing to do. He was so bored he decided to take a walk downtown. Around one corner he found a sign that read "Town Museum." He could not imagine what would be in a museum of his town. He did not think there was anything interesting to display. But he went inside to see.

Victor was in the museum for hours. He found out that there had been a rich silver mine near the town in the 1880s, and that there had been a massive explosion which was reported in national newspapers. New safety rules for all mines resulted from the accident.

The town had also been the state capital for a short time right after statehood was granted. This was soon after the railroad had reached the town and new settlers arrived by the hundreds.

"Wow!" Victor said. "I had no idea my town was so amazing!"

✔ How does Victor change in the passage?

✔ Name one thing Victor discovers about his town.

Name: _____ Date: _____

Victor Discovers History

11	Victor had no interest in history and did not see any
22	value in learning about the past. "The past is past," he
31	would often proclaim. "I should only be concerned with
35	what is happening now."
46	One Saturday Victor had nothing to do. He was so bored
57	he decided to take a walk downtown. Around one corner he
67	found a sign that read "Town Museum." He could not
79	imagine what would be in a museum of his town. He did
89	not think there was anything interesting to display. But he
93	went inside to see.
104	Victor was in the museum for hours. He found out that
117	there had been a rich silver mine near the town in the 1880s,
127	and that there had been a massive explosion which was
136	reported in national newspapers. New safety rules for all
141	mines resulted from the accident.
153	The town had also been the state capital for a short time
163	right after statehood was granted. This was soon after the
173	railroad had reached the town and new settlers arrived by
175	the hundreds.
185	"Wow!" Victor said. "I had no idea my town was
187	so amazing!"

 How does Victor change in the passage?

 Name one thing Victor discovers about his town.

Words Read	–	Errors	=	WCPM

☐ **Fall (110 WCPM)**
☐ **Winter (127 WCPM)**
☐ **Spring (139 WCPM)**

WCPM	/	Words Read	=	Accuracy %

PROSODY				
	L1	L2	L3	L4
Reading in Phrases	O	O	O	O
Pace	O	O	O	O
Syntax	O	O	O	O
Self-correction	O	O	O	O
Intonation	O	O	O	O

Super Spots

A leopard has spots for more than one reason. The leopard's spots are dark brown and shaped like flowers. They help the big cat hide from its prey. In forests and grasslands, the spots break up the shape of the leopard. Other animals cannot easily see the leopard.

Another reason for the spots is communication. A leopard has a white spot on the tip of its tail and on the backs of its ears. These spots help leopards find each other in tall grass.

Even black leopards have spots. These cats live in the dark rain forests of Southeast Asia. They look solid black. But their spots can be seen from the right angle.

Jaguars and cheetahs are other big cats with spots. The spots of all three cats are about the same color. But the spots are different shapes. Jaguar spots are also like flowers, but they are bigger than leopard spots. Jaguar spots also have dots in the center. Cheetahs have solid spots that are evenly spread across its body.

✔ How do leopards use spots to communicate?

✔ What is the major difference between the spots of big cats?

Name: _____ Date: _____

Super Spots

10	A leopard has spots for more than one reason. The
19	leopard's spots are dark brown and shaped like flowers.
31	They help the big cat hide from its prey. In forests and
41	grasslands, the spots break up the shape of the leopard.
48	Other animals cannot easily see the leopard.
57	Another reason for the spots is communication. A leopard
73	has a white spot on the tip of its tail and on the backs of its
84	ears. These spots help leopards find each other in tall grass.
94	Even black leopards have spots. These cats live in the
104	dark rain forests of Southeast Asia. They look solid black.
114	But their spots can be seen from the right angle.
124	Jaguars and cheetahs are other big cats with spots. The
137	spots of all three cats are about the same color. But the spots
147	are different shapes. Jaguar spots are also like flowers, but
157	they are bigger than leopard spots. Jaguar spots also have
168	dots in the center. Cheetahs have solid spots that are evenly
172	spread across its body.

✔ How do leopards use spots to communicate?

✔ What is the major difference between the spots of big cats?

Words Read	–	Errors	=	WCPM

☐ **Fall (110 WCPM)**
☐ **Winter (127 WCPM)**
☐ **Spring (139 WCPM)**

WCPM	/	Words Read	=	Accuracy %

PROSODY				
	L1	L2	L3	L4
Reading in Phrases	O	O	O	O
Pace	O	O	O	O
Syntax	O	O	O	O
Self-correction	O	O	O	O
Intonation	O	O	O	O

Rare Air

You can't see it, but clean air is an important and often rare resource. Nearly every living thing needs air to live. If air becomes dirty because of pollution, plants can die. People and animals can become sick.

Air pollution is often from smoke. In the 1200s in England, people complained about smoke when coal was first burned. Today, people burn oil and natural gas to heat their homes and operate their cars. Air pollution also comes from businesses, such as electrical plants.

When you can see hazy brown air, you know that it's dirty. Polluted air traps gases. When these gases cannot escape, they raise the temperature of Earth. People cannot breathe easily when the air is bad. Their eyes become red, and noses and lungs are irritated. They can develop asthma and other breathing problems.

There are ways to control air pollution. But they are costly. Many businesses do not want to pay a lot of money. Customers do not want to pay more for the products they buy.

✔️ Why is clean air important?

✔️ What problem does the author point out about controlling air pollution?

Name: _____ Date: _____

Rare Air

12	You can't see it, but clean air is an important and often
22	rare resource. Nearly every living thing needs air to live.
32	If air becomes dirty because of pollution, plants can die.
38	People and animals can become sick.
48	Air pollution is often from smoke. In the 1200s in
56	England, people complained about smoke when coal was
67	first burned. Today, people burn oil and natural gas to heat
77	their homes and operate their cars. Air pollution also comes
83	from businesses, such as electrical plants.
94	When you can see hazy brown air, you know that it's
103	dirty. Polluted air traps gases. When these gases cannot
112	escape, they raise the temperature of Earth. People cannot
123	breathe easily when the air is bad. Their eyes become red,
133	and noses and lungs are irritated. They can develop asthma
137	and other breathing problems.
147	There are ways to control air pollution. But they are
159	costly. Many businesses do not want to pay a lot of money.
169	Customers do not want to pay more for the products
171	they buy.

✔ Why is clean air important?

✔ What problem does the author point out about controlling air pollution?

Words Read	–	Errors	=	WCPM

☐ **Fall (110 WCPM)**
☐ **Winter (127 WCPM)**
☐ **Spring (139 WCPM)**

WCPM	/	Words Read	=	Accuracy %

PROSODY				
	L1	L2	L3	L4
Reading in Phrases	O	O	O	O
Pace	O	O	O	O
Syntax	O	O	O	O
Self-correction	O	O	O	O
Intonation	O	O	O	O

Bright Stars

The Bayville Bright Stars played baseball, but none of them were stars. Each player had been rejected by another, better team.

The Bayville Bright Stars were definitely a team. The players liked each other, and they worked well together. As they organized their team, they discovered that each team member had one skill. Shawn could run fast while José could throw a baseball a long distance. Taylor was capable of watching the whole field to see what everyone was doing. Vera was good at shortstop; this was the one position she could play well. None of the Bright Stars were excellent players, but they were consistently good. Best of all, the team loved to play baseball.

The team decided to let each player choose his best position. They practiced often until their first game was scheduled. They didn't win that game, but at least they scored.

In the last game of the season, the Bright Stars finally demonstrated what they could do. They beat the best team by one run and shocked everyone. No team could have been happier with a win.

☑ How were the Bayville Bright Stars formed?

☑ Why does the narrator believe the Bayville Bright Stars are a good team?

Name: _____ Date: _____

Bright Stars

9	The Bayville Bright Stars played baseball, but none of
19	them were stars. Each player had been rejected by another,
21	better team.
30	The Bayville Bright Stars were definitely a team. The
40	players liked each other, and they worked well together. As
49	they organized their team, they discovered that each team
59	member had one skill. Shawn could run fast while José
69	could throw a baseball a long distance. Taylor was capable
79	of watching the whole field to see what everyone was
90	doing. Vera was good at shortstop; this was the one position
101	she could play well. None of the Bright Stars were excellent
111	players, but they were consistently good. Best of all, the
116	team loved to play baseball.
126	The team decided to let each player choose his best
134	position. They practiced often until their first game
144	was scheduled. They didn't win that game, but at least
146	they scored.
157	In the last game of the season, the Bright Stars finally
167	demonstrated what they could do. They beat the best team
178	by one run and shocked everyone. No team could have been
182	happier with a win.

✔ How were the Bayville Bright Stars formed?

✔ Why does the narrator believe the Bayville Bright Stars are a good team?

Words Read	–	Errors	=	WCPM

☐ **Fall (110 WCPM)**
☐ **Winter (127 WCPM)**
☐ **Spring (139 WCPM)**

WCPM	/	Words Read	=	Accuracy %

PROSODY				
	L1	L2	L3	L4
Reading in Phrases	O	O	O	O
Pace	O	O	O	O
Syntax	O	O	O	O
Self-correction	O	O	O	O
Intonation	O	O	O	O

The Hidden Door

Zoe and Carl thought their new home was the oddest place. The big, rambling house squatted like a toad in the middle of a large field. It had been built in the mid-1800s as part of a large farm. It had many rooms and wandering hallways. Sometimes a hall would come to an abrupt stop. Stairs ended at a solid wall.

After several weeks, Zoe and Carl thought they knew everything about the old house. But their parents had one more surprise.

"Have you found the hidden door in the library?" their father asked.

The twins gazed around the room, seeing only tall shelves filled with books. Their father walked over to one bookcase and reached up under a shelf. They heard a click, and a part of the bookcase moved forward. There was a door behind it.

"We've discovered that this house used to be a part of the Underground Railroad before the Civil War. Escaped slaves from the South would stay in the rooms behind this bookcase. No one would find them behind the hidden door," the twins' mother explained.

✔ What is the house's biggest surprise?

✔ How is the house a part of history?

Name: _____ Date: _____

The Hidden Door

10	Zoe and Carl thought their new home was the oddest
21	place. The big, rambling house squatted like a toad in the
34	middle of a large field. It had been built in the mid-1800s as
45	part of a large farm. It had many rooms and wandering
55	hallways. Sometimes a hall would come to an abrupt stop.
61	Stairs ended at a solid wall.
70	After several weeks, Zoe and Carl thought they knew
80	everything about the old house. But their parents had one
82	more surprise.
92	"Have you found the hidden door in the library?" their
94	father asked.
103	The twins gazed around the room, seeing only tall
113	shelves filled with books. Their father walked over to one
124	bookcase and reached up under a shelf. They heard a click,
135	and a part of the bookcase moved forward. There was a
138	door behind it.
150	"We've discovered that this house used to be a part of the
158	Underground Railroad before the Civil War. Escaped slaves
168	from the South would stay in the rooms behind this
177	bookcase. No one would find them behind the hidden
182	door," the twins' mother explained.

✔ What is the house's biggest surprise?

✔ How is the house a part of history?

Words Read	–	Errors	=	WCPM

☐ **Fall (110 WCPM)**
☐ **Winter (127 WCPM)**
☐ **Spring (139 WCPM)**

WCPM	/	Words Read	=	Accuracy %

PROSODY				
	L1	L2	L3	L4
Reading in Phrases	O	O	O	O
Pace	O	O	O	O
Syntax	O	O	O	O
Self-correction	O	O	O	O
Intonation	O	O	O	O

A Closer Look

Megan felt as though she had landed on another planet. She was spending the summer with her aunt and uncle who lived on a large ranch in Wyoming. Megan had come from a busy city in California.

On her first day, Megan went outside and gazed at the landscape. The land seemed completely empty as it stretched for miles.

"There's nothing here," Megan complained.

"Just wait," her aunt said and smiled.

Megan did wait, but nothing seemed to happen. Then one day, Megan's aunt and uncle took her for a ride to a mountain meadow where Megan saw beautiful wildflowers, but that was all.

And then over the wildflowers flitted tiny hummingbirds. Their wings moved in a blur. Megan's aunt explained that they were Rufous hummingbirds. Then she pointed up in the sky where Megan saw a mass of fluttering insects. They turned out to be Monarch butterflies migrating to Wyoming from their winter home in Mexico.

"In the fall the elk herds migrate," Megan's uncle said. "There is always something to see if you look closer."

✔ What is Megan's problem at the start of the passage?

✔ What lesson does Megan learn?

Name: _____ Date: _____

A Closer Look

10	Megan felt as though she had landed on another planet.
21	She was spending the summer with her aunt and uncle who
33	lived on a large ranch in Wyoming. Megan had come from a
37	busy city in California.
48	On her first day, Megan went outside and gazed at the
56	landscape. The land seemed completely empty as it
59	stretched for miles.
64	"There's nothing here," Megan complained.
71	"Just wait," her aunt said and smiled.
80	Megan did wait, but nothing seemed to happen. Then
93	one day, Megan's aunt and uncle took her for a ride to a
100	mountain meadow where Megan saw beautiful wildflowers,
104	but that was all.
112	And then over the wildflowers flitted tiny hummingbirds.
122	Their wings moved in a blur. Megan's aunt explained that
131	they were Rufous hummingbirds. Then she pointed up in
142	the sky where Megan saw a mass of fluttering insects. They
151	turned out to be Monarch butterflies migrating to Wyoming
157	from their winter home in Mexico.
167	"In the fall the elk herds migrate," Megan's uncle said.
177	"There is always something to see if you look closer."

✔ What is Megan's problem at the start of the passage?

✔ What lesson does Megan learn?

Words Read	–	Errors	=	WCPM

☐ **Fall (110 WCPM)**
☐ **Winter (127 WCPM)**
☐ **Spring (139 WCPM)**

WCPM	/	Words Read	=	Accuracy %

PROSODY

	L1	L2	L3	L4
Reading in Phrases	O	O	O	O
Pace	O	O	O	O
Syntax	O	O	O	O
Self-correction	O	O	O	O
Intonation	O	O	O	O

The Seashore

There are many fun activities to choose from when you visit the seashore. The beaches, boardwalks, and ocean waters offer many things to do. You can build sandcastles, swim, surf, collect shells, or play games.

Lots of people like to collect seashells. Miles of sandy shores invite a walk along the water's edge. You will find that the waves push many shells onto the sand. Soft-bodied sea animals, called mollusks, use these shells for protection.

The ocean can cool you off on a hot day. Swimming and surfing are two ways to enjoy the water. Riding waves on a surfboard can be lots of fun! However, it is important for swimmers and surfers to be careful. Big waves or strong tides can make a fun activity unsafe.

If you like to play games, be sure to visit the beach and boardwalk. You can join a beach ballgame. You can also watch and cheer on the players. Most boardwalk games cost money but offer prizes if you win.

Paid passes are needed on many beaches. Often you can prepay for a whole season of fun. Then you can return to the seashore anytime. Everyone should go to the seashore!

👆 What is the author's view of the seashore?

👆 What are mollusks?

Name: _____ Date: _____

The Seashore

10	There are many fun activities to choose from when you
18	visit the seashore. The beaches, boardwalks, and ocean
28	waters offer many things to do. You can build sandcastles,
35	swim, surf, collect shells, or play games.
45	Lots of people like to collect seashells. Miles of sandy
56	shores invite a walk along the water's edge. You will find
67	that the waves push many shells onto the sand. Soft-bodied
76	sea animals, called mollusks, use these shells for protection.
88	The ocean can cool you off on a hot day. Swimming and
100	surfing are two ways to enjoy the water. Riding waves on a
111	surfboard can be lots of fun! However, it is important for
121	swimmers and surfers to be careful. Big waves or strong
128	tides can make a fun activity unsafe.
141	If you like to play games, be sure to visit the beach and
151	boardwalk. You can join a beach ballgame. You can also
161	watch and cheer on the players. Most boardwalk games cost
168	money but offer prizes if you win.
178	Paid passes are needed on many beaches. Often you can
191	prepay for a whole season of fun. Then you can return to the
199	seashore anytime. Everyone should go to the seashore!

✓ What is the author's view of the seashore?

✓ What are mollusks?

Words Read	–	Errors	=	WCPM

☐ **Fall (110 WCPM)**
☐ **Winter (127 WCPM)**
☐ **Spring (139 WCPM)**

WCPM	/	Words Read	=	Accuracy %

PROSODY				
	L1	L2	L3	L4
Reading in Phrases	O	O	O	O
Pace	O	O	O	O
Syntax	O	O	O	O
Self-correction	O	O	O	O
Intonation	O	O	O	O

Alicia's Dilemma

Alicia had a dog, a miniature schnauzer named Rosie that she had grown up with. Now Alicia had a little sister, Marta, who also loved the dog. But Marta was always sick with red, itchy eyes and a runny nose. Lately, she was getting ear infections.

"Your sister is allergic to your pooch," Dr. Hurtago said to Alicia one day when her mom had taken Marta to the doctor's office.

"Rosie is a member of our family," said Alicia's mom. "But Marta cannot be sick all the time."

The girls went home and embraced Rosie, which caused Marta to start sniffling all over again.

The next day after school, Alicia went to see Rosie's veterinarian. "I love Rosie, but she can't stay with us. She needs another home; it has to be someplace where I could visit her," Alicia explained.

The vet looked thoughtfully at her. "My sister loves schnauzers, and she just moved into town. She has been thinking about getting a dog, so this may be perfect."

"Could I visit and take Rosie for walks?" Alicia asked.

"I'm sure you could," said the vet with a smile.

✔ What is Alicia's dilemma?

✔ How does the veterinarian help Alicia?

Name: _____ Date: _____

Alicia's Dilemma

10	Alicia had a dog, a miniature schnauzer named Rosie that
22	she had grown up with. Now Alicia had a little sister, Marta,
33	who also loved the dog. But Marta was always sick with
44	red, itchy eyes and a runny nose. Lately, she was getting
46	ear infections.
56	"Your sister is allergic to your pooch," Dr. Hurtago said
68	to Alicia one day when her mom had taken Marta to the
70	doctor's office.
80	"Rosie is a member of our family," said Alicia's mom.
88	"But Marta cannot be sick all the time."
97	The girls went home and embraced Rosie, which caused
104	Marta to start sniffling all over again.
114	The next day after school, Alicia went to see Rosie's
125	veterinarian. "I love Rosie, but she can't stay with us. She
136	needs another home; it has to be someplace where I could
140	visit her," Alicia explained.
149	The vet looked thoughtfully at her. "My sister loves
159	schnauzers, and she just moved into town. She has been
169	thinking about getting a dog, so this may be perfect."
179	"Could I visit and take Rosie for walks?" Alicia asked.
189	"I'm sure you could," said the vet with a smile.

✓ What is Alicia's dilemma?

✓ How does the veterinarian help Alicia?

Words Read	–	Errors	=	WCPM

☐ **Fall (110 WCPM)**
☐ **Winter (127 WCPM)**
☐ **Spring (139 WCPM)**

WCPM	/	Words Read	=	Accuracy %

PROSODY

	L1	L2	L3	L4
Reading in Phrases	O	O	O	O
Pace	O	O	O	O
Syntax	O	O	O	O
Self-correction	O	O	O	O
Intonation	O	O	O	O

Making Perfume

Lin loved the smell of flowers and forest pine needles. She loved the smell of oranges and lemons.

Lin wondered how people made perfumes and got smells out of things in nature. So her mother took her to a perfume factory to see. A tour guide told them many things about perfumes.

The guide said that perfumes are made from oils. The oils once came from flowers, leaves, fruits, roots, and seeds. Oils from these sources are still used. But scientists can now make many of the same smells in their labs. They also make new smells that are not found in nature.

Lin watched people extracting oils. Some oils were squeezed out while others were boiled out. Some people were putting flower petals on big, flat trays. They covered the petals with pork fat that could pull out the sweet smells.

The guide said that as many as 300 different smells can go into one perfume. People who make perfumes must have a good sense of smell. They must also know how to put different smells together.

Lin thought about her sense of smell. She wondered if some day she might be able to make perfumes.

☑ Why does Lin's mother take her to the factory?

☑ How can smells that are not found in nature be found in perfumes?

Name: _____ Date: _____

Making Perfume

10	Lin loved the smell of flowers and forest pine needles.
18	She loved the smell of oranges and lemons.
26	Lin wondered how people made perfumes and got
39	smells out of things in nature. So her mother took her to a
50	perfume factory to see. A tour guide told them many things
52	about perfumes.
63	The guide said that perfumes are made from oils. The oils
73	once came from flowers, leaves, fruits, roots, and seeds. Oils
83	from these sources are still used. But scientists can now
95	make many of the same smells in their labs. They also make
103	new smells that are not found in nature.
111	Lin watched people extracting oils. Some oils were
120	squeezed out while others were boiled out. Some people
130	were putting flower petals on big, flat trays. They covered
142	the petals with pork fat that could pull out the sweet smells.
153	The guide said that as many as 300 different smells can
163	go into one perfume. People who make perfumes must have
175	a good sense of smell. They must also know how to put
178	different smells together.
188	Lin thought about her sense of smell. She wondered if
197	some day she might be able to make perfumes.

✔ Why does Lin's mother take her to the factory?

✔ How can smells that are not found in nature be found in perfumes?

Words Read	–	Errors	=	WCPM

☐ **Fall (110 WCPM)**
☐ **Winter (127 WCPM)**
☐ **Spring (139 WCPM)**

WCPM	/	Words Read	=	Accuracy %

PROSODY				
	L1	L2	L3	L4
Reading in Phrases	O	O	O	O
Pace	O	O	O	O
Syntax	O	O	O	O
Self-correction	O	O	O	O
Intonation	O	O	O	O

Carrie Chapman Catt

Women and men in the United States did not always share a right to vote. Men were in charge of voting, and women had no role in government. Susan B. Anthony tried to change the law. She fought hard for women's right to vote. This did not happen while Anthony was alive.

A woman named Carrie Chapman Catt joined Susan B. Anthony in the fight for women's rights. Catt was offended by the way women were treated. She felt that granting women the right to vote could not be delayed any longer.

Catt became part of a woman's group that discussed such topics as peace and women's rights. Catt told the group that women must have a part in making decisions. So she started a plan to bring women together. The women recognized that Catt was smart and her speeches were convincing. They agreed to help.

Catt organized marches and got women to write letters. This helped them reach many others. Several states began to allow women to vote. Finally, in 1920, women were granted the right to vote by the United States government. They had won their fight, and Catt had made a mark on history.

What did Catt work to achieve?

How did Catt convince other women to join her cause?

Name: _____ Date: _____

Carrie Chapman Catt

10	Women and men in the United States did not always
22	share a right to vote. Men were in charge of voting, and
32	women had no role in government. Susan B. Anthony tried
43	to change the law. She fought hard for women's right to
52	vote. This did not happen while Anthony was alive.
61	A woman named Carrie Chapman Catt joined Susan B.
71	Anthony in the fight for women's rights. Catt was offended
81	by the way women were treated. She felt that granting
92	women the right to vote could not be delayed any longer.
101	Catt became part of a woman's group that discussed
111	such topics as peace and women's rights. Catt told the
121	group that women must have a part in making decisions.
132	So she started a plan to bring women together. The women
141	recognized that Catt was smart and her speeches were
146	convincing. They agreed to help.
155	Catt organized marches and got women to write letters.
165	This helped them reach many others. Several states began to
175	allow women to vote. Finally, in 1920, women were granted
186	the right to vote by the United States government. They had
197	won their fight, and Catt had made a mark on history.

✔ What did Catt work to achieve?

✔ How did Catt convince other women to join her cause?

Words Read	–	Errors	=	WCPM

☐ **Fall (110 WCPM)**
☐ **Winter (127 WCPM)**
☐ **Spring (139 WCPM)**

WCPM	/	Words Read	=	Accuracy %

PROSODY

	L1	L2	L3	L4
Reading in Phrases	O	O	O	O
Pace	O	O	O	O
Syntax	O	O	O	O
Self-correction	O	O	O	O
Intonation	O	O	O	O

Changing Views of Earth

As you watch the moon and stars at night or see the sun rise and set, it's easy to imagine that the sky revolves around Earth. This was what people long ago thought. They believed that Earth was the center of the universe.

When some ancient Greek astronomers suggested that Earth revolved around the sun, others thought this idea was wrong. Astronomers long ago did not have telescopes to prove their ideas.

In the 1500s and 1600s, astronomers began to use telescopes, which had been invented by the Dutch. Galileo Gallilei was one of the most famous of these astronomers. He believed his observations of the skies proved that Earth revolved around the sun. He had seen moons orbiting the planet Jupiter. So he knew that not everything in space circled Earth. Galileo was criticized for his ideas. Many people were not ready to accept that Earth did not have the most important place in the universe.

As years passed, astronomers had better equipment. They also said that Earth orbited the sun. At last, everyone had to agree. The proof was too strong. And then a new idea was proposed. The sun was not the center of the universe, either!

👆 What did people long ago believe about Earth?

👆 How did telescopes affect people's views about the universe?

Name: _____ Date: _____

Changing Views of the Earth

13	As you watch the moon and stars at night or see the sun
24	rise and set, it's easy to imagine that the sky revolves
34	around Earth. This was what people long ago thought. They
43	believed that Earth was the center of the universe.
50	When some ancient Greek astronomers suggested that
60	Earth revolved around the sun, others thought this idea was
69	wrong. Astronomers long ago did not have telescopes to
72	prove their ideas.
81	In the 1500s and 1600s, astronomers began to use
90	telescopes, which had been invented by the Dutch. Galileo
100	Gallilei was one of the most famous of these astronomers.
110	He believed his observations of the skies proved that Earth
120	revolved around the sun. He had seen moons orbiting the
130	planet Jupiter. So he knew that not everything in space
139	circled Earth. Galileo was criticized for his ideas. Many
151	people were not ready to accept that Earth did not have the
157	most important place in the universe.
164	As years passed, astronomers had better equipment.
175	They also said that Earth orbited the sun. At last, everyone
187	had to agree. The proof was too strong. And then a new
198	idea was proposed. The sun was not the center of the
200	universe, either!

✔ What did people long ago believe about Earth?

✔ How did telescopes affect people's views about the universe?

Words Read	–	Errors	=	WCPM

☐ **Fall (110 WCPM)**
☐ **Winter (127 WCPM)**
☐ **Spring (139 WCPM)**

WCPM	/	Words Read	=	Accuracy %

PROSODY				
	L1	L2	L3	L4
Reading in Phrases	O	O	O	O
Pace	O	O	O	O
Syntax	O	O	O	O
Self-correction	O	O	O	O
Intonation	O	O	O	O

The Bridge

Once there was a village that was nestled high in the mountains. The only way to reach the village was to cross a rushing river and travel up a steep and rocky path that twisted around the mountains. The river was dangerous. The path was narrow and difficult to walk on, but the villagers liked it that way. The villagers did not welcome strangers, although they were polite when one arrived. And the world went on, leaving the village behind.

One day gold was discovered in the mountains around the village. Suddenly, strangers were everywhere, climbing the steep path and digging into the mountainsides. Many miners were hurt as they looked for gold. They fell from the path and slid down the mountain. They became lost in the path's twists and turns. Some disappeared and were never seen again.

At last, people in the valleys decided they must build a bridge across the river and make the path straight. When it was finished, the path to the village and into the mountains was much safer. New people came and moved into the village. They built homes and started businesses. The world had arrived, and the village was forever changed.

👆 How does the discovery of gold change the village?

👆 Why do the people in the valleys build a bridge?

Name: _____ Date: _____

The Bridge

11	Once there was a village that was nestled high in the
23	mountains. The only way to reach the village was to cross a
34	rushing river and travel up a steep and rocky path that
42	twisted around the mountains. The river was dangerous.
53	The path was narrow and difficult to walk on, but the
63	villagers liked it that way. The villagers did not welcome
72	strangers, although they were polite when one arrived. And
80	the world went on, leaving the village behind.
89	One day gold was discovered in the mountains around
96	the village. Suddenly, strangers were everywhere, climbing
105	the steep path and digging into the mountainsides. Many
117	miners were hurt as they looked for gold. They fell from the
128	path and slid down the mountain. They became lost in the
137	path's twists and turns. Some disappeared and were never
139	seen again.
150	At last, people in the valleys decided they must build a
161	bridge across the river and make the path straight. When it
172	was finished, the path to the village and into the mountains
182	was much safer. New people came and moved into the
191	village. They built homes and started businesses. The world
199	had arrived, and the village was forever changed.

✓ How does the discovery of gold change the village?

✓ Why do the people in the valleys build a bridge?

Words Read	–	Errors	=	WCPM

☐ **Fall (110 WCPM)**

☐ **Winter (127 WCPM)**

☐ **Spring (139 WCPM)**

WCPM	/	Words Read	=	Accuracy %

PROSODY				
	L1	L2	L3	L4
Reading in Phrases	O	O	O	O
Pace	O	O	O	O
Syntax	O	O	O	O
Self-correction	O	O	O	O
Intonation	O	O	O	O

Seed Treasures

Many people think of treasure as gold, silver, and precious gems. However, gardeners know that their treasure is seeds. They especially value seeds that are known as *heirlooms*.

An heirloom is something valuable. It is handed down from generation to generation. Heirloom seeds come from plants that people have been growing for a long time. Some heirloom plants were first cultivated by Native Americans hundreds of years ago.

Besides age, heirloom seeds are thought to be "true-to-type." This means that the seeds will produce a plant like the one they came from. Most vegetables grown today are from hybrid plants. The seeds from these plants are often not true-to-type. They may not even grow. If they do, the vegetables often are not like those that came from the parent plant.

Many gardeners also like heirloom seeds because of quality. These gardeners want tomatoes that taste like real tomatoes. They do not want tomatoes that taste like something else. They want sweet and juicy corn. They do not want something that looks good but has little taste.

👆 What are heirloom seeds?

👆 Why are heirloom seeds considered "true-to-type"?

Name: _____ Date: _____

Seed Treasures

9	Many people think of treasure as gold, silver, and
16	precious gems. However, gardeners know that their
25	treasure is seeds. They especially value seeds that are
28	known as *heirlooms*.
37	An heirloom is something valuable. It is handed down
45	from generation to generation. Heirloom seeds come from
56	plants that people have been growing for a long time. Some
64	heirloom plants were first cultivated by Native Americans
68	hundreds of years ago.
78	Besides age, heirloom seeds are thought to be "true-to-
89	type." This means that the seeds will produce a plant like
99	the one they came from. Most vegetables grown today are
109	from hybrid plants. The seeds from these plants are often
122	not true-to-type. They may not even grow. If they do, the
132	vegetables often are not like those that came from the
134	parent plant.
142	Many gardeners also like heirloom seeds because of
151	quality. These gardeners want tomatoes that taste like real
160	tomatoes. They do not want tomatoes that taste like
170	something else. They want sweet and juicy corn. They do
180	not want something that looks good but has little taste.

✔ What are heirloom seeds?

✔ Why are heirloom seeds considered "true-to-type"?

Words Read	–	Errors	=	WCPM

☐ **Fall (110 WCPM)**
☐ **Winter (127 WCPM)**
☐ **Spring (139 WCPM)**

WCPM	/	Words Read	=	Accuracy %

PROSODY				
	L1	L2	L3	L4
Reading in Phrases	O	O	O	O
Pace	O	O	O	O
Syntax	O	O	O	O
Self-correction	O	O	O	O
Intonation	O	O	O	O

The Fox

The sun was about to set, so the fennec fox knew that it was about time to hunt for food. He poked his nose out of his underground den. Then his whole head emerged.

Anyone watching might think that a much larger animal lived there. The fox's ears were at least half the length of his 12-inch body. The fox treasured his ears because they helped to keep him cool in the searing desert heat. He also was proud of his long, thick hair. It also protected him from the hot sun and kept him warm at night. *It looks good, too,* the fox thought.

Out on the sand, the fox roamed. He was not picky about food. He would eat plants, rodents, eggs, small reptiles, and insects. If he found water, he might drink some, but he did not need it. He could survive without water for a long time.

At last, the fox sensed a reptile nest. He used his hairy feet to dig up the eggs. He finished his tasty meal before the other foxes in his community found out he had a wonderful treat. Then it was back to his cool den under the sand as the sun began to rise.

✔ Why does the fox think highly of his ears?

✔ Why does the fox not search for water?

Name: _____ Date: _____

The Fox

13	The sun was about to set, so the fennec fox knew that it
26	was about time to hunt for food. He poked his nose out of
34	his underground den. Then his whole head emerged.
43	Anyone watching might think that a much larger animal
56	lived there. The fox's ears were at least half the length of his
66	12-inch body. The fox treasured his ears because they helped
78	to keep him cool in the searing desert heat. He also was
90	proud of his long, thick hair. It also protected him from the
103	hot sun and kept him warm at night. *It looks good, too,* the
105	fox thought.
117	Out on the sand, the fox roamed. He was not picky about
127	food. He would eat plants, rodents, eggs, small reptiles, and
139	insects. If he found water, he might drink some, but he did
151	not need it. He could survive without water for a long time.
163	At last, the fox sensed a reptile nest. He used his hairy
176	feet to dig up the eggs. He finished his tasty meal before the
187	other foxes in his community found out he had a wonderful
201	treat. Then it was back to his cool den under the sand as the
205	sun began to rise.

✓ Why does the fox think highly of his ears?

✓ Why does the fox not search for water?

Words Read	–	Errors	=	WCPM

☐ **Fall (110 WCPM)**
☐ **Winter (127 WCPM)**
☐ **Spring (139 WCPM)**

WCPM	/	Words Read	=	Accuracy %

PROSODY				
	L1	L2	L3	L4
Reading in Phrases	O	O	O	O
Pace	O	O	O	O
Syntax	O	O	O	O
Self-correction	O	O	O	O
Intonation	O	O	O	O

Saving Up

My class planned a trip to the aquarium. We decided to raise money for everyone's admission ticket. We earned the money by having a Good-to-Eat Sale at school.

Each morning for a week everyone brought in something that was both delicious and healthy. We had a wide assortment of treats to sell. I brought some enormous bran muffins. Miss Hansen brought in granola bar cookies. Other students brought raisins, carrot sticks, and bananas. We set up our table where the school buses and cars dropped off their passengers. Each morning, we arranged the goods on the table so they looked tempting.

As students were dropped off, they saw the delicious foods. Everyone was surprised to see what was for sale. No one could pass our table without stopping and buying something. The sale was a huge success. We earned enough money for everyone to attend the class trip. The class cannot wait to see all of the sharks and the rare fish at the aquarium.

☑ What is a Good-to-Eat Sale?

☑ What text evidence shows that the sale was a success?

Name: _____ Date: _____

Saving Up

11	My class planned a trip to the aquarium. We decided to
20	raise money for everyone's admission ticket. We earned the
30	money by having a Good-to-Eat Sale at school.
39	Each morning for a week everyone brought in something
49	that was both delicious and healthy. We had a wide
59	assortment of treats to sell. I brought some enormous bran
68	muffins. Miss Hansen brought in granola bar cookies. Other
77	students brought raisins, carrot sticks, and bananas. We set
88	up our table where the school buses and cars dropped off
97	their passengers. Each morning, we arranged the goods on
103	the table so they looked tempting.
112	As students were dropped off, they saw the delicious
123	foods. Everyone was surprised to see what was for sale. No
132	one could pass our table without stopping and buying
142	something. The sale was a huge success. We earned enough
153	money for everyone to attend the class trip. The class cannot
167	wait to see all of the sharks and the rare fish at the aquarium.

✓ What is a Good-to-Eat Sale?

✓ What text evidence shows that the sale was a success?

Words Read	–	Errors	=	WCPM

☐ **Fall (127 WCPM)**
☐ **Winter (140 WCPM)**
☐ **Spring (150 WCPM)**

WCPM	/	Words Read	=	Accuracy %

PROSODY				
	L1	L2	L3	L4
Reading in Phrases	O	O	O	O
Pace	O	O	O	O
Syntax	O	O	O	O
Self-correction	O	O	O	O
Intonation	O	O	O	O

Fruit Fun

Ellen's favorite pastime was making things, so she was delighted when her aunt sent her a box of modeling clay. The clay was so soft and gooey. Ellen could press and mold it into all kinds of shapes.

Ellen started by creating different kinds of fruits. First, she molded apples, bananas, and oranges. Then she created some pears, plums, grapefruit, peaches, and lemons. She arranged her best pieces of fruit in a fancy china bowl. When her mother saw the bowl, she was amazed at how real the fruit looked. That gave Ellen and her mother an idea. They placed the pretty bowl in the center of the dining room table.

That evening when Dad arrived home, he immediately noticed the fruit bowl. "Those peaches look so ripe and delicious!" Dad exclaimed.

Ellen started laughing so hard she couldn't stop.

"What are you laughing at?" Dad demanded. He reached out and selected the prettiest peach. Right away he realized why Ellen was laughing.

"You completely fooled me," he said. "This peach certainly looks good enough to eat."

✔ What gift does Ellen receive?

✔ Why is Ellen laughing at the end of the passage?

Name: _____ Date: _____

Fruit Fun

9	Ellen's favorite pastime was making things, so she was
20	delighted when her aunt sent her a box of modeling clay.
32	The clay was so soft and gooey. Ellen could press and mold
38	it into all kinds of shapes.
47	Ellen started by creating different kinds of fruits. First,
56	she molded apples, bananas, and oranges. Then she created
64	some pears, plums, grapefruit, peaches, and lemons. She
75	arranged her best pieces of fruit in a fancy china bowl.
86	When her mother saw the bowl, she was amazed at how
97	real the fruit looked. That gave Ellen and her mother an
109	idea. They placed the pretty bowl in the center of the dining
111	room table.
119	That evening when Dad arrived home, he immediately
129	noticed the fruit bowl. "Those peaches look so ripe and
132	delicious!" Dad exclaimed.
140	Ellen started laughing so hard she couldn't stop.
149	"What are you laughing at?" Dad demanded. He reached
159	out and selected the prettiest peach. Right away he realized
163	why Ellen was laughing.
171	"You completely fooled me," he said. "This peach
177	certainly looks good enough to eat."

✔ What gift does Ellen receive?

✔ Why is Ellen laughing at the end of the passage?

Words Read	–	Errors	=	WCPM

☐ **Fall (127 WCPM)**
☐ **Winter (140 WCPM)**
☐ **Spring (150 WCPM)**

WCPM	/	Words Read	=	Accuracy %

PROSODY				
	L1	L2	L3	L4
Reading in Phrases	O	O	O	O
Pace	O	O	O	O
Syntax	O	O	O	O
Self-correction	O	O	O	O
Intonation	O	O	O	O

The Clay Men

Long ago a Chinese emperor believed he would live forever. When he was just a boy, he told workers to start making soldiers from clay. He felt these clay fighters would always keep him safe.

Each clay soldier was the same size as a real man, and each one was unique. They looked like the soldiers in the emperor's own army. Because the workers spent so much time on them, the clay men appeared ready to fight when ordered.

The emperor lived a long time ago. At the time, China sent ships filled with dazzling silk to many lands. Many countries paid well to have Chinese silks. They dressed in fine robes and held big festivals and feasts. The Chinese emperor was interested only in his clay army.

The ruler hid his clay fighters. He did not want anyone to find them. But in 1974, workers digging on the land found the underground rooms where thousands of the clay men were hidden. Now people can go to China to see them. It is a great sight.

👆 Why did the emperor want a clay army?

👆 How were the soldiers rediscovered?

Name: _____   Date: _____

The Clay Men

9	Long ago a Chinese emperor believed he would live
21	forever. When he was just a boy, he told workers to start
31	making soldiers from clay. He felt these clay fighters would
35	always keep him safe.
46	Each clay soldier was the same size as a real man,
56	and each one was unique. They looked like the soldiers
65	in the emperor's own army. Because the workers spent
77	so much time on them, the clay men appeared ready to fight
79	when ordered.
90	The emperor lived a long time ago. At the time, China
100	sent ships filled with dazzling silk to many lands. Many
110	countries paid well to have Chinese silks. They dressed in
120	fine robes and held big festivals and feasts. The Chinese
128	emperor was interested only in his clay army.
140	The ruler hid his clay fighters. He did not want anyone to
151	find them. But in 1974, workers digging on the land found
160	the underground rooms where thousands of the clay men
173	were hidden. Now people can go to China to see them. It is
176	a great sight.

✔ Why did the emperor want a clay army?

✔ How were the soldiers rediscovered?

Words Read	–	Errors	=	WCPM

☐ **Fall (127 WCPM)**
☐ **Winter (140 WCPM)**
☐ **Spring (150 WCPM)**

WCPM	/	Words Read	=	Accuracy %

PROSODY				
	L1	L2	L3	L4
Reading in Phrases	O	O	O	O
Pace	O	O	O	O
Syntax	O	O	O	O
Self-correction	O	O	O	O
Intonation	O	O	O	O

The Octopus

The octopus is a smart animal. It is also unusual. The octopus has a large head, eyes, and eight arms. It also has many tricks it can use to escape predators and other dangers.

One trick is to hide right in front of a predator. To do this the octopus uses special muscles and pigment cells on its skin. It changes itself to match the colors, patterns, and textures of its surroundings.

A predator may see where the octopus is hiding. Then the octopus has another trick. It releases black ink in a cloud. The predator cannot see the octopus escape. The ink also makes it difficult for a predator to smell the octopus.

The octopus is also a fast swimmer. If it is grabbed by an arm, the octopus will lose the arm and swim away. The arm will grow back later. The octopus has a sharp beak as well. It will bite hard to protect itself, and its saliva is poisonous. So predators will likely try an easier target.

✔ What text evidence supports the author's view that the octopus is smart?

✔ What happens if an octopus loses an arm?

Name: _____ Date: _____

The Octopus

10	The octopus is a smart animal. It is also unusual.
20	The octopus has a large head, eyes, and eight arms.
31	It also has many tricks it can use to escape predators
34	and other dangers.
48	One trick is to hide right in front of a predator. To do this
58	the octopus uses special muscles and pigment cells on its
68	skin. It changes itself to match the colors, patterns, and
72	textures of its surroundings.
83	A predator may see where the octopus is hiding. Then the
94	octopus has another trick. It releases black ink in a cloud.
104	The predator cannot see the octopus escape. The ink also
114	makes it difficult for a predator to smell the octopus.
127	The octopus is also a fast swimmer. If it is grabbed by an
139	arm, the octopus will lose the arm and swim away. The arm
152	will grow back later. The octopus has a sharp beak as well. It
164	will bite hard to protect itself, and its saliva is poisonous. So
171	predators will likely try an easier target.

 What text evidence supports the author's view that the octopus is smart?

 What happens if an octopus loses an arm?

Words Read	–	Errors	=	WCPM

☐ **Fall (127 WCPM)**
☐ **Winter (140 WCPM)**
☐ **Spring (150 WCPM)**

WCPM	/	Words Read	=	Accuracy %

PROSODY				
	L1	L2	L3	L4
Reading in Phrases	O	O	O	O
Pace	O	O	O	O
Syntax	O	O	O	O
Self-correction	O	O	O	O
Intonation	O	O	O	O

Lightning

Lightning is the bright flash of light you see during a storm. It is usually followed by thunder. A storm can be ten miles away and still cause lightning.

Lightning is electricity that is suddenly discharged. This release of energy heats the air. The air then rapidly expands with a loud boom of thunder. A bolt of lightning may travel across the sky or hit the ground. The electric current may then move along the ground.

Weather forecasters monitor lightning as they follow storms. They estimate that there are about 100,000 thunderstorms every year in the United States. These storms produce about 25 million lightning strikes. Earth may be hit by more than 100 lightning bolts every second.

Lightning is dangerous. Anyone who is outside when thunder is heard should immediately find shelter. Inside, any contact with water should be avoided during a storm. This is because water easily conducts electricity that comes from lightning. It is always better to think first about safety.

✔️ How are lightning and thunder different?

✔️ Why is it a good idea to avoid contact with water during a lightning storm?

Name: _____ Date: _____

Lightning

11	Lightning is the bright flash of light you see during a
23	storm. It is usually followed by thunder. A storm can be ten
29	miles away and still cause lightning.
37	Lightning is electricity that is suddenly discharged. This
48	release of energy heats the air. The air then rapidly expands
60	with a loud boom of thunder. A bolt of lightning may travel
71	across the sky or hit the ground. The electric current may
76	then move along the ground.
83	Weather forecasters monitor lightning as they follow
91	storms. They estimate that there are about 100,000
100	thunderstorms every year in the United States. These storms
110	produce about 25 million lightning strikes. Earth may be hit
118	by more than 100 lightning bolts every second.
126	Lightning is dangerous. Anyone who is outside when
134	thunder is heard should immediately find shelter. Inside,
144	any contact with water should be avoided during a storm.
153	This is because water easily conducts electricity that comes
164	from lightning. It is always better to think first about safety.

✔ How are lightning and thunder different?

✔ Why is it a good idea to avoid contact with water during a lightning storm?

Words Read	–	Errors	=	WCPM

☐ **Fall (127 WCPM)**
☐ **Winter (140 WCPM)**
☐ **Spring (150 WCPM)**

WCPM	/	Words Read	=	Accuracy %

PROSODY				
	L1	L2	L3	L4
Reading in Phrases	O	O	O	O
Pace	O	O	O	O
Syntax	O	O	O	O
Self-correction	O	O	O	O
Intonation	O	O	O	O

In the Deep Ocean

In the deepest parts of the ocean, there is no light. Yet there is life. Creatures who live deep in the ocean have adapted to the lack of light. Here are just a few of these strange creatures.

There are transparent jellyfish that float through the water. They look like glass. Many are dotted with a chemical that glows.

Fangtooth fish prowl the bottom. They are only about six inches long. But they look fierce with big heads, wide mouths, and long, sharp teeth.

Giant tube worms cluster around a deep ocean vent. Hot water heated deep in the earth gushes from the vent. The worms live on chemicals in the hot water.

Like most deep sea creatures, the blobfish moves slowly, eating whatever floats by. From the front, it has a face that looks like a blob with a big nose and mouth and tiny eyes.

Anglerfish are all teeth and spines. One of these spines dangles from the head like a fishing pole with a bright knob on the end that is bait to attract other fish.

✔ What is lacking in the deepest parts of the ocean?

✔ Why do you find tube worms around ocean vents?

Name: _____ Date: _____

In the Deep Ocean

12	In the deepest parts of the ocean, there is no light. Yet
23	there is life. Creatures who live deep in the ocean have
36	adapted to the lack of light. Here are just a few of these
38	strange creatures.
46	There are transparent jellyfish that float through the
57	water. They look like glass. Many are dotted with a chemical
59	that glows.
69	Fangtooth fish prowl the bottom. They are only about six
79	inches long. But they look fierce with big heads, wide
84	mouths, and long, sharp teeth.
94	Giant tube worms cluster around a deep ocean vent. Hot
105	water heated deep in the earth gushes from the vent. The
113	worms live on chemicals in the hot water.
122	Like most deep sea creatures, the blobfish moves slowly,
134	eating whatever floats by. From the front, it has a face that
147	looks like a blob with a big nose and mouth and tiny eyes.
157	Anglerfish are all teeth and spines. One of these spines
169	dangles from the head like a fishing pole with a bright knob
179	on the end that is bait to attract other fish.

✔ What is lacking in the deepest parts of the ocean?

✔ Why do you find tube worms around ocean vents?

Words Read	–	Errors	=	WCPM

☐ **Fall (127 WCPM)**
☐ **Winter (140 WCPM)**
☐ **Spring (150 WCPM)**

WCPM	/	Words Read	=	Accuracy %

PROSODY				
	L1	L2	L3	L4
Reading in Phrases	O	O	O	O
Pace	O	O	O	O
Syntax	O	O	O	O
Self-correction	O	O	O	O
Intonation	O	O	O	O

Strange Partners

Wolf was desperate. A falling tree had trapped his brother in a hole. Brother Wolf did not seem to be injured, but the tree could not be moved. Brother Wolf would starve unless someone would help.

At the farm, Wolf approached Horse cautiously. They had been enemies for a long time, and Horse likely would deny any request from Wolf.

"Please, Horse," the Wolf pleaded. "Can we put aside our problems for a bit? I cannot move the tree that traps my brother, and I need your help. In return, I promise that we will hunt no one that lives on this farm."

"Why should I believe you?" Horse snorted.

"There is no good reason for you to, but I ask you to try," Wolf said.

Horse agreed to take a chance and followed Wolf to the forest. He found Wolf's brother trapped as he said. Horse was strong and able to push the tree aside while Wolf dug in the ground to make it easier to move. When his brother was free, Wolf thanked Horse for being his partner.

☙ What is Wolf's problem?

☙ Why does Horse find it hard to believe Wolf at first?

Name: _____ Date: _____

Strange Partners

9	Wolf was desperate. A falling tree had trapped his
21	brother in a hole. Brother Wolf did not seem to be injured,
32	but the tree could not be moved. Brother Wolf would starve
36	unless someone would help.
45	At the farm, Wolf approached Horse cautiously. They had
56	been enemies for a long time, and Horse likely would deny
60	any request from Wolf.
70	"Please, Horse," the Wolf pleaded. "Can we put aside our
82	problems for a bit? I cannot move the tree that traps my
94	brother, and I need your help. In return, I promise that we
103	will hunt no one that lives on this farm."
110	"Why should I believe you?" Horse snorted.
124	"There is no good reason for you to, but I ask you to try,"
126	Wolf said.
137	Horse agreed to take a chance and followed Wolf to the
147	forest. He found Wolf's brother trapped as he said. Horse
160	was strong and able to push the tree aside while Wolf dug in
172	the ground to make it easier to move. When his brother was
180	free, Wolf thanked Horse for being his partner.

✔ What is Wolf's problem?

✔ Why does Horse find it hard to believe Wolf at first?

Words Read	–	Errors	=	WCPM

☐ **Fall (127 WCPM)**
☐ **Winter (140 WCPM)**
☐ **Spring (150 WCPM)**

WCPM	/	Words Read	=	Accuracy %

PROSODY				
	L1	L2	L3	L4
Reading in Phrases	O	O	O	O
Pace	O	O	O	O
Syntax	O	O	O	O
Self-correction	O	O	O	O
Intonation	O	O	O	O

A Message from the Past

Lucy and Karla were excited because their class was going on a trip. They were going to visit a natural history museum. There was a new exhibit at the museum about ancient Egypt. The girls were fascinated by the Egyptian picture writing called *hieroglyphics*.

After the trip, Karla wanted to find out more. She went to the library and checked out several books on ancient Egypt. She also searched the internet with her mother for information. On the internet, she even found a site where she could write her own message in hieroglyphics.

The next time Karla saw Lucy, she showed her a message in hieroglyphics. "This is very mysterious," Karla said. "It's a message from the past that has your name in it."

Lucy studied the message and then began to laugh. "This message is not from the past; it's from you," she chuckled.

"How do you know?" Karla asked, surprised.

"I've been studying hieroglyphics, too," Lucy explained. "You meant to say that 'Lucy is a friend', but you called me a 'frond' instead." They both laughed.

👆 What are hieroglyphics?

👆 How does Lucy know the message is not ancient?

Name: _____ Date: _____

A Message from the Past

9	Lucy and Karla were excited because their class was
21	going on a trip. They were going to visit a natural history
31	museum. There was a new exhibit at the museum about
40	ancient Egypt. The girls were fascinated by the Egyptian
44	picture writing called *hieroglyphics*.
56	After the trip, Karla wanted to find out more. She went to
66	the library and checked out several books on ancient Egypt.
75	She also searched the internet with her mother for
85	information. On the internet, she even found a site where
93	she could write her own message in hieroglyphics.
104	The next time Karla saw Lucy, she showed her a message
113	in hieroglyphics. "This is very mysterious," Karla said. "It's
124	a message from the past that has your name in it."
134	Lucy studied the message and then began to laugh. "This
145	message is not from the past; it's from you," she chuckled.
152	"How do you know?" Karla asked, surprised.
159	"I've been studying hieroglyphics, too," Lucy explained.
172	"You meant to say that 'Lucy is a friend', but you called me
178	a 'frond' instead." They both laughed.

 What are hieroglyphics?

 How does Lucy know the message is not ancient?

Words Read	–	Errors	=	WCPM

☐ **Fall (127 WCPM)**
☐ **Winter (140 WCPM)**
☐ **Spring (150 WCPM)**

WCPM	/	Words Read	=	Accuracy %

PROSODY				
	L1	L2	L3	L4
Reading in Phrases	O	O	O	O
Pace	O	O	O	O
Syntax	O	O	O	O
Self-correction	O	O	O	O
Intonation	O	O	O	O

The Rules of Baseball

Fly balls, ground outs, and home runs are things that make us think of baseball. Baseball has been played for many years. In fact, the rules that baseball players use today were created in 1845.

Baseball games played before these rules were set used bats, baseballs, and bases, too. Players hit the ball with a bat and ran around the bases, just like today. But players used to hit the runners with the ball. Soon they realized this could harm a runner. So one of the new rules said that a player must tag out the runner as he runs to base, which is how the game is played today.

Players were not looking for fame; they just loved playing baseball. But they felt their game must have rules. One baseball club made a list of rules. One of these rules stated that if a player swings at a ball and misses three times, he is out.

The first baseball game played with the new set of rules was scheduled and played in 1846. The players still had fun and most everyone admitted that the new rules were helpful. This is how baseball got its rules.

👍 How was baseball before 1845 the same as it is today?

👍 How was baseball before 1845 different than today?

Name: _____ Date: _____

The Rules of Baseball

10	Fly balls, ground outs, and home runs are things that
20	make us think of baseball. Baseball has been played for
31	many years. In fact, the rules that baseball players use today
35	were created in 1845.
44	Baseball games played before these rules were set used
56	bats, baseballs, and bases, too. Players hit the ball with a bat
67	and ran around the bases, just like today. But players used
78	to hit the runners with the ball. Soon they realized this
91	could harm a runner. So one of the new rules said that a
104	player must tag out the runner as he runs to base, which is
110	how the game is played today.
119	Players were not looking for fame; they just loved
129	playing baseball. But they felt their game must have rules.
141	One baseball club made a list of rules. One of these rules
153	stated that if a player swings at a ball and misses three
157	times, he is out.
168	The first baseball game played with the new set of rules
179	was scheduled and played in 1846. The players still had fun
188	and most everyone admitted that the new rules were
196	helpful. This is how baseball got its rules.

✓ How was baseball before 1845 the same as it is today?

✓ How was baseball before 1845 different than today?

Words Read	–	Errors	=	WCPM

☐ **Fall (127 WCPM)**
☐ **Winter (140 WCPM)**
☐ **Spring (150 WCPM)**

WCPM	/	Words Read	=	Accuracy %

PROSODY				
	L1	L2	L3	L4
Reading in Phrases	O	O	O	O
Pace	O	O	O	O
Syntax	O	O	O	O
Self-correction	O	O	O	O
Intonation	O	O	O	O

My Country

Wangari Muta Maathai was a force for change in Africa. She was a champion for human rights and for democracy. She also fought for the environment and conservation. She wanted to preserve the beauty of her native Kenya. For her efforts, Maathai was awarded the Nobel Prize in 2004.

As part of her work for the environment, Maathai started the Green Belt Movement in Kenya. The focus of the movement was to organize women's groups to plant trees. Since 1976, women have planted more than 20 million trees on farms and schools across the country. Several African countries have since joined the Green Belt Movement.

Maathai was also influential in the fight to protect public land. In 2010, she joined the Karura Forest Environmental Education Trust. In that same year, she founded an institute. The plan for the institute was to support research on how to use the land wisely. One of the goals was to find ways to help people conserve as well as use land. Another goal focused on resolving conflicts over land resources.

In September of 2011, Maathai died at the age of 71. Many people honor her by continuing to fight for the land and for the people.

✔ What is the author's view of Maathai?

✔ What was a result of the Green Belt Movement?

Name: _____ Date: _____

My Country

10	Wangari Muta Maathai was a force for change in Africa.
20	She was a champion for human rights and for democracy.
29	She also fought for the environment and conservation. She
40	wanted to preserve the beauty of her native Kenya. For her
49	efforts, Maathai was awarded the Nobel Prize in 2004.
59	As part of her work for the environment, Maathai started
69	the Green Belt Movement in Kenya. The focus of the
78	movement was to organize women's groups to plant trees.
88	Since 1976, women have planted more than 20 million trees
97	on farms and schools across the country. Several African
105	countries have since joined the Green Belt Movement.
115	Maathai was also influential in the fight to protect public
124	land. In 2010, she joined the Karura Forest Environmental
134	Education Trust. In that same year, she founded an institute.
146	The plan for the institute was to support research on how to
159	use the land wisely. One of the goals was to find ways to
169	help people conserve as well as use land. Another goal
176	focused on resolving conflicts over land resources.
187	In September of 2011, Maathai died at the age of 71.
198	Many people honor her by continuing to fight for the land
202	and for the people.

☝ What is the author's view of Maathai?

☝ What was a result of the Green Belt Movement?

Words Read	–	Errors	=	WCPM

☐ **Fall (127 WCPM)**
☐ **Winter (140 WCPM)**
☐ **Spring (150 WCPM)**

	PROSODY			
	L1	L2	L3	L4
Reading in Phrases	O	O	O	O
Pace	O	O	O	O
Syntax	O	O	O	O
Self-correction	O	O	O	O
Intonation	O	O	O	O

WCPM	/	Words Read	=	Accuracy %

The Stilt House

While searching for a place to settle, a group of people long ago came upon a beautiful lake. They all agreed that the lake and the surrounding shores would be a perfect spot to build their village, so that is what they did. They gathered materials from the trees and created their homes in the traditional style of their culture.

When the hot months of summer came, rain fell heavily, and the water in the lake steadily rose. It flooded into the rooms, ruining the floors, the food, and the bed mats. At last, the water receded. The people repaired and cleaned their homes and continued on with life.

But the next year the rains came and the lake rose again. "What shall we do?" the people cried. They did not want to move away.

"Raise your houses," an old man said. At first, no one knew what the old man meant, but then a young woman said, "He means to put our houses on stilts." And that is what they did.

Today, in many parts of the world you can see houses on stilts. They are built near any place where the water may rise during the rainy season.

✔ What is the problem the settlers encountered in the summer months?

✔ What is the solution to this problem?

Name: _____ Date: _____

The Stilt House

11	While searching for a place to settle, a group of people
22	long ago came upon a beautiful lake. They all agreed that
33	the lake and the surrounding shores would be a perfect spot
44	to build their village, so that is what they did. They
54	gathered materials from the trees and created their homes in
60	the traditional style of their culture.
70	When the hot months of summer came, rain fell heavily,
82	and the water in the lake steadily rose. It flooded into the
93	rooms, ruining the floors, the food, and the bed mats. At
102	last, the water receded. The people repaired and cleaned
109	their homes and continued on with life.
121	But the next year the rains came and the lake rose again.
133	"What shall we do?" the people cried. They did not want to
135	move away.
146	"Raise your houses," an old man said. At first, no one
157	knew what the old man meant, but then a young woman
169	said, "He means to put our houses on stilts." And that is
172	what they did.
184	Today, in many parts of the world you can see houses on
195	stilts. They are built near any place where the water may
200	rise during the rainy season.

 What is the problem the settlers encountered in the summer months?

 What is the solution to this problem?

Words Read	–	Errors	=	WCPM

☐ **Fall (127 WCPM)**
☐ **Winter (140 WCPM)**
☐ **Spring (150 WCPM)**

WCPM	/	Words Read	=	Accuracy %

PROSODY				
	L1	L2	L3	L4
Reading in Phrases	O	O	O	O
Pace	O	O	O	O
Syntax	O	O	O	O
Self-correction	O	O	O	O
Intonation	O	O	O	O

Hand Talk

Jordan stared at the two students talking at the next table in the cafeteria. They weren't talking, exactly. Their hands were moving in a blur of gestures, and their mouths were moving. However, they weren't speaking.

Jordan did not want to be rude, but he was so curious that he had to ask them what they were doing. One of the two students said, "We are talking to each other with sign language." Her words sounded a little different. She smiled and pointed to one ear. "I'm deaf," she said.

"Can I learn sign language?" Jordan asked. The girl watched his mouth form the question then nodded, "Yes."

In the next few weeks, Jordan met with the two students every lunch hour. They taught him that sign language does not spell out every letter in a word. It uses gestures to indicate concepts. For example, he found out that pointing to himself then crossing his fisted hands and forearms in front of his body, and pointing to another person is a way to say "I love you." Jordan was thrilled to learn a second language, especially an animated yet quiet language.

👆 What does Jordan not understand at the start of the passage?

👆 How does Jordan teach himself a second language?

Name: _____ Date: _____

Hand Talk

11	Jordan stared at the two students talking at the next table
20	in the cafeteria. They weren't talking, exactly. Their hands
31	were moving in a blur of gestures, and their mouths were
36	moving. However, they weren't speaking.
48	Jordan did not want to be rude, but he was so curious
61	that he had to ask them what they were doing. One of the
72	two students said, "We are talking to each other with sign
81	language." Her words sounded a little different. She smiled
90	and pointed to one ear. "I'm deaf," she said.
99	"Can I learn sign language?" Jordan asked. The girl
108	watched his mouth form the question then nodded, "Yes."
119	In the next few weeks, Jordan met with the two students
129	every lunch hour. They taught him that sign language does
141	not spell out every letter in a word. It uses gestures to
150	indicate concepts. For example, he found out that pointing
160	to himself then crossing his fisted hands and forearms in
173	front of his body, and pointing to another person is a way to
184	say "I love you." Jordan was thrilled to learn a second
191	language, especially an animated yet quiet language.

✔ What does Jordan not understand at the start of the passage?

✔ How does Jordan teach himself a second language?

Words Read	–	Errors	=	WCPM

☐ **Fall (127 WCPM)**
☐ **Winter (140 WCPM)**
☐ **Spring (150 WCPM)**

WCPM	/	Words Read	=	Accuracy %

PROSODY

	L1	L2	L3	L4
Reading in Phrases	O	O	O	O
Pace	O	O	O	O
Syntax	O	O	O	O
Self-correction	O	O	O	O
Intonation	O	O	O	O

Strong Senses

As scientists learn more about the human brain, they are discovering that it is not as rigid as they once thought. Now they know that the brain can change in response to what a person experiences. This idea gives hope to people who suffer brain injuries.

An example of how the brain can redirect itself is how other senses may become stronger when one sense is lost. A blind person may develop acute hearing. Blindness may also result in a better sense of touch. A deaf person's sense of sight may improve. Touch may also become better. A deaf musician may play an instrument by feeling the vibrations in the music. To make these changes in the senses, the brain creates new connections. These connections go around the damaged area.

The brain can also trick the senses. Many people who lose a limb can still feel the missing part. A part of the brain near the area that used to process signals from the missing part seems to take over. That is why people may think that they still feel missing fingers when they touch their faces.

The brain is still a mystery in many ways. But scientists are learning more all the time.

What is the main idea of the passage?

Name one example of the way the brain might redirect itself.

Name: _____ Date: _____

Strong Senses

10	As scientists learn more about the human brain, they are
22	discovering that it is not as rigid as they once thought. Now
34	they know that the brain can change in response to what a
43	person experiences. This idea gives hope to people who
46	suffer brain injuries.
57	An example of how the brain can redirect itself is how
67	other senses may become stronger when one sense is lost.
76	A blind person may develop acute hearing. Blindness may
88	also result in a better sense of touch. A deaf person's sense
99	of sight may improve. Touch may also become better. A deaf
108	musician may play an instrument by feeling the vibrations
120	in the music. To make these changes in the senses, the brain
128	creates new connections. These connections go around the
130	damaged area.
141	The brain can also trick the senses. Many people who lose
155	a limb can still feel the missing part. A part of the brain near
166	the area that used to process signals from the missing part
178	seems to take over. That is why people may think that they
187	still feel missing fingers when they touch their faces.
198	The brain is still a mystery in many ways. But scientists
204	are learning more all the time.

✔ What is the main idea of the passage?

✔ Name one example of the way the brain might redirect itself.

Words Read	−	Errors	=	WCPM

☐ **Fall (127 WCPM)**
☐ **Winter (140 WCPM)**
☐ **Spring (150 WCPM)**

WCPM	/	Words Read	=	Accuracy %

PROSODY				
	L1	L2	L3	L4
Reading in Phrases	O	O	O	O
Pace	O	O	O	O
Syntax	O	O	O	O
Self-correction	O	O	O	O
Intonation	O	O	O	O

The Trash Band

In a village in Paraguay, a bright light shines on the future of a group of young people. These children are musicians. They and their families are very poor. They survive by sorting through a mountain of garbage to find things that can be recycled and sold.

A man named Favio Chavez wanted to give the children a chance. He wanted to teach them how to play music. Chavez knew that none of the children's families would ever have enough money to buy instruments. So he had a wild idea. The children would make their own instruments using materials they recycled from the garbage dump.

Now twenty children perform in the "Recycled Orchestra." They have cellos made from rusty cans and violins made from bowls with strings tightened by forks. Bottle caps became keys on a saxophone, and old X-rays became drum heads.

The orchestra plays music written by classic composers such as Mozart. They also play modern music. The Recycled Orchestra is becoming widely known. They now play concerts in many places. The orchestra has brought the young musicians into a brighter future.

👉 What was Chavez's idea?

👉 What is the "Recycled Orchestra"?

Name: _____ Date: _____

The Trash Band

11	In a village in Paraguay, a bright light shines on the
21	future of a group of young people. These children are
30	musicians. They and their families are very poor. They
40	survive by sorting through a mountain of garbage to find
47	things that can be recycled and sold.
57	A man named Favio Chavez wanted to give the children
68	a chance. He wanted to teach them how to play music.
77	Chavez knew that none of the children's families would
88	ever have enough money to buy instruments. So he had a
97	wild idea. The children would make their own instruments
105	using materials they recycled from the garbage dump.
112	Now twenty children perform in the "Recycled
121	Orchestra." They have cellos made from rusty cans and
130	violins made from bowls with strings tightened by forks.
141	Bottle caps became keys on a saxophone, and old X-rays
144	became drum heads.
152	The orchestra plays music written by classic composers
162	such as Mozart. They also play modern music. The Recycled
170	Orchestra is becoming widely known. They now play
179	concerts in many places. The orchestra has brought the
185	young musicians into a brighter future.

 What was Chavez's idea?

 What is the "Recycled Orchestra"?

Words Read	–	Errors	=	WCPM

☐ **Fall (127 WCPM)**
☐ **Winter (140 WCPM)**
☐ **Spring (150 WCPM)**

WCPM	/	Words Read	=	Accuracy %

PROSODY				
	L1	L2	L3	L4
Reading in Phrases	O	O	O	O
Pace	O	O	O	O
Syntax	O	O	O	O
Self-correction	O	O	O	O
Intonation	O	O	O	O

Worth Saving

Every day on her way to school, Rosa passed a huge old oak tree that grew in the center of the road. It seemed to her like an old friend who would always be there.

One day Rosa's father said that the town planned to cut down the old oak tree because it was in danger of falling. Rosa was horrified. Her father said he would help her figure out what to do.

Rosa and her father found a tree expert who could tell them about the old tree. He had a technique to find out how old the tree was without harming it. He later informed them that the tree was probably over 300 years old.

"That tree was here when George Washington was alive!" Rosa exclaimed. "He may have even ridden past it."

Rosa wrote a letter to the newspaper telling what she imagined about George Washington and the tree. Many people read the letter, and they started a campaign to save the tree. So the tree was strengthened with cables instead of being cut down. Everyone agreed that it was a part of history worth saving.

✔️ What text evidence supports the idea that the tree is important to Rosa?

✔️ How does Rosa save the tree?

Name: _____ Date: _____

Worth Saving

12	Every day on her way to school, Rosa passed a huge old
26	oak tree that grew in the center of the road. It seemed to her
35	like an old friend who would always be there.
46	One day Rosa's father said that the town planned to cut
58	down the old oak tree because it was in danger of falling.
69	Rosa was horrified. Her father said he would help her figure
73	out what to do.
84	Rosa and her father found a tree expert who could tell
97	them about the old tree. He had a technique to find out how
108	old the tree was without harming it. He later informed them
117	that the tree was probably over 300 years old.
126	"That tree was here when George Washington was alive!"
135	Rosa exclaimed. "He may have even ridden past it."
145	Rosa wrote a letter to the newspaper telling what she
153	imagined about George Washington and the tree. Many
164	people read the letter, and they started a campaign to save
175	the tree. So the tree was strengthened with cables instead of
186	being cut down. Everyone agreed that it was a part of
189	history worth saving.

✓ What text evidence supports the idea that the tree is important to Rosa?

✓ How does Rosa save the tree?

Words Read	–	Errors	=	WCPM

☐ **Fall (127 WCPM)**
☐ **Winter (140 WCPM)**
☐ **Spring (150 WCPM)**

WCPM	/	Words Read	=	Accuracy %

PROSODY				
	L1	L2	L3	L4
Reading in Phrases	O	O	O	O
Pace	O	O	O	O
Syntax	O	O	O	O
Self-correction	O	O	O	O
Intonation	O	O	O	O

The Park Wins

Henry often rode his bicycle on the path by the river near his house. He enjoyed watching the ducks and geese along the shore, but there was no place to stop. "This town needs a park by the river," Henry grumbled.

Henry talked to his grandmother. She thought that all of the property along the river was privately owned so there wouldn't be any place to put a park.

"What about that land where the oil tanks used to be? No one seems to be using it since the tanks were torn down," Henry suggested.

Henry and his grandmother went to town hall to investigate the property. They found out that the owner wanted to sell the property, and there were grants from scenic groups that could be used to purchase it for a park.

"This is our chance to get a park!" Henry exclaimed. They spread the news to everyone in town. Some people were excited at the possibility of a park, and others were against it. Finally, the town scheduled a day for the people to vote. When all the votes were counted, the park won. It wasn't long before people had a place where they could go to enjoy the river.

What does Henry want to accomplish?

Why do Henry and his grandmother go to town hall?

Name: _____ Date: _____

The Park Wins

12	Henry often rode his bicycle on the path by the river near
22	his house. He enjoyed watching the ducks and geese along
34	the shore, but there was no place to stop. "This town needs
41	a park by the river," Henry grumbled.
51	Henry talked to his grandmother. She thought that all of
61	the property along the river was privately owned so there
69	wouldn't be any place to put a park.
80	"What about that land where the oil tanks used to be?
92	No one seems to be using it since the tanks were torn
95	down," Henry suggested.
104	Henry and his grandmother went to town hall to
113	investigate the property. They found out that the owner
123	wanted to sell the property, and there were grants from
135	scenic groups that could be used to purchase it for a park.
145	"This is our chance to get a park!" Henry exclaimed.
155	They spread the news to everyone in town. Some people
166	were excited at the possibility of a park, and others were
177	against it. Finally, the town scheduled a day for the people
188	to vote. When all the votes were counted, the park won.
199	It wasn't long before people had a place where they could
204	go to enjoy the river.

 What does Henry want to accomplish?

 Why do Henry and his grandmother go to town hall?

Words Read	–	Errors	=	WCPM

☐ **Fall (127 WCPM)**
☐ **Winter (140 WCPM)**
☐ **Spring (150 WCPM)**

WCPM	/	Words Read	=	Accuracy %

PROSODY

	L1	L2	L3	L4
Reading in Phrases	O	O	O	O
Pace	O	O	O	O
Syntax	O	O	O	O
Self-correction	O	O	O	O
Intonation	O	O	O	O

Weekend Treat

I usually sleep late on weekends, but last Saturday morning was different. Our neighbor, Mr. Konkus, invited us to go to our local park to watch hot air balloons take off. I got up really early; I already was eating breakfast as the sun came up.

When we arrived at the park, I couldn't believe it. The balloons were beautiful, and each had a propane heater warming the air in the bag. The heaters were so loud that I could barely hear Mr. Konkus when he asked if I wanted to go up in a balloon.

I asked my parents, and they said it was okay. In fact, my mom decided to come with me. The two of us climbed into the gondola. (That's the wicker basket that hangs under the balloon.) The pilot turned up the heater, and our ride began.

I was shivering with excitement as I looked at the giant opening of the red and blue balloon above my head. The wind carried the balloon away from the park. However, the pilot soon steered us to a grassy field, and our descent to the ground was gentle. The chase truck came to pick us up; Dad was waiting in the back. I told my parents that I'd get up early every Saturday to do that again!

⚲ What gets the narrator to wake up early on the weekend?

⚲ Who goes on the balloon ride?

Name: _____ Date: _____

Weekend Treat

9	I usually sleep late on weekends, but last Saturday
17	morning was different. Our neighbor, Mr. Konkus, invited
31	us to go to our local park to watch hot air balloons take off.
43	I got up really early; I already was eating breakfast as the
46	sun came up.
57	When we arrived at the park, I couldn't believe it. The
66	balloons were beautiful, and each had a propane heater
79	warming the air in the bag. The heaters were so loud that I
91	could barely hear Mr. Konkus when he asked if I wanted to
96	go up in a balloon.
109	I asked my parents, and they said it was okay. In fact, my
121	mom decided to come with me. The two of us climbed into
131	the gondola. (That's the wicker basket that hangs under the
142	balloon.) The pilot turned up the heater, and our ride began.
153	I was shivering with excitement as I looked at the giant
164	opening of the red and blue balloon above my head. The
174	wind carried the balloon away from the park. However, the
187	pilot soon steered us to a grassy field, and our descent to the
199	ground was gentle. The chase truck came to pick us up; Dad
212	was waiting in the back. I told my parents that I'd get up
219	early every Saturday to do that again!

 What gets the narrator to wake up early on the weekend?

What goes on the balloon ride?

Words Read	−	Errors	=	WCPM

☐ **Fall (127 WCPM)**
☐ **Winter (140 WCPM)**
☐ **Spring (150 WCPM)**

WCPM	/	Words Read	=	Accuracy %

PROSODY				
	L1	L2	L3	L4
Reading in Phrases	O	O	O	O
Pace	O	O	O	O
Syntax	O	O	O	O
Self-correction	O	O	O	O
Intonation	O	O	O	O

Invention of the Wheel

Exactly when the wheel was invented is not known. But ancient clay tablets have been found that show a drawing of a potter's wheel. These tablets are estimated to be about 5,500 years old. It seems that wheels did not appear as part of a vehicle until around 4,000 years ago. They can be seen on Egyptian chariots.

Wheels are such a basic and important part of human life that you may think every culture created them. Yet, the Inca, Aztec, and Maya civilizations did not appear to use the wheel for manufacture or transportation.

Archaeologists speculate people may have first used logs to make it easier to pull sleds carrying loads. They would have dragged the sled from one rolling log to the next.

Finally, people figured out how to cut a round wheel from a log. They attached two wheels to a sled to make a cart. For wheels to work, another invention was critical. That was an axle that connected to wheels and allowed them to turn. At some point, someone made a fixed axle. A fixed axle does not turn. Instead, it is attached to the cart frame. Only the wheels revolve, so carts could turn corners more smoothly. Since then, the basic wheel has not changed.

✔ Which ancient cultures did not use the wheel?

✔ Why was the invention of the fixed axle so important?

Name: _____ Date: _____

Invention of the Wheel

10	Exactly when the wheel was invented is not known. But
21	ancient clay tablets have been found that show a drawing of
31	a potter's wheel. These tablets are estimated to be about
43	5,500 years old. It seems that wheels did not appear as part
55	of a vehicle until around 4,000 years ago. They can be seen
58	on Egyptian chariots.
69	Wheels are such a basic and important part of human life
80	that you may think every culture created them. Yet, the Inca,
90	Aztec, and Maya civilizations did not appear to use the
95	wheel for manufacture or transportation.
103	Archaeologists speculate people may have first used logs
114	to make it easier to pull sleds carrying loads. They would
125	have dragged the sled from one rolling log to the next.
126	Finally, people figured out how to cut a round wheel
136	from a log. They attached two wheels to a sled to make a
149	cart. For wheels to work, another invention was critical.
158	That was an axle that connected to wheels and allowed
168	them to turn. At some point, someone made a fixed axle.
180	A fixed axle does not turn. Instead, it is attached to the cart
192	frame. Only the wheels revolve, so carts could turn corners
203	more smoothly. Since then, the basic wheel has not changed.

Which ancient cultures did not use the wheel?

Why was the invention of the fixed axle so important?

Words Read	–	Errors	=	WCPM

☐ **Fall (127 WCPM)**
☐ **Winter (140 WCPM)**
☐ **Spring (150 WCPM)**

WCPM	/	Words Read	=	Accuracy %

PROSODY				
	L1	L2	L3	L4
Reading in Phrases	O	O	O	O
Pace	O	O	O	O
Syntax	O	O	O	O
Self-correction	O	O	O	O
Intonation	O	O	O	O

Beyond the Invention

Many famous inventors have made history with their inventions. They include Thomas Edison and the light bulb, Alexander Graham Bell and the telephone, the Wright brothers and the airplane, and Ada Lovelace and the computer program.

Inventors think about what might be possible to meet people's needs. They may bring together the ideas of others with their own. But what happens to an invention after it has been invented?

People adjust, add to, and fine-tune things, and this activity is called "tweaking." These people make modifications to improve an invention and take it way beyond the original. For example, Steve Jobs changed the design of computers to make them easier to use. He took the beginnings of a portable phone and turned it into a much smaller device. New phones will do so much more than just take and make calls.

Another modifier was Henry Ford. He took the first automobiles and turned them into vehicles that the average person could afford. He did this by using the assembly line.

So look at inventions and ask, "What more can be done?"

✔ What happens when you tweak something?

✔ What is the main idea of this article?

Name: _____ Date: _____

Beyond the Invention

8	Many famous inventors have made history with their
17	inventions. They include Thomas Edison and the light bulb,
25	Alexander Graham Bell and the telephone, the Wright
34	brothers and the airplane, and Ada Lovelace and the
36	computer program.
45	Inventors think about what might be possible to meet
55	people's needs. They may bring together the ideas of others
66	with their own. But what happens to an invention after it
69	has been invented?
79	People adjust, add to, and fine-tune things, and this
86	activity is called "tweaking." These people make
95	modifications to improve an invention and take it way
104	beyond the original. For example, Steve Jobs changed the
116	design of computers to make them easier to use. He took the
127	beginnings of a portable phone and turned it into a much
138	smaller device. New phones will do so much more than just
142	take and make calls.
151	Another modifier was Henry Ford. He took the first
160	automobiles and turned them into vehicles that the average
171	person could afford. He did this by using the assembly line.
182	So look at inventions and ask, "What more can be done?"

✔ What happens when you tweak something?

✔ What is the main idea of this article?

Words Read	–	Errors	=	WCPM

☐ **Fall (127 WCPM)**
☐ **Winter (140 WCPM)**
☐ **Spring (150 WCPM)**

WCPM	/	Words Read	=	Accuracy %

PROSODY

	L1	L2	L3	L4
Reading in Phrases	O	O	O	O
Pace	O	O	O	O
Syntax	O	O	O	O
Self-correction	O	O	O	O
Intonation	O	O	O	O

The Story Rug

The Navajo woman sat in front of her loom and searched her imagination. She was about to begin weaving a new rug from the wool of her sheep. She had carefully carded and spun the wool and dyed the white yarn red, cream, green, and yellow. The colors had come from plants she had gathered herself. She also had brown, black, and white yarn that she had left the natural colors of the sheep. These preparations took a long time, but the woman was pleased with the results. She wanted to create a traditional rug made in the old way.

So what story would the rug tell? She decided to show the traditional life of her people and of some Navajo who still desired to live in the old ways.

Over the next few weeks, the rug grew as images of corn, bean, and squash plants took shape. These were important plants to the Navajo. In the center appeared a six-sided Hogan, the traditional home made of logs. In the corners, the woman wove the images of four sacred mountains. Finally, the rug was finished. Not only was it a work of art, it was an amazing narrative as well.

👆 What story does the rug show?

👆 Why does the Navajo woman choose this story?

Name: _____ Date: _____

The Story Rug

11	The Navajo woman sat in front of her loom and searched
22	her imagination. She was about to begin weaving a new rug
33	from the wool of her sheep. She had carefully carded and
44	spun the wool and dyed the white yarn red, cream, green,
54	and yellow. The colors had come from plants she had
64	gathered herself. She also had brown, black, and white yarn
75	that she had left the natural colors of the sheep. These
85	preparations took a long time, but the woman was pleased
96	with the results. She wanted to create a traditional rug made
100	in the old way.
111	So what story would the rug tell? She decided to show
122	the traditional life of her people and of some Navajo who
130	still desired to live in the old ways.
142	Over the next few weeks, the rug grew as images of corn,
151	bean, and squash plants took shape. These were important
162	plants to the Navajo. In the center appeared a six-sided
172	Hogan, the traditional home made of logs. In the corners,
181	the woman wove the images of four sacred mountains.
194	Finally, the rug was finished. Not only was it a work of art,
201	it was an amazing narrative as well.

✔ What story does the rug show?

✔ Why does the Navajo woman choose this story?

Words Read	–	Errors	=	WCPM

☐ **Fall (127 WCPM)**
☐ **Winter (140 WCPM)**
☐ **Spring (150 WCPM)**

WCPM	/	Words Read	=	Accuracy %

PROSODY

	L1	L2	L3	L4
Reading in Phrases	O	O	O	O
Pace	O	O	O	O
Syntax	O	O	O	O
Self-correction	O	O	O	O
Intonation	O	O	O	O

Cave Painter

About 60,000 years ago an artist approached a large and deep cave in an area now called France. He carried several items of his craft. He had charcoal and mineral-laced clay in different colors. He also had a torch he would light once he got into the cave.

The artist had important work to do to help his clan and family. The large animals they hunted had become scarce. If the upcoming hunt was not successful, the artist's family might starve.

In the cave, the artist felt along the rough, rocky walls until he found a place that he knew would work. He lit his torch and began to mix paint on small flat rocks. The smoke from the torch made it somewhat difficult to see the wall, but the artist had done this many times in the past. He could almost close his eyes and see the pictures he would create.

The artist painted large bulls and deer with tall horns. He used the grooves and bulges in the rock to make the animals seem to leap from the walls. As he applied the colors, the animals came alive with power and strength. Finally, the artist placed his own hand on the painting and drew around the fingers to create a handprint. Now perhaps the animals would come.

What does the artist create?

What does the artist hope his art will do?

Name: _____ Date: _____

Cave Painter

10	About 60,000 years ago an artist approached a large and
21	deep cave in an area now called France. He carried several
33	items of his craft. He had charcoal and mineral-laced clay in
45	different colors. He also had a torch he would light once he
49	got into the cave.
61	The artist had important work to do to help his clan and
70	family. The large animals they hunted had become scarce.
80	If the upcoming hunt was not successful, the artist's family
82	might starve.
93	In the cave, the artist felt along the rough, rocky walls
106	until he found a place that he knew would work. He lit his
118	torch and began to mix paint on small flat rocks. The smoke
129	from the torch made it somewhat difficult to see the wall,
142	but the artist had done this many times in the past. He could
153	almost close his eyes and see the pictures he would create.
164	The artist painted large bulls and deer with tall horns. He
176	used the grooves and bulges in the rock to make the animals
188	seem to leap from the walls. As he applied the colors, the
197	animals came alive with power and strength. Finally, the
208	artist placed his own hand on the painting and drew around
218	the fingers to create a handprint. Now perhaps the animals
220	would come.

✔ What does the artist create?

✔ What does the artist hope his art will do?

Words Read	–	Errors	=	WCPM

☐ Fall (127 WCPM)
☐ Winter (140 WCPM)
☐ Spring (150 WCPM)

WCPM	/	Words Read	=	Accuracy %

PROSODY				
	L1	L2	L3	L4
Reading in Phrases	O	O	O	O
Pace	O	O	O	O
Syntax	O	O	O	O
Self-correction	O	O	O	O
Intonation	O	O	O	O

Rosa Parks

In the early 1960s, the struggle for civil rights in the United States focused on equal treatment in work, housing, and daily life for African Americans. The movement began in earnest with one person who made all the difference.

Rosa Parks was a 42-year-old seamstress in 1955. When she boarded a public bus on December 1 in Montgomery City, she was on her way home. She sat behind the ten seats reserved for white people in the front of the bus. Those ten seats were quickly filled. Then a white man got on the bus. The driver told Mrs. Parks and three other African Americans to give up their seats. Mrs. Parks was tired and without planning to she said no. As a result, she was arrested and convicted of a crime. She had violated a law that separated white and black people. Mrs. Parks challenged and appealed her conviction.

Mrs. Parks became a spark for the civil rights movement. Activists soon started a boycott of public buses. More African Americans than whites rode the buses, so the bus companies were soon threatened. The boycott lasted for over a year until the Supreme Court ruled that the law of segregation was not legal. The government ordered buses to be integrated.

✔ Why was Rosa Parks arrested?

✔ What effect did Rosa Parks's stand have?

Name: _____ Date: _____

Rosa Parks

11	In the early 1960s, the struggle for civil rights in the
20	United States focused on equal treatment in work, housing,
29	and daily life for African Americans. The movement began
39	in earnest with one person who made all the difference.
50	Rosa Parks was a 42-year-old seamstress in 1955. When
60	she boarded a public bus on December 1 in Montgomery
73	City, she was on her way home. She sat behind the ten seats
85	reserved for white people in the front of the bus. Those ten
97	seats were quickly filled. Then a white man got on the bus.
106	The driver told Mrs. Parks and three other African
117	Americans to give up their seats. Mrs. Parks was tired and
128	without planning to she said no. As a result, she was
139	arrested and convicted of a crime. She had violated a law
147	that separated white and black people. Mrs. Parks
152	challenged and appealed her conviction.
162	Mrs. Parks became a spark for the civil rights movement.
171	Activists soon started a boycott of public buses. More
181	African Americans than whites rode the buses, so the bus
189	companies were soon threatened. The boycott lasted for
200	over a year until the Supreme Court ruled that the law
209	of segregation was not legal. The government ordered buses
212	to be integrated.

✓ Why was Rosa Parks arrested?

✓ What effect did Rosa Parks's stand have?

Words Read	–	Errors	=	WCPM

☐ **Fall (127 WCPM)**
☐ **Winter (140 WCPM)**
☐ **Spring (150 WCPM)**

WCPM	/	Words Read	=	Accuracy %

PROSODY				
	L1	L2	L3	L4
Reading in Phrases	O	O	O	O
Pace	O	O	O	O
Syntax	O	O	O	O
Self-correction	O	O	O	O
Intonation	O	O	O	O

Someone Once Lived Here

Lee planned to spend the summer with his cousin who had just moved with her family out into the country. His aunt and uncle had bought a farm where they planned to grow pumpkins and other vegetables.

When Lee arrived, his cousin Kiko excitedly told him that there were many places to explore. They were soon outside and on their way.

After hiking up a large hill and down into a small valley, Lee spied something ahead. "That looks like a stone wall," he said.

When they got closer, Kiko exclaimed, "It's not just a wall! It's an old house!"

The cousins examined the remains of the small stone house. They discovered a piece of an old bowl that had a blue design painted on it.

Kiko and Lee displayed the piece of pottery and described their find to Kiko's parents. Everyone was intrigued about the ruins.

At the local library, Lee and Kiko found documentation that showed the house was probably built in the early 1700s and was likely the first farmhouse on the land. Kiko was thrilled to find out that her new home had such history!

✔ Where is Lee spending the summer?

✔ What do Lee and Kiko find in the stone house?

Name: _____ Date: _____

Someone Once Lived Here

10	Lee planned to spend the summer with his cousin who
21	had just moved with her family out into the country. His
32	aunt and uncle had bought a farm where they planned to
37	grow pumpkins and other vegetables.
47	When Lee arrived, his cousin Kiko excitedly told him that
57	there were many places to explore. They were soon outside
61	and on their way.
73	After hiking up a large hill and down into a small valley,
83	Lee spied something ahead. "That looks like a stone wall,"
85	he said.
95	When they got closer, Kiko exclaimed, "It's not just a
100	wall! It's an old house!"
109	The cousins examined the remains of the small stone
121	house. They discovered a piece of an old bowl that had a
126	blue design painted on it.
135	Kiko and Lee displayed the piece of pottery and
143	described their find to Kiko's parents. Everyone was
147	intrigued about the ruins.
156	At the local library, Lee and Kiko found documentation
167	that showed the house was probably built in the early 1700s
178	and was likely the first farmhouse on the land. Kiko was
189	thrilled to find out that her new home had such history!

 Where is Lee spending the summer?

 What do Lee and Kiko find in the stone house?

Words Read	–	Errors	=	WCPM

☐ **Fall (127 WCPM)**
☐ **Winter (140 WCPM)**
☐ **Spring (150 WCPM)**

WCPM	/	Words Read	=	Accuracy %

PROSODY				
	L1	L2	L3	L4
Reading in Phrases	O	O	O	O
Pace	O	O	O	O
Syntax	O	O	O	O
Self-correction	O	O	O	O
Intonation	O	O	O	O

Changing the Game

Soccer is an ancient game that has been played in various forms and many places throughout history. Through the years, the game has changed. The soccer ball has also gone through many changes.

The ancient Chinese, Greeks, Romans, and Egyptians all played kicking games. The ball was made of various material including cloth, animal skulls, and pig or cow bladders. These balls were obviously not a regular shape so no one knew exactly where they would go when kicked. This unpredictability made for an interesting game with the ball flying off in many directions.

By 1836, vulcanized rubber became available. The pig bladder was replaced by a rubber bladder that helped the ball hold its shape. The outside of the ball was made of leather. By 1872, an official size and weight had been set for the ball. The measurements remain the same today.

People are still trying to improve the design of the soccer ball. The perfect ball would be waterproof, fast, and accurate. It also needs to feel soft so it doesn't hurt players' heads. The soccer ball of the future may still look the same, but it will be more high tech.

👆 How did early soccer balls make the game unpredictable?

👆 In the author's view, what would be a perfect soccer ball?

Name: _____ Date: _____

Changing the Game

11	Soccer is an ancient game that has been played in various
19	forms and many places throughout history. Through the
30	years, the game has changed. The soccer ball has also gone
33	through many changes.
41	The ancient Chinese, Greeks, Romans, and Egyptians all
50	played kicking games. The ball was made of various
59	material including cloth, animal skulls, and pig or cow
69	bladders. These balls were obviously not a regular shape so
79	no one knew exactly where they would go when kicked.
88	This unpredictability made for an interesting game with the
94	ball flying off in many directions.
102	By 1836, vulcanized rubber became available. The pig
112	bladder was replaced by a rubber bladder that helped the
124	ball hold its shape. The outside of the ball was made of
136	leather. By 1872, an official size and weight had been set for
144	the ball. The measurements remain the same today.
155	People are still trying to improve the design of the soccer
164	ball. The perfect ball would be waterproof, fast, and
176	accurate. It also needs to feel soft so it doesn't hurt players'
188	heads. The soccer ball of the future may still look the same,
195	but it will be more high tech.

✔ How did early soccer balls make the game unpredictable?

✔ In the author's view, what would be a perfect soccer ball?

Words Read	–	Errors	=	WCPM

☐ **Fall (127 WCPM)**
☐ **Winter (140 WCPM)**
☐ **Spring (150 WCPM)**

WCPM	/	Words Read	=	Accuracy %

PROSODY				
	L1	L2	L3	L4
Reading in Phrases	O	O	O	O
Pace	O	O	O	O
Syntax	O	O	O	O
Self-correction	O	O	O	O
Intonation	O	O	O	O